T0374570

"*A New Song* is far more than a collection of essays. It invites readers into a conversation of Hebrew poetry with some of the best and most diverse conversation partners in the field. With sensitivity to the intersections of poetry and theology, composition and reception, and reading and response, the depth of these essays reflects the depths of the poetry they explore. I will be recommending this book to students and scholars alike!"

ELIZABETH H. P. BACKFISH, William Jessup University

"If you can read only one book on biblical poetry this year—even this decade—this should be it. The range is vast, the depth profound. Leading voices from across the world are gathered together in one place, curated carefully and most ably by the editorial team. What isn't here? Here readers will learn about poetry in all parts of the Old Testament/Hebrew Bible, while gaining new insights into prosody and performance, lament and dance, translation and reception, art and image, communication and ethics, liturgy and illness—among others! A stunning collection; worth owning, yes, but much, much more: worth digesting."

BRENT A. STRAWN, Duke University

A New Song

A New Song

Biblical Hebrew Poetry

as Jewish and Christian Scripture

EDITORS STEPHEN D. CAMPBELL,
RICHARD G. ROHLFING JR., AND RICHARD S. BRIGGS

STUDIES IN
**SCRIPTURE
& BIBLICAL**
THEOLOGY

LEXHAM
ACADEMIC

A New Song: Biblical Hebrew Poetry as Jewish and Christian Scripture
Studies in Scripture and Biblical Theology

Copyright 2023 Stephen D. Campbell, Richard G. Rohlfing Jr., and Richard S. Briggs

Lexham Academic, an imprint of Lexham Press
1313 Commercial Street, Bellingham, WA 98225
LexhamPress.com

Print ISBN 9781683596912
Digital ISBN 9781683596929
Library of Congress Control Number 2022951702

Lexham Editorial: Derek R. Brown, Katy Smith, Abigail Stocker, Mandi Newell
Cover Design: Brittany Schrock
Typesetting: ProjectLuz.com

A New Song

Sing a new song to the Lord,
sing through the skin of your teeth,
sing in the code of your blood,
sing with a throat full of earth,

sing to the quick of your nails,
sing from the knots of your lungs,
sing like a dancer on coals,
sing as a madman in tongues,

sing as if singing made sense,
sing in the caves of your heart,
sing like you want them to dance,
sing through the shades of your past,

sing what you never could say,
sing at the fulcrum of joy,
sing without need of reply.

Michael Symmons Roberts

Contents

List of Contributors

RICHARD S. BRIGGS is the prior of the Community of St Cuthbert at St Nics Church, Durham, and visiting research fellow in Old Testament at Cranmer Hall, St John's College, Durham University.

JASON BYASSEE is the senior pastor of Timothy Eaton Memorial Church in Toronto, Ontario, and author and editor of numerous books, series, and articles.

STEPHEN D. CAMPBELL is the academic director at Aquila Theological Institute and Pastor of the International Baptist Church of Bonn, Germany.

ELLEN F. DAVIS is the Amos Ragan Kearns Distinguished Professor of Bible and Practical Theology at Duke Divinity School.

JUNE F. DICKIE is a postdoctoral researcher, University of Kwazulu-Natal.

DAVID G. FIRTH is the academic dean and tutor in Old Testament at Trinity College, Bristol.

SUSAN GILLINGHAM is professor of the Hebrew Bible at Worcester College, Oxford and research associate on the Faculty of Theology and Religion at the University of Pretoria, South Africa.

JOHN GOLDINGAY is a senior professor of Old Testament and the David Allan Hubbard Professor Emeritus of Old Testament at Fuller Theological Seminary.

C.T.R. HAYWARD is a retired professor of Hebrew Bible at Durham University.

KATIE M. HEFFELFINGER is the deputy director and lecturer in biblical studies and hermeneutic at the Church of Ireland Theological Institute.

SHAI HELD is president, dean, and chair in Jewish Thought at Hadar Institute.

MICHEAL O'SIADHAIL is an Irish poet and author of many books of poetry including *The Gossamer Wall* and *The Five Quintets*.

RICHARD G. ROHLFING JR. is the lead pastor of Faith Legacy Church in Sacramento, CA, and adjunct professor at Western Seminary and William Jessup University.

BENJAMIN D. SOMMER is a professor of Bible at the Jewish Theological Seminary of America and a senior fellow at the Shalom Hartman Institute.

YISCA ZIMRAN is a lecturer in biblical studies at Bar Ilan University.

Abbreviations

AB	Anchor Bible
AJSL	*American Journal of Semitic Languages and Literatures*
ANE	Ancient Near East(ern)
ANEM	Ancient Near East Monographs
ANTC	Abingdon New Testament Commentary
AOTC	Abingdon Old Testament Commentaries
AThR	*Anglican Theology Review*
BBR	*Bulletin for Biblical Research*
BCOTWP	Baker Commentary on the Old Testament: Wisdom and Psalms
BECNT	Baker Exegetical Commentary on the New Testament
BETL	Bibliotheca Ephemeridum Theologicarum Lovaniensium
Bib	*Biblica*
BibInt	*Biblical Interpretation*
BIOSCS	*Bulletin of the International Organization for Septuagint and Cognate Studies*
BIS	Biblical Interpretation Series
BJS	Brown Judaic Studies
BR	*Biblical Research*
BSac	*Bibliotheca Sacra*
BT	*The Bible Translator*
BTB	*Biblical Theology Bulletin*
BZ	*Biblische Zeitschrift*
CBQ	*Catholic Biblical Quarterly*
CBQMS	Catholic Biblical Quarterly Monograph Series
CI	*Critical Inquiry*
ETL	*Ephemerides theologicae louvanienses*
EvQ	*Evangelical Quarterly*
ExAud	*Ex Auditu*
FOTL	Forms of the Old Testament Literature

HBT	*Horizons in Biblical Theology*
HKAT	Handkommentar zum Alten Testament
HSM	Harvard Semitic Monographs
IBC	Interpretation Bible Commentary
ICC	International Critical Commentary
Int	*Interpretation*
JANES	*Journal of the Ancient Near Eastern Society*
JAOS	*Journal of the American Oriental Society*
JBL	*Journal of Biblical Literature*
JBQ	*Jewish Bible Quarterly*
JETS	*Journal of the Evangelical Theological Society*
JNSL	*Journal of Northwest Semitic Languages*
JPS	Jewish Publication Society
JQR	*Jewish Quarterly Review*
JSem	*Journal of Semitics*
JSNTSup	Journal for the Study of the New Testament: Supplement Series
JSOT	*Journal for the Study of the Old Testament*
JSOTSup	Journal for the Study of the Old Testament: Supplement Series
JSS	*Journal of Semitic Studies*
JTS	*Journal of Theological Studies*
LNTSSup	Library of New Testament Studies Supplement Series
MLBS	Mercer Library of Biblical Studies
MNTC	Moffatt New Testament Commentary
MT	Masoretic Text
NAC	New American Commentary
NIB	*New Interpreter's Bible*
NICNT	New International Commentary on the New Testament
NICOT	New International Commentary on the Old Testament
NovT	*Novum Testamentum*
OBO	Orbis biblicus et Orientalis
OBT	Overtures to Biblical Theology
OTE	*Old Testament Essays*
OTS	Old Testament Studies
PMLA	*Proceedings of the Modern Language Association*
PRSt	*Perspectives in Religious Studies*
RevExp	*Review and Expositor*
RTR	*Reformed Theological Review*

SBLDS	Society of Biblical Literature Dissertation Series
SBLSP	*Society of Biblical Literature Seminar Papers*
SBLSymS	Society of Biblical Literature Symposium Series
SJ	Studia Judaica
SP	Sacra Pagina
ST	*Studia Theologica*
SwJT	*Southwestern Journal of Theology*
TDOT	*Theological Dictionary of the Old Testament*. Edited by G. Johannes Botterweck, Hene Ringgren, and Heinz-Josef Fabry
TJ	*Trinity Journal*
TNTC	Tyndale New Testament Commentaries
TynBul	*Tyndale Bulletin*
UCOP	University of Cambridge Oriental Publications
VE	*Vox Evangelica*
VT	*Vetus Testamentum*
VTSup	Supplement to Vetus Testamentum
WBC	Word Biblical Commentary
WCJS	*World Congress of Jewish Studies*
WUNT	Wissenschaftliche Untersuchungen zum Neuen Testament
ZAW	*Zeitschrift für die alttestamentliche Wissenschaft*

ANCIENT SOURCES

1 En.	1 Enoch
ʿAbod. Zar.	Avodah Zarah
Abraham	Philo, On the Life of Abraham
Alleg. Interp.	Philo, Allegorical Interpretation
b.	Babylonian Talmud
Eccl. Rab.	Ecclesiastes Rabbah
Exod. Rab.	Exodus Rabbah
Gen. Rab.	Genesis Rabbah
Jub.	Jubilees
L.A.B.	Liber antiquitatum biblicarum (Pseudo-Philo)
Lev. Rab.	Leviticus Rabbah
LXX	Septuagint
Meg.	Megillah
Mek. Isa.	Mekilta Isaiah

Midr. Prov.	*Midrash Proverbs*
Midr. Pss.	*Midrash Psalms*
Migration	Philo, *On the Migration of Abraham*
Names	Philo, *On the Change of Names*
Ned.	*Nedarim*
Num. Rab.	*Numbers Rabbah*
Pesiq. Rab.	*Pesiqta Rabbati*
Pesiq. Rab Kah.	*Pesiqta of Rab Kahana*
Pirqe R. El.	*Pirqe Rabbi Eliezer*
QG	Philo, *Questions and Answers on Genesis*
S. Eli. Rab.	*Seder Eliyahu Rabbah*
S. Eli. Zut.	*Seder Eliyahu Zuta*
Sanh.	*Sanhedrin*
Song. Rab.	*Song of Songs Rabbah*
t.	Tosefta
T. Ab.	*Testament of Abraham*
T. Job	*Testament of Job*
T. Naph.	*Testament of Naphtali*
Tanḥ Gen.	*Tanḥuma Genesis*
Tanḥ. Lev.	*Tanḥuma Leviticus*
Tg. Hos.	*Targum Hosea*
Tg. Neof.	*Targum Neofiti*
Tg. Onq.	*Targum Onqelos*
Tg. Ps.-J.	*Targum Pseudo-Jonathan*
y.	Jerusalem Talmud

Acknowledgements

The main contributions to this volume have grown out of papers first given at a conference entitled *New Song: Biblical Hebrew Poetry as Jewish and Christian Scripture for the 21st Century*, held at Ushaw College on the edge of Durham, England, on June 24–25, 2019. We would like to thank all those who took part in the conference, and the wonderful collegial experience over those two days of sharing thoughts and reflections on biblical Hebrew poetry in the lives of Jewish and Christian believers.

The conference was organized by Stephen Campbell, Jean Luah, and Richard Rohlfing, and they would like to thank in particular Theresa Phillips at Durham University's Centre for Catholic Study. She provided invaluable logistical support and wisdom that was essential to the conference that resulted in this volume. We would also like to thank the staff at Ushaw College where the conference took place. We must also recognize those who financially supported the event, including the Centre for Catholic Studies at Durham University; Ushaw College; the Centre for the Study of Jewish Culture, Society, and Politics; and Logos Bible Software.

In addition, the editors would like to thank Derek Brown and all those at Lexham who have helped to turn this project into the book you now hold in your hands. We are grateful to Walter Moberly—a scholar and friend—who gave so much support and counsel that should publicly be recognized. It is a particular pleasure to welcome into the conversation our three respondents—Susan Gillingham, Micheal O'Siadhail, and Jason Byassee—who in their different but complementary ways help to continue the conversation in this volume. Michael Symmons Roberts offered a poetry reading at the conference, and helped us broaden our horizons beyond the normal round of academic papers. We are delighted to be able to include selections of his work here.

As editors, we are also each grateful to family and friends who have sustained us through the editing of this volume with wise counsel and practical support.

We are grateful for the permissions granted to reprint the following poems in this volume:

The poems "A New Song" (p. vii), "Choreography" (pp. 200-201), and "Manumission" (p. 244) by Michael Symmons Roberts are reprinted by permission from Penguin Random House.

The poem "Stretching" (p. 208) by Michael O'Siadhail is reprinted by permission by Bloodaxe Books.

The poem "93" (p. 208) by Maria Apichella is reprinted by permission from Black Spring Press / Eyewear Publishing.

The poem "Transit" (p. 244) by Michael O'Siadhail is reprinted by permission from Bloodaxe Books. The German translation is from Horst Heiderhoff Verlag. The Norwegian translation is from Solum Bokvennen. The Japanese translation is from Shichigatsudoo (July House).

The poem "43 - Dear Inmost Soul" (p. 204) by Edward Clarke is reprinted by permission from Paraclete Press.

The poem "Darkness/Wings" (pp. 206-7) by Jacqueline Osherow is reprinted by permission from Grove Atlantic.

Introduction

This book brings together a diverse roster of Jewish and Christian scholars to explore the reading of biblical Hebrew poetic texts within the context—and for the benefit—of contemporary communities of faith. These are worked examples, each paper representing a discrete interpretive sounding of a poetic text's "wonderous depth."

The genesis of this volume is firmly rooted in the beauty of Durham, the medieval market town in the northeast of England, which is home to Durham University. The University's Department of Theology and Religion and the medieval setting of the city, with commanding presence of the nearly one-thousand-year-old cathedral, helped to create a unique environment for constructive projects such as this. It was within this context of faithful and creative engagement with the Bible that the ideas for this volume began to grow, first into a conference organized by then PhD students Stephen D. Campbell, Richard G. Rohlfing, Jr., Kelsie Gayle Rodenbiker, and Jean K.C. Luah. Ultimately, the organizers became convinced that this conference was a conversation worth sharing and decided to pursue publication. We are very thankful for all the editors at Lexham Press, but especially for Derek Brown, who is a poet himself. He quickly caught the vision of the project and encouraged its development.

Poetry, by its very nature invites—indeed requires—multiple reflections to more fully engage with the subject matter. Therefore, we sought contributors from a diversity of backgrounds to participate in the original conference; similarly so for the responses that were commissioned for this volume. The essay contributions in this volume come from scholars from the United States, the Republic of Ireland, the UK, South Africa, and Israel. What they have in common is a deliberate attempt to locate themselves at the intersection of the academy and communities of faith.

Though large expanses of biblical Hebrew poetry go unexplored, a dip into each respective section of the *Tanakh* is observed. It is our hope that the range of selected texts, traditions, and angles of approach on display will work together to underscore shared challenges and shared rewards. The demands of these ancient and enigmatic texts are many. They foster interpretive flexibility and beckon us into greater personal and corporate humility. We need all conceivable interpretive tools at our disposal. We also urgently need one another.

In chapter one British biblical scholar and Anglican minister John Goldingay looks to the puzzling poetry found in the Testament of Jacob (Gen 49:2-27). His paper seeks to sidestep the many difficulties that modern critical scholarship has identified with this text by taking more account of the fact that the Testament is a piece of poetry. For Goldingay, this fact means that readers must engage with poetic devices such as paronomasia, repetition, ambiguity, allusiveness, asyndesis, jerkiness, and ellipsis, and ask about their effect, rather than seeking to resolve them. The implications of Goldingay's analysis extend well beyond Genesis 49, offering an important introduction to the genre of poetry and its many devices for constructing and conveying meaning.

In chapter two Catholic scholar of Old Testament and ancient Judaism C.T.R. Hayward turns his careful attention to the Song of the Sea (Exodus 15). Both Jews and Christians have long recognized liturgical possibilities in this Song, and Hayward thoughtfully explores the Song's place in the synagogue service and, in the pre-Vatican II Catholic liturgy. The presence of the Song in these traditional liturgies reveals much of how the worshipers view this poem, and its relevance to their own situation.

In chapter three Australian-born, British biblical scholar David Firth explores Hannah's Song from three related angles. Similar to the essay by Hayward, this study is important in that it addresses a poem embedded in narrative. Yet, Firth first considers this text as a discrete poem which displays certain poetic features, all contributing to its overall theme of the reversal of fortunes in a Yahweh's world. Second, and emerging from this, Firth recognizes and explores this poem's ethical perspective on human power structures. Finally, Firth reflects on how the poem is now integrated into the books of Samuel, providing a hermeneutical key through which the book's own ethics can be understood. Using these three angles shows how the poem has been used and therefore also how it continues to form the ethical perspective of the communities who continue to read it today.

In chapter four North American biblical scholar Ellen Davis turns a keen eye to Psalms 38 and 42-43. She illustrates the distinctive value of lament psalms as religious literature, namely their sustained and possibly unique potential for eliciting a response, for generating the involvement of those who repeat or pray them, for changing the conversation from the abstract and technocratic to something that is profoundly humane. Davis considers the theological aesthetics of lament, by looking at Psalm 38 through the eyes of the 17th-century poet-preacher John Donne, the American contemporary poet Gregory Orr, and a piece of lament in the form of contemporary dance. As Davis argues, the poet, preacher, and the dancer, who must reckon regularly with the ineffable power of silence in their artistic performances, may be more adept than most biblical scholars at intuiting how this lament may conduce to human healing and wholeness.

In chapter five South African Bible translator and researcher June Dickie addresses three genres of psalms from a contemporary, reader-response approach to translation. She begins by orienting the reader to the current state of affairs in Bible translation and shows that the notion of "translation" has changed over the years and now frequently includes oral/performance translations and those using other media apart from written text. After this introduction, Dickie presents findings from an empirical study. First, Zulu youth compose and perform their own translations of two praise psalms; secondly, AIDS-sufferers to compose their own laments following the form of biblical lament; and third, a wisdom psalm is "translated" into other media by creative performance-artists. The study shows that contemporary South Africans are finding these ancient texts to speak with emotion, imagination, beauty, and power in a way that makes them memorable.

In chapter six North American Jewish biblical scholar Benjamin D. Sommer turns to the long-debated nature of biblical poetic parallelism. Sommer argues that this important debate has not given sufficient attention to the relationship between our understanding of the biblical poetic line and the function of biblical poems as scripture. Sommer therefore address Psalms 27 and 114 to discuss how theories of prosody help to shape a reading of these poems. In particular, he addresses the religious significance that emerges more clearly from these poems in light of attention to questions of prosody.

In chapter seven, Rabbi Shai Held turns his attention to Psalm 88, undoubtedly one of the darkest and bleakest poems in the Bible. Although this poem is often held up as paradigmatic of the psalms of lament, it differs from most other laments in fundamental ways. Most crucially, the core arc of the lament, the movement from lament to praise, is entirely absent from the psalm. In this essay, Shai Held offers a bold and honest exploration of the ways in which Psalm 88 is even darker and bleaker than many readers tend to see (or are willing to acknowledge). He reflects on whether and how contemporary readers (and pray-ers) might be able to stand inside this psalm, characterized as it is by the psalmist's chronic illness and belief that God forsook him long ago and that his life has been defined by that forsakenness.

In chapter eight North American biblical scholar Katie M. Heffelfinger (now based in the Republic of Ireland) offers a helpful discussion of the nature of biblical prophetic poetry in light of its tendency to convey truth through encounter, emotion, and ambiguity. This tendency has implications for our expectations about what it might mean to be addressed by God. For Heffelfinger, the prophetic poetry of Second Isaiah is a useful point of entry into an examination for such encounter, as it is both intensely poetic and heavily dominated by poems that present themselves as spoken in the LORD's voice. The voice readers hear is emotional and intensely personal. It is not best approached through abstract theological principles, but through the very relationality it offers. By setting this divine discourse in poetic form, this prophetic text offers a rich and varied experience that by their very nature as poetic texts insist that relationship with God invites us into a realm in which mystery, paradox, emotion, and imagination are profoundly relevant. Heffelfinger then examines Isaiah 45:9–25 attending to its poetic self-presentation, highlighting the ways in which it makes meaning through imagery, tension, ambiguity, and the emotional range of its speaking voice and considering the particular demands this chapter makes up on the imagination of the receptive hearer. Heffelfinger then concludes by considering the implications of this approach to reading for contemporary communities of faith, particularly in terms of the nature of Scripture and faithful response to it.

In chapter nine Israeli biblical scholar Yisca Zimran takes up a synchronic-literary reading of the book of Hosea, particularly the "Assyria-Egypt" motif. Through such a reading, Zimran sheds light on the prophetic book as a complete work, with cohesive significance that exceeds the meaning of each individual unit. As Zimran shows, a synchronic reading of the book of Hosea enables involvement of the reader in the interpretive process, and allows a new understanding of the prophecy, based on a sequential reading of individual prophecies, and the interpretive influence one unit has on another. The result is a sequential process of the relationship between God and his nation, which doesn't necessarily emerge from the reading of the isolated units. As Zimran argues, the broader relationship created by this reading of the book enables the reader to place God's relationship with humanity or the nation in a broader context, relatable in all times.

Similarly, the three commissioned responses come from a variety of vantages: Rev. Canon Professor Susan Gillingham (Oxford), brings her expertise and love of Reception History and the Psalter to bear on the (possibly) liturgical phrase "New Song," a phrase that occurs only in the psalter; world-renowned Irish poet, Micheal O'Siadhail, turns his expert eye to the very nature of poetry; and Methodist pastor-theologian Jason Byassee (Vancouver School of Theology) offers an intimate account of the original conference in Durham.

Between the essays and responses lies a brief interlude of "new songs," this volume's own embedded poetry. These poems are dialogue, art interpreting art, poetic *lectio divina*, a contemporary wrestling with the biblical text and thus, inevitably, the divine. The bulk of these poems were written by those in attendance at the 2019 New Song conference. They include poems from world-renowned poets as well as a few more fledgling voices. We intend this as an encouragement to *all* readers, to lift their own voice and sing these old songs new.

Stephen D. Campbell and Richard Rohlfing Jr.

Part One

—

Biblical Hebrew Poetry as Jewish and Christian Scripture

1

On Reading Genesis 49: How Hebrew Poetry Communicates Then and Now

John Goldingay

Coincidentally, some while ago Raymond de Hoop and Jean-Daniel Macchi both published substantial monographs on the Testament of Jacob in the same year.[1] Between them the volumes come to well over a thousand pages. Both were concerned to discuss the many detailed exegetical problems in the poem and to establish its origin.

On the question of origin, they came to quite different conclusions. De Hoop located the key stages in the creation of the chapter in the pre-monarchic and Solomonic period, while Macchi argued systematically for its origin in the Persian period. Both scholars present plausible cases for their conclusions; both are able to do so because they necessarily construct a big picture from a small number of dots. In both cases one is tempted to infer that the critical traditions from which the scholars come play a key role in generating the big picture. That is, the one issues from the mid-twentieth century tradition of dating things in the united monarchy, the other from the late-twentieth century tradition of dating things in the Persian period (it is dispiriting to have to think that our views on critical questions may thus mainly reflect the traditions within which we work, and it makes one wonder what we think we are doing when we undertake this kind of study, and whether we should simply acknowledge that the origin and background of Genesis 49 is a mystery).

---

1. R. de Hoop, *Genesis 49 in its Literary and Historical Context*, OTS 39 (Leiden: Brill 1998); Jean-Daniel Macchi, *Israël et ses tribus selon Genèse 49*, OBO 171 (Fribourg im Breisgau: Akademische Verlagsbuchhandlung; Göttingen: Vandenhoeck & Ruprecht, 1999).

Related questions arise from the detailed studies of the sayings within Jacob's Testament. More than one commentator on Genesis observes ruefully that there is nothing like a scholarly consensus on the interpretation of aspects of the chapter (with no sense of irony over the fact that one generation's scholarly consensus is the next generation's out-of-date misconception). A major reason why de Hoop's study occupies 695 pages is that he seeks to consider all the scholarly suggestions about the detailed interpretation of the chapter. Amusingly, he fails; Gary Rendsburg in his review of the monograph[2] notes two of his own studies that de Hoop does not mention. But how can we make progress in understanding the Testament if there are so many possibilities?

POETRY AND RHETORIC

In relation to both questions, the dating one and the exegetical one, we may reduce the problem by taking more account of the fact that the Testament of Jacob is a piece of poetry and a piece of rhetoric.

[2]Assemble and listen, sons of Jacob,

   listen to Israel your father.

הִקָּבְצוּ וְשִׁמְעוּ בְּנֵי יַעֲקֹב

וְשִׁמְעוּ אֶל־יִשְׂרָאֵל אֲבִיכֶם

[3]Reuben: you, my firstborn,

   my strength and the initiation of my vigor,

Excellence in high position

   and excellence in strength.

[4]Turbulence like water: you are not to excel,

because you climbed your father's big bed.

Thereby you polluted—

   one who climbed my couch!

רְאוּבֵן בְּכֹרִי אַתָּה

כֹּחִי וְרֵאשִׁית אוֹנִי

יֶתֶר שְׂאֵת

וְיֶתֶר עָז

פַּחַז כַּמַּיִם אַל־תּוֹתַר

כִּי עָלִיתָ מִשְׁכְּבֵי אָבִיךָ

אָז חִלַּלְתָּ

יְצוּעִי עָלָה

[5]Simeon and Levi, brothers,

   their blades, tools of violence:

[6]In their council my person is not to come,

   in their congregation my soul is not to join.

שִׁמְעוֹן וְלֵוִי אַחִים

כְּלֵי חָמָס מְכֵרֹתֵיהֶם

בְּסֹדָם אַל־תָּבֹא נַפְשִׁי

בִּקְהָלָם אַל־תֵּחַד כְּבֹדִי

2. Gary Rendsburg, review of R. de Hoop, *Genesis 49 in its Literary and Historical Context*; *JSS* 47 (2002): 138–41.

Because in their anger they killed someone,

   in their pleasure they hamstrung an ox.

7Cursed be their anger because it was strong,

   their outburst because it was tough!

I will divide them in Jacob,

   disperse them in Israel.

8Judah: you,

   your brothers will confess you.

Your hand on your enemies' neck,

   your father's sons will bow down to you.

9A lion cub, Judah

   (from prey, son, you've gone up):

He has bent down, lain, like a lion,

   like a cougar—who would rouse him?

10The staff will not leave from Judah,

   the scepter from between his feet,

until there comes tribute to him

   and the obedience of the peoples to him.

11Tying his donkey to a vine,

   the offspring of his she-donkey to a choice vine,

he has washed his clothing in wine,

   his garment in grape-blood:

12darker of eyes than wine,

   whiter of teeth than milk.

13Zebulun: toward the shore of the seas he will dwell,

   toward the shore for ships, him,

   his flank at Sidon.

14Issachar: a donkey, sturdy,

   lying among the sheepfolds.

15He has seen a resting place, how good it was,

   and the region, how beautiful.

But he has bent his shoulder to the burden,

   become a conscript servant.

כִּי בְאַפָּם הָרְגוּ אִישׁ

וּבִרְצֹנָם עִקְּרוּ שׁוֹר

אָרוּר אַפָּם כִּי עָז

וְעֶבְרָתָם כִּי קָשָׁתָה

אֲחַלְּקֵם בְּיַעֲקֹב

וַאֲפִיצֵם בְּיִשְׂרָאֵל

יְהוּדָה אַתָּה

יוֹדוּךָ אַחֶיךָ

יָדְךָ בְּעֹרֶף אֹיְבֶיךָ

יִשְׁתַּחֲווּ לְךָ בְּנֵי אָבִיךָ

גּוּר אַרְיֵה יְהוּדָה

מִטֶּרֶף בְּנִי עָלִיתָ

כָּרַע רָבַץ כְּאַרְיֵה

וּכְלָבִיא מִי יְקִימֶנּוּ

לֹא־יָסוּר שֵׁבֶט מִיהוּדָה

וּמְחֹקֵק מִבֵּין רַגְלָיו

עַד כִּי יָבֹא שִׁילֹה [שִׁילוֹ קרי]

וְלוֹ יִקְּהַת עַמִּים

אֹסְרִי לַגֶּפֶן עירה [עִירוֹ קרי]

וְלַשֹּׂרֵקָה בְּנִי אֲתֹנוֹ

כִּבֵּס בַּיַּיִן לְבֻשׁוֹ

וּבְדַם־עֲנָבִים סותה [סוּתוֹ קרי]

חַכְלִילִי עֵינַיִם מִיָּיִן

וּלְבֶן שִׁנַּיִם מֵחָלָב

זְבוּלֻן לְחוֹף יַמִּים יִשְׁכֹּן

וְהוּא לְחוֹף אֳנִיֹּת

וְיַרְכָתוֹ עַל־צִידֹן

יִשָּׂשכָר חֲמֹר גָּרֶם

רֹבֵץ בֵּין הַמִּשְׁפְּתָיִם

וַיַּרְא מְנֻחָה כִּי טוֹב

וְאֶת־הָאָרֶץ כִּי נָעֵמָה

וַיֵּט שִׁכְמוֹ לִסְבֹּל

וַיְהִי לְמַס־עֹבֵד

¹⁶Dan: his people will govern   דָּן יָדִין עַמּוֹ

  as one of the clans of Israel.   כְּאַחַד שִׁבְטֵי יִשְׂרָאֵל

¹⁷May Dan be a snake by the road,   יְהִי־דָן נָחָשׁ עֲלֵי־דֶרֶךְ

  a viper by the path,   שְׁפִיפֹן עֲלֵי אֹרַח

one that bites the horse's heels   הַנֹּשֵׁךְ עִקְּבֵי־סוּס

  so its rider falls backwards: וַיִּפֹּל רֹכְבוֹ אָחוֹר

    ¹⁸for your deliverance I have waited, YHWH.   לִישׁוּעָתְךָ קִוִּיתִי יְהוָה

¹⁹Gad: an attacker will attack him,   גָּד גְּדוּד יְגוּדֶנּוּ

  but he himself will attack their heel.   וְהוּא יָגֻד עָקֵב

²⁰From Asher: rich his bread,   מֵאָשֵׁר שְׁמֵנָה לַחְמוֹ

  and he, one who will give a king's delicacies.   וְהוּא יִתֵּן מַעֲדַנֵּי־מֶלֶךְ

²¹Naphtali: a hind set free;   נַפְתָּלִי אַיָּלָה שְׁלֻחָה

  it gives fawns of the fold.   הַנֹּתֵן אִמְרֵי־שָׁפֶר

²²A son, a wild donkey, Joseph,   בֵּן פֹּרָת יוֹסֵף

  a son, a wild donkey: בֵּן פֹּרָת

its daughters by a spring,   עֲלֵי־עָיִן בָּנוֹת

  it has stridden by a terrace.   צָעֲדָה עֲלֵי־שׁוּר

²³People made things bitter for him and fought,   וַיְמָרֲרֻהוּ וָרֹבּוּ

  archers were hostile towards him.   וַיִּשְׂטְמֻהוּ בַּעֲלֵי חִצִּים

²⁴But his bow stayed firm,   וַתֵּשֶׁב בְּאֵיתָן קַשְׁתּוֹ

  his arms and his hands were agile,   וַיָּפֹזּוּ זְרֹעֵי יָדָיו

from the hands of the Strong Man of Jacob,   מִידֵי אֲבִיר יַעֲקֹב

  from there, the Shepherd, the Stone of Israel,   מִשָּׁם רֹעֶה אֶבֶן יִשְׂרָאֵל

²⁵from God, your Father, so he will help you,   מֵאֵל אָבִיךָ וְיַעְזְרֶךָּ

  and Shadday, so he will bless you,   וְאֵת שַׁדַּי וִיבָרְכֶךָּ

with blessings of the heavens above,   בִּרְכֹת שָׁמַיִם מֵעָל

  blessings of the deep lying below.   בִּרְכֹת תְּהוֹם רֹבֶצֶת תָּחַת

Blessings of the breasts and the womb,   בִּרְכֹת שָׁדַיִם וָרָחַם

²⁶your father's blessings—   בִּרְכֹת אָבִיךָ

They have been stronger than the blessings of those who   גָּבְרוּ עַל־בִּרְכֹת הוֹרַי

                                      [conceived me,

beyond the desirable things on the age-long hills.

They will come on Joseph's head,

  on the brow of one set apart among his brothers.

עַד־תַּאֲוַת גִּבְעֹת עוֹלָם

תִּהְיֶיןָ לְרֹאשׁ יוֹסֵף

וּלְקָדְקֹד נְזִיר אֶחָיו

[27]Benjamin: a wolf who will maul,

  in the morning will eat prey,

  and towards the evening will divide spoil."

בִּנְיָמִין זְאֵב יִטְרָף

בַּבֹּקֶר יֹאכַל עַד

וְלָעֶרֶב יְחַלֵּק שָׁלָל

My translation assumes that the Testament is rhythmic poetry and that it works with the conventions of Hebrew verse in mostly comprising a series of short self-contained sentences that divide into two parts with two or three or four stresses in each part. We could haggle over some of the details, as well as over the framework assumption, though I do not think they affect the burden of my paper. I will refer to the parts of a line as cola. The second colon commonly restates the first or complements it or explains a question raised by it or simply completes it. In Genesis 49 there are two or three tricola, and there is also one colon with five stresses, as the Masoretes punctuate it. In the translation I have worked with the Masoretic Text's punctuation in the sense that I have followed the way it uses maqqephs and thus the way it generates the rhythm in the lines. I have resisted the temptation to revise this aspect of its punctuation even though a bit of revision could produce a text that is neater and would thus please me more. While most lines are syntactically self-contained, some involve enjambment, where either a line is syntactically incomplete or it leads into another line that cannot stand on its own.

While the sayings about individual people and about the clans that trace their ancestry back to these individuals all take poetic form, beyond that feature, they vary. They differ in how far they focus on the individual and how far they focus on the clan, and they differ in length from two or three cola to eighteen or nineteen. The length of the Judah and Joseph sections coheres with the prominence of these individuals in Genesis 37–50 and with the prominence of these clans in Israel, but for the other sayings there is no evident explanation for the variation in length. Perhaps the variety reflects their being of separate origin among the clans, or perhaps a single poet composed them in their varied forms.

Poetry in the Hebrew Scriptures switches easily between the second person and the third person; in Genesis 49 the switch happens within the Judah and Joseph declarations (the Reuben declaration is second person, the others are entirely third person). Using the second person means that rhetorically the poetry directly addresses the people named. Conversely, using the third person means that it speaks about these people to others who are listening because the declaration has significance for them, and/ or it puts the people who are the subjects into the position of seeming to overhear statements that are actually about them. For related reasons Jacob himself can switch between speaking as "I" and referring to himself as "he."

These rhetorical features relate to a question that intrigues me. Whatever the poem's date, how do we think it was delivered to people and received by them? It is less of a question if Genesis and prophetic books came into being through the work of Second Temple scribes working like us in our studies. If their work was then read by anyone else, it was presumably by other scribes or by people like students studying Torah in a yeshiva. But if somehow the message of the prophets and the stories in Genesis, for instance, reached ordinary people, how did they reach them?

I assume that in some way written text and oral communication complemented each other. I infer from the rhythmic nature of Hebrew poetry that the messages were chanted in some way, and I invite my students to imagine prophets like Amos like rap artists, which helps the imagination in this connection. One of the features of rap is that artists can vary the number of words in a line as long as they keep the rhythm going. The analogy with rap thus helps one to see how prophets could have chanted their messages while varying the length of lines and cola–they just had to keep the rhythm going. Did someone rap Jacob's Testament?

Simeon	and Levi,	brothers,	
their blades	tools of	violence:	
In their council	my person	is not	to come,
in their congregation	my soul	is not	to join.
Because	in their anger	they killed	someone,
in their pleasure	they hamstrung	an ox.	
Cursed	their anger	because it was	strong,
their outburst	because it was	tough!	
I will divide them	in Jacob,		
disperse them	in Israel.		

I have a vivid memory of listening as an undergraduate to Gwynne Henton Davies declaim Isaiah's song about the vineyard, in his preacherly Welsh Hebrew, and I will not mind if my students remember my rapping Amos.

ALLUSIVENESS, ANAPHORA

What about the many exegetical questions in Genesis 49? I do not suggest that the appeal to poetry can solve all the questions about them, and specifically not the enigmatic *'ad kî yābō' šîlōh*; in the translation I follow what Rashi calls the midrashic interpretation—Rashi himself goes with the Targum in taking the literal interpretation to be a messianic one.

But in connection with the poetic nature of the Testament, I make five comments. And in connection with each of them I note other examples, which come from Jeremiah because I happen to be working on Jeremiah at the moment.

First, poetry may not be syntactically neat; it may be allusive and elliptical. It may not provide grammatical links between phrases, and it may thus leave the audience to provide them if it is to understand the lines. That requirement is, then, one of the ways in which the audience has to involve itself with the message, and it means we should resist the suggestion that we need to tidy the text up and make it easier to read. Thus Jacob's comments about Reuben, *excellence in high position, excellence in strength*, and then *turbulence like water*, hang loosely onto the description of Reuben that precedes and that follows. In content, the two phrases about excellence belong with what precedes and the phrase about turbulence belongs with what follows, which is the way the Masoretes have divided the verses. Jacob's point is that despite the excellence of Reuben's position and his energy, Reuben's turbulence means he will not *excel* in the future. But in form, the three noun phrases belong together. The form and the meaning thus work against each other. Typically, poetry sucks us into one direction, then discomforts us.[3]

In Jacob's closing line about Reuben, his curt condemnation refers to Reuben polluting his bed. The plural word for "bed" suggests its size, and the repetition of the verb "climbed" draws further attention to the impressive nature of this bed; normally one lies "down" on a mat on the floor. But within this final line about Reuben, Jacob moves from second person to third person, in a way that does not strictly clash with Hebrew

---

3. Kathleen Scott Goldingay, in a comment on a draft of this paper.

or English grammar but is nevertheless subtle and requires close atten-tiveness. It does tempt scholars into emending it.

Jeremiah, too, can be elliptical, and in Jeremiah, too, an odd implica-tion of poetry's elliptical nature is to make one more respectful of the text as it comes down to us, and resistant to the temptation to rewrite it. In connection with some particular elliptical words (8:13), William McKane comments, "since their sense is so suspect, they should be delet-ed."[4] My reaction is the opposite: if a line's sense is difficult, it deserves close attention.

Jeremiah's declaration about a woman surrounding a man (31:22) is an example. It may be an aphorism, which as such then parallels the elliptical nature of many aphorisms in Proverbs, whose puzzling nature derives in part from our not knowing their context and background. In a study of Ecclesiastes, Elsa Tamez includes a list of Hispanic aphorisms which can seem obscure to someone from a different background, but she has the cultural background that enables her to explain them for the reader.[5] In connection with the Scriptures, attention to the language of elliptical texts against the background of related texts may be illuminating. In the line about a woman surrounding a man, Jeremiah's reference to Yahweh creating a new thing could properly make one think about the signifi-cance of that language in Isaiah 40–55. Jeremiah's use of the verb šābab could properly make one think of his own use of the verb šûb. For the modern student of Jeremiah, reading in light of modern thinking about women and men can produce interesting results in the interpretation of this declaration, though they may not be results that Jeremiah would rec-ognize. Yet perhaps one should recognize that speaking elliptically gives the audience permission to discover things from one's words that one did not put there. The point parallels the observation that once something is put into writing and is put out there, the author loses control of its meaning. The great advantage of prose is its capacity for precision and clarity, but it thereby sacrifices suggestiveness. The great advantage of poetry is the reverse. How wise of God to inspire both prose and poetry within the Scriptures!

---

4. William McKane, *A Critical and Exegetical Commentary on Jeremiah*, 2 vols. (London: Bloomsbury; repr., 2014) 1:189.
5. Elsa Tamez, *When Horizons Close: Rereading Ecclesiastes*, trans. Margaret Wilde (Maryknoll: Orbis, 2000), 146–154.

The effect of allusiveness on a poem's original hearers may be to encourage attention, so that the audience is more deeply affected by the message when it becomes more explicit or direct. In his message about Egypt, Jeremiah begins:

> Get ready breastplate and shield,
>   advance for battle ...
> Why have I seen—
>   they are shattered,
>   they are falling back. (46:3–5)

While the actual scriptural text provides people with an introduction telling them that the poem is about Egypt and that it relates to the imminent battle of Carchemish, Judahites listening to Jeremiah in the temple courtyards might initially have no idea of what it refers to, though they might be aware that a decisive event was imminent and might know that its result would be decisively important for them. Yahweh is then giving them some insight about it. But Jeremiah does not make clear who is commissioning these warriors, whether it is he, their commander, or Yahweh—though it does not matter too much; the point is the actual commission. Nor does Jeremiah make clear whose warriors are being commissioned or whose warriors are running for their lives—for instance, Babylon's or Egypt's. Which way the listeners understood it would make a difference to their potential response. Some people would be glad to hear of the comeuppance of the Egyptian army and king that had defeated and killed Josiah. On the other hand, it was the Egyptians who had put Jehoiakim on the throne, and official Judahite policy was likely pro-Egyptian, and people who were inclined to see the Egyptians as potential allies and supporters would not welcome the idea of an Egyptian defeat. So the message works with the allusiveness that often characterizes prophecy when it expresses itself in poetry. It makes people listen and requires them to listen on if they are to get the point. The exhortation compares with some other exhortations to Judah itself (4:5–6; 6:1–6), which are ironic in a different direction as they urge Judah to prepare to be attacked.

Second, that same line about Reuben from which we started illustrates how Hebrew poetry likes anaphora, or more simply, repetition. A suspicion of repetition can generate suggestions about emending the biblical text, like a suspicion of ellipsis, but the suspicion is again inappropriate. Anaphora can be a means of heightening impact. *Excellence* in high position and *excellence* in strength, Jacob exclaims about Reuben, and he then goes on that Reuben is not to *excel*, which adds to the devastating implications of his statement. "You would have been worthy of the birthright, the dignity of the priesthood and the kingship," Pseudo-Jonathan comments. "But because you sinned, my son, the birthright was given to Joseph, the kingship to Judah, and the priesthood to Levi." The repetition adds to the impact.

A famous example in Jeremiah:

> I looked at the earth, and here empty and void;
> and to the heavens, and their light was not there.
> I looked at the mountains, and here, shaking;
> and all the hills rocked.
> I looked, and here, humanity was not there,
> and every bird in the heavens—they had flown. (4:23–25)

There was no need to repeat the verb *I looked*, but the effect is to keep taking us inside the experience of Jeremiah's looking and to imagine what he is imagining. The repetition makes it harder for us to be distanced from the scene that Jeremiah portrays.

PARONOMASIA, DOUBLE MEANINGS

Third, Hebrew poetry can be sophisticated in its use of paronomasia. In Jacob's address, Judah, *Yəhûdâ*, is one whom his brothers will confess or recognize or praise, *yādâ*. Dan will govern, *dîn*. Gad will be the victim and the initiator of attack, *gādad* or *gûd*. Paronomasia opens the poet's eyes and opens the audience's eyes to things that we might otherwise not see or to links that we would otherwise not make. Judah's brothers do in due course recognize him, by recognizing David. Dan had seemed to lose out in the allocation of land to the clans, but in the end he triumphs. Gad, too, has a hard time with the vulnerability of its land east of the Jordan.

Jeremiah is fond of a particular form of paronomasia that uses an idiom whereby one combines the infinitive form of a verb with its finite form and thus emphasizes the actuality of what the expression refers to. But on several occasions, he combines the infinitive of one verb with the finite form of a different but similar verb; commentators are then again sometimes inclined to "correct" his formulations. "I will gather and finish them off," he says (8:13), *'āsōp 'ăsîpēm*; more literally, "in gathering, I will finish them off." Gathering is an appropriate image in the context, because he goes on to talk about grapes and figs. But gathering is often a sinister metaphor, for death, and thus it links neatly with the verb that suggests bringing about the end of something.

Fourth, Hebrew poetry likes to play with double meanings. So is *turbulence* a critique of Reuben, as the Septuagint suggests, or is it a warning about Reuben's fate, as the Vulgate and the Targums suggest? Maybe it is both. In the saying about Simeon and Levi, perhaps something similar applies to the word that I translate *blades*. For this word the Sheffield Dictionary notes four possible alternative meanings: counsel, weapon, staff, and beguilement. If the word could be understood as having any of these meanings, they would not be inappropriate.

The beginning of the Reuben verses note that Reuben inherited an abundance of energy and forcefulness from Jacob because he was Jacob's firstborn; he is thus the first fruit of his father's manly strength, *rē'šît 'ônî*. One could half-expect a first child to be full of such dynamism and vitality, but there are also temptations attaching to the position of number one, and Reuben fell for them. In light of what follows, one might imagine Jacob also being aware of the other possible meaning of *rē'šît 'ônî*, "the initiation of my trouble" (Vulg., Aq, Sym).

Jeremiah promises,

> The waywardness of Israel will be looked for, but there will
> be none,
>> and the wrongdoings of Judah, but they will not be found,
>> because I will pardon whomever I let remain. (50:20)

Does Jeremiah mean there is no waywardness to be found because all waywardness will be pardoned? Or is the promise that no waywardness will be manifested, as a result of the creative potential of being pardoned and restored?

A recurrent example from Jeremiah comes when he comments on the way Judah's lifestyle is bringing disaster upon it, and adds,

> This is your *rā'â*, because it is *mār*,
>> because it has reached right to your heart. (4:18)

The word *rā'â* usefully has the ambiguity of the English word *bad*; there is a neat play on this ambiguity in the question why bad things happen to good people. *Rā'â* covers both the bad things that people do and the bad things that happen to people, and it points to the insight that often the bad things that we do issue in bad things happening to us. The Tanakh recognizes that life does not always work out that way, but often it does, and Jeremiah sees this dynamic in Judah in his time. In the comment I quoted, is Jeremiah talking about the people's bad life or their bad fate? The effect of his language is to make them think about that question and about the implications of the two sides to the meaning of *rā'â*. His words play on the link between dire behavior or nature and dire trouble— perhaps because he treats direness as one thing, and can move between behavior and fate as aspects of the one thing. The ambiguous nature of his words is heightened by the description of the *rā'â* as *mār*, as bitterness or as something bitter. There is one other passage where Jeremiah uses the word *mār*, in 2:19, again in association with *ra'*. Like *ra'*, bitterness can be a description of the harshness and toughness of wrongdoers or of the harshness or toughness of what happens to them as a result of their wrongdoing. Yet further, in the comment I quoted, Jeremiah has just referred to the rebelliousness that is expressed in Judah's wrong-doing, and "rebel" is the verb *mārâ*. Rebellion is bitter in its execution and bitter in its results for the rebel. For Judah, it is so in the way it has "reached right to your heart" or your mind. Is there something dire and bitter about the very heart of Judah's life? Or is there something dire and bitter about the way the results of its wrongdoing reach the very heart of its life? It would be less confusing for Western readers to think of the dire trouble as being bitter and of the dire behavior or nature as reaching as far as the mind or heart, but Jeremiah does not encourage this distinction. The nature and life of Jerusalem has found its organic outworking in the calamity that has come to it. Actions simply issue in consequences, which are aspects of the same reality.

METAPHOR

In Jacob's Testament, the most complex double meaning comes in the Joseph blessing. This example also takes me, fifthly, into the fact that poetry likes metaphor—indeed, arguably it is the key feature that distinguishes poetry from rhythmic prose. In Jeremiah, I am inclined to see more of the text as poetry than other interpreters do, but I acknowledge that this distinction between poetry and rhythmic prose is tricky to make. It seems likely that the distinction is sharper in our minds than it was in (say) Jeremiah's, and that part of our problem is the need to decide how to lay out a written, printed text.

Jeremiah's poetry makes extensive use of metaphor and simile. It is a major way in which he does his thinking, not just his communicating. Arguably, it is necessarily so. There are few things one can say literally about God and his relationship with us; we are bound to use metaphor in this connection. Metaphor does more than add to the impact of an idea. It makes ideas possible. It makes it possible to think and see things, and it then makes it possible to communicate them. Metaphor makes it possible to speak about things that we could not otherwise speak of. Metaphor also makes it possible to say more about things that we could otherwise speak of, as we speak of one thing we know in terms of another thing that we know. When poetry uses an image, it encourages the listener to reflect on the imagery. It opens up possibilities. Words in prose are more inclined to have tight, defined meaning. Words in poetry are more open.

Jeremiah (like Hosea) manifests an extravagant profusion of his metaphorical thinking and language.

- God is king, and in different ways both the world and Israel are the people he governs. People must bow down before him. He has a cabinet. He sends messengers. He is commander-in-chief and sends his (heavenly and earthly) armies to bring trouble to rebels. He exercises authority. He makes pacts. He may listen to intercession.
- God is guide. He points out the path for people to walk. They must go after him rather than go after other guides (gods).
- God is master. People must serve him, and not other masters.
- God is builder, but also destroyer.
- God is shepherd. He provides.
- God is father. He begets children. He adopts children. Israel belongs to his household. He passes on a domain.
- God is husband. He marries a wife. He commits himself to faithfulness and expects faithfulness. He is lord. He is jealous and he objects to his wife whoring and committing adultery. He divorces.
- God is teacher. He expects attentiveness and obedience.
- God is farmer. He plants vines, olives, and figs. He looks for fruit. He plants trees and fells them. He irrigates or withholds irrigation. He controls access to his garden and resents its invasion and attack. But he can devastate it if it fails to produce fruit. He has a farmhand.

In Jacob's Testament, the first line about Joseph repeats itself, as the
Reuben verses do. The repetition gives the audience chance to absorb
the intriguing description of Joseph as a son who is *pōrāt*. The Septuagint
and the Vulgate and the Targums take *pōrāt* as a participle from *pārâ* that
qualifies *bēn* and means fruitful, but the form is anomalous and the feminine is odd. Which makes one wonder if the word is a noun. But *pōrāt*
might also make you think of Ephraim. Back in Genesis 41, when Ephraim
was born, Joseph already linked his name with the verb *pārâ*: it suggested
fruitfulness. Directly or overtly, then, Jacob speaks here of Joseph, but (as
Luther put it) Ephraim is hiding between the formulation of his words.[6]

When Jacob then comes to talk about Joseph's "daughters," BDB takes
the "daughters" to be the branches of that fruitful tree, but *bānôt* never
elsewhere refers to plants, only to animate beings. So "daughters" might
make people think again about that word *pōrāt* and remember that a *pere'*
is a wild donkey, so that a *pōrāt* could be a wild she-donkey who would
naturally have daughters. The Joseph clan is a female donkey, which is
evidently not an insult, not least because donkeys are really important;
they are the equivalent of a pick-up truck. This understanding fits the
animal imagery that is used to characterize many of the clans. The metaphor of daughters might then refer to the villages in Joseph's territory;
they would be equivalent to Judah's daughters, which appear elsewhere.
But within the poem, as young donkeys, they suggest that Joseph (especially in the person of Ephraim) has the energy and agility that ranges
free by springs and by the walled terraces that stretch along mountain
slopes. Outlining these possibilities is complicated and hard to assimilate
when presented orally, though in a way that problem is useful because
it links with another question that intrigues me. How does one think
about the communication of Hebrew poetry with its subtlety, ambiguity,
ellipsis, and paronomasia? When one listens to a poem for the first time,
one may "get" aspects of it, but one will get more when one hears it again
and then again; the same dynamic will apply to reading it by oneself. Did
Israelite prophets and poets—or scribes—hope that people would have
their words ringing in their heads as they went away and that they might
see more of their implications as the words stayed with them? Or did they

---

6. Martin Luther, *Lectures on Genesis 45–50*, vol. 8 of *Luther's Works*, ed. Jaroslav Pelikan
and Helmut T. Lehmann, American ed. (Philadelphia: Muehlenberg and Fortress; St.
Louis: Concordia, 1955–1986), 295.

assume that they themselves would deliver their poems on a number of occasions, so that people might pick up more the second and third time?

In this Testament "Father Jacob" introduces himself as a teacher instructing his sons and laying out the fruit of his insight for them. He thus parallels "Father Solomon" in Proverbs 1–9, who also speaks as a teacher laying out his insight for his sons. The actual authors of these poems hide discretely behind Jacob and Solomon; they draw attention away from themselves and seek to enhance the impact of their teaching by inviting their audiences to collude with them in imagining it on the lips of these key figures. The fact that both teachers speak in poetry makes for some memorability and allows the average line to look at its subject from two angles and to sustain interest. But Solomon's poetry in Proverbs 1–9 works by being simple and univocal. There may be double meanings (the strange woman may be an allegorical figure) but the surface meaning is clear and important. Jacob's poetry is denser, and it thrives on being equivocal. While Jacob does speak as a father-teacher, in the opening verse of the chapter he announces that he is going to declare what is to happen in days to come, which makes him sound more like a prophet, and prophets often do speak in dense and puzzling ways.

Jacob is as much like Jeremiah as like Solomon. Jeremiah is more puzzling than (say) Amos, he likes paronomasia and ellipse and ambiguity as Jacob does, and he likes animal imagery as Jacob does. I have assumed that some of the impasse over Jacob's poetry (as over aspects of Jeremiah) derives from the assumption that Jacob surely spoke univocally. And there are advantages in being easy to understand. But it is also possible to make things too easy for people, with the result that they get it at one level but at another level fail to get it, and sometimes the necessity of working hard to understand ultimately helps understanding. When Jacob is difficult to understand, the answer may be to work with the puzzles and the ambiguities rather than seeking to eliminate them. I do not see why both subtle, elusive poetry and straightforward, plain poetry should not have been directed at the same people at the same time, as we ourselves may profit from being addressed plainly and univocally, and also elusively and puzzlingly. The Jeremiah scroll alternates between the univocal and the allusive, whether or not Jeremiah himself was responsible for both.

POETRY EXPRESSING CONVICTIONS

If Jacob's poetic rhetoric was designed to get some convictions home to people, what were those convictions? If we seek to express the implications of his Testament in prosaic terms, what results? If we cannot know what period it comes from, does the poem itself indicate what it might be designed to do for Israel in *any* of the possible periods? One might say that the question underlying the Testament is, how should Israel think of the situation and experience of the twelve clans? The Testament mediates between the persons of the twelve sons and the destiny of the clans that will grow from them. It implies that their destiny relates sometimes to the action of their ancestors, though also sometimes to aspects of their political situation, and sometimes to factors in their geographical position. Genesis has referred to the actions or experiences of Reuben, Simeon, Levi, Joseph, and Judah. Their actions or experiences are the main background to Jacob's declarations about the first three brothers, and they are part of the background in connection with Judah and Joseph. For the six brothers who come between Judah and Joseph, Jacob's declarations relate to the geographical and/or political positions of the clans that will issue from them; the clan's geographical and political position is also the other consideration that applies to Joseph. For Benjamin the declaration relates to his clan's later action, though this consideration also applies to Judah.

One way or another, the Testament thus provides some account of the way:

- Reuben fails to have the prominence that one would expect.
- Simeon and Levi disappear geographically from the number of the clans.
- Judah provides Israel with its leadership.
- Zebulun's territory lies between the two seas.
- Issachar has fine territory in Jezreel but has to submit to the Canaanites there.
- Dan has to fight for territory in the southwest and then in the north.
- Gad has to defend itself from its rivals for territory east of the Jordan.
- Asher has rich country on the northwest coast.
- Naphtali has broad rolling pastures to the north.
- Joseph thrives in a way that manifests the persistence its ancestor showed.

- Benjamin is especially violent, though the comparison with a wolf need not be pejorative.

Genesis 49 is a highpoint in Genesis, and Genesis as a whole does not simply transcribe events but tells stories that have varying relationships to actual events. One might compare Genesis 49 with Genesis 1, which gives us no information on the literal, concrete process whereby God brought the world into being but does give us information on what God was doing, in bringing the world into being. Or one might compare Genesis 49 with Daniel 11, which expresses itself as talk about the future but is nearly all talk about the past: giving an account of the past in the form of prophecy makes clear that the sequence of events was under God's control. Much of Genesis 49 reflects the actual experience of the twelve clans, which is projected back into Jacob's awareness to express how it was not chance but part of a bigger picture, part of a coherent broader story that goes back to the ancestor who gave Israel its name. In Genesis, it was no ordinary human being who passed on what seemed to be revelations from God. It was Israel's original father figure. Further, while some of Jacob's words are statements, sometimes he expresses his own commitment or prayers or hopes; and prophecy regularly presupposes the assumption that what actually happens will depend on an interaction between God's declarations of intent and people's response to them.

In this connection, what Jacob had to say to each clan was significant for all the clans.

- Reuben needed to learn that one act whereby he grossly flouted society's proper values in the realm of family and sex could have disastrous results for his clan. The same applied to Simeon and Levi in the realm of violence. (Outside the framework of the Testament, Levi found that God could use its violence and make Levi his servant.) The other clans might be wise to learn from Simeon and Levi's story.
- The clans as a whole would properly acknowledge Judah for the achievements that stemmed from its violence, and for its marvelous flourishing, and so would the peoples who submitted to Judah. Outside the framework of the Testament, they did submit, in David's day, though Judah's hegemony and flourishing did not last, so that for a later audience, Jacob's words would raise

the question whether that hegemony and flourishing would return—as prophets said they would.

- There is an overlapping point to be made about Joseph. Joseph the man has already had to deal with hostility but has survived and triumphed through his firmness and agility and the support and blessing of God, which will also issue in blessing in the future that parallels Judah's. Again, outside the framework of the Testament, they did issue in blessing in the flourishing of the northern kingdom, though this blessing, too, did not last—but prophets again said that it would return.
- Zebulun, Issachar, Dan, Asher, Naphtali, and Benjamin would have futures which involved an interaction between their geographical position with its blessings, their political position with its threats, and their personal qualities with their potentials. The lines about these clans include the ones that look least directly relevant to the other clans, but the truth that this fact hints at is that the life and the fate, the blessings and the sufferings, of each clan matter to all the clans. They are a family.

The inclusion of Jacob's Testament in the Torah implies that it continued to be significant for the people of God. It is indeed a high point in Genesis, a climax to the book, a sometimes-enigmatic poem that is animated and vibrant, thought-provoking and suggestive, significant and challenging.

2

Shirat Ha-Yam (the Song of the Sea) in Jewish and Christian Liturgical Tradition

C.T.R. Hayward

Nahum Sarna rightly describes *Shirat Ha-Yam* (The Song at the Sea) as "a spontaneous, lyrical outpouring of emotion on the part of the people who experienced the great events of the Exodus";[1] and one answer to the question of "how to read Hebrew poetry within communities of faith today" is provided by some of those communities themselves: we might read such poetry in the setting of liturgical worship. Indeed, liturgical use of biblical poetry might also enable faithful readers or reciters to find "meaning for today" in those texts, by setting them alongside other Scriptural and non-Scriptural information hallowed by the religious memories of the worshipers, regularly repeated and internalized in the thoughts and ritual actions of their several communities. The striking poetic form, and the equally striking contents, of *Shirat Ha-Yam* ensured from the outset that it was a composition that would always attract attention;[2] and its intricate language, seamlessly intertwining tantalizing references to events

---

1. See Nahum M. Sarna, *The JPS Torah Commentary: Exodus* (Philadelphia: Jewish Publication Society of America, 1991), 75. For the importance of emotion in the religious performance of texts in Jewish antiquity, see now the insightful and significant observations of Angela Kim Harkins, "The Performative Reading of the *Hodayot*: The Arousal of Emotions and the Exegetical Generation of Texts," *JSP* 21 (2011): 55–71; idem, "The Emotional Re-Experiencing of the Hortatory Narratives Found in the Admonition of the *Damascus Document*," *DSD* 22 (2015): 285–307.
2. See the classic study of Judah Goldin, *The Song at the Sea* (New Haven: Yale University Press, 1971); Robert B. Alter, *The Art of Biblical Poetry* (New York: Basic Books, 1985),

past, present, and future demand and still demand from the attentive
worshiper that perceptiveness and heightened awareness required by
all who would appreciate fine poetry.

Jews and Catholics through the ages have found no difficulty in allot-
ting liturgical roles to *The Song at the Sea*. This brief essay cannot explore
those roles exhaustively, but will confine itself to considering the song's
place in the synagogue service in the course of the daily morning Psalm,
Pᵉsuqei de Zimra, and the citations of Exodus 15:11 and 18 in the prayer
'ezrat 'aboteinu following the recital of *Shema'*. In the Catholic liturgy, from
antiquity until the early twentieth century, the canticle *Cantemus Domino*
was sung each Thursday as part of the Office of Lauds;[3] and the first three
verses of Exodus 15 are sung at the Easter Vigil ceremonies, following the
reading of Exodus 14:24-31, the account of the crossing of the sea.[4] The
canticle at Lauds is given in the version of St. Jerome's Vulgate; but the
verses set for the Easter Vigil derive from a Latin translation earlier than
St. Jerome's time, the *Vetus Latina*, which in most respects represents a
rendering into Latin of the Old Greek (Septuagint) version.[5] The presence
of the song in these traditional liturgies reveals a good deal about how
the worshipers view this poem, and its relevance to their own situation.

In what follows, we need to be aware of a simple, but somewhat limiting fact of liturgical scholarship. Whereas Christians wrote down prayers
and liturgical formulae from a comparatively early date, Jews (famously)

50-54; James L. Kugel, *Traditions of the Bible: A Guide to the Bible as it Was at the Start of
the Common Era* (Cambridge: Harvard University Press, 1998), 588-612.

3. For the re-ordering of the Breviary as ordered by Pius X in 1911, see Pierre Batiffol,
History of the Roman Breviary, trans. Atwell M.Y. Baylay (London: Longmans, Green,
1912), 317-30.

4. The Office of Lauds referred to in this essay indicates the service used in the Roman
Church until the major reform of the Breviary promulgated by Pius X in 1911: an
English translation of the whole pre-1911 Breviary was made by John, Marquess of
Bute, *The Roman Breviary: Reformed by Order of the Holy Oecumenical Council of Trent*,
2 vols (Edinburgh and London: Blackwood, 1879). The traditional Easter Vigil liturgy
designates Exod 15:1-3 as a *tract*, that is, an extended or "drawn out" text to be chant-
ed by the cantors: the musical settings of tracts, although somewhat formulaic, are
often complex and demanding, requiring considerable expertise in performance. The
Latin text is cited from *Officium Majoris Hebdomadae et Octavae Paschae* (Regensburg:
Pustet, 1923).

5. See David L. Everson, *The Vetus Latina and the Vulgate of the Book of Exodus* (Leiden:
Brill, 2014); and for a general survey of recent research into the Old Latin, see Pierre-
Maurice Bogaert, "The Latin Bible," in *The New Cambridge History of the Bible. From the
Beginnings to 600*, ed. J. Carleton Paget and Joachim Schaper (Cambridge: Cambridge
University Press, 2013), 505-14.

had no comprehensive "Prayer Book" giving a continuous form of the synagogue service until Rav Amram Gaon produced his *Seder* in the ninth century CE.[6] There is much, therefore, that we simply do not know, and this needs to be recognized. At the same time, this paper is not primarily concerned with the history of liturgy, so we shall attempt to work with what is known, or what can (more or less) firmly be discerned, from the texts we have. These texts leave little doubt that behind the present liturgical traditions lies a long history of engagement with this song and its meaning, which sometimes Jews and Christians share, and which at other times serve to distinguish the two religions. Important in this Jewish-Christian shared experience of the song is the version of the Greek Septuagint, which must first, and all too briefly, demand our attention.

THE SONG AT THE SEA IN THE
OLD GREEK (SEPTUAGINT) VERSION

What is probably the oldest Jewish interpretation of the song known to us is preserved in the Septuagint, the Greek translation of what became the Old Testament of the Christians.[7] Of the many distinctive characteristics of this translation, we can mention only those most important for our purposes. First, it regularly uses a single Greek word for what in the Hebrew are two differing expressions. So, for example, the Hebrew verbs *rāmāh* ("throw upwards") and *yārāh* ("throw downwards") are both translated "he threw" (vv. 1 and 4); the verbs *tᵉšlach* ("you sent") and *nāšaptā* ("you blew") are both rendered as "you sent" (vv. 7 and 10); in verse 8, the graphic verbs *nitstsᵉbû* ("they stood") and *qāpᵉ'û* ("they were congealed")

---

6. It is of interest to note that Rav Amram, resident at Sura in Babylonia, produced his *Seder* in reply to a request from scholars in Barcelona. Much debate attends the original form and contents of the *Seder*, which was used, re-used, and significantly changed over the years: see Stefan C. Reif, *Judaism and Hebrew Prayer: New Perspectives on Jewish Liturgical History* (Cambridge: Cambridge University Press, 1993), 185-87; for the text, see E.D. Goldschmidt, *Seder Rav Amram Gaon* (Jerusalem: Mosad Rav Kook, 1971) [Hebrew]. For the text of the synagogue service, we have used *The Complete Art Scroll Siddur*, trans. Rabbi Nosson Scherman, 2nd ed. (New York: Mesorah Publications, 2003).
7. For the Greek text of LXX, we have used the edition of John W. Wevers, *Septuaginta: Vetus Testamentum Graecum Auctoritate Scientiarum Gottingensis editum II.1: Exodus* (Göttingen: Vandenhoeck & Ruprecht, 1991). The Greek translation of the Pentateuch is dated by most scholars to c. 280-250 BCE: see Jennifer M. Dines, *The Septuagint* (London: T&T Clark, 2004), 41-42, 50-51.

appear as "were solidified"; and the single noun *tromos*, "trembling," does duty for Hebrew *rā'ad* ("trembling") and *pachad* ("dread") in verses 15 and 16. These, and other examples of the same translational procedure, serve to give the Greek version of the poem a particular cohesiveness, the purpose of which becomes clearer in light of two further translational peculiarities, namely repeated references to glory, and a stress on divine action. "Glory" words appear seven times, doing duty for a variety of Hebrew expressions.[8] For example, in verse 1 "for He is highly exalted," *kî gā'ōh gā'āh*, becomes "for gloriously He has been glorified"; the ambiguous Hebrew *we'anwēhû* of the following verse is taken as "and I shall glorify Him";[9] and the *tehillōt* "praises" of verse 11 become "glories." The Lord is the principal actor. The Hebrew of verse 4 declares that the Egyptians "were sunk" in the sea, whereas LXX insist that "He," that is, the Lord, "drowned" or threw them into the sea, and the next verse says that "He" (the Lord) covered them, the Hebrew declaring that the deeps covered them. Famous is the LXX's reconstruction of verse 3, which tells us that "the Lord is *breaking* wars" in place of the Hebrew "the Lord is a man of war." The Greek also echoes its version of verse 3 in its translation of verse 7, "and in the vastness of your glory you *broke* the enemies."

In its Jewish-Greek dress, therefore, the song confronts us as a tightly organized, mighty assertion of the Lord's glory, that is, his reputation, his majesty, his splendor before the nations, especially the Egyptians. This is underscored by the fact that the Greek word *doxa* is first used by the LXX translators with reference to the Lord in this poem; and thereafter the Lord's "glory" will be used to speak of his presence in the tabernacle and the priestly service. Here we might pause to notice explicit reference to the sanctuary in the song, at verses 13 and 17. Might the LXX, therefore, imply that the song was sung liturgically? Scholars have long noted that

---

8. On the LXX's use of "glory" in this poem, see Alain le Boulluec and Pierre Sandevoir, *La Bible d'Alexandrie*, 2 volumes: *L'Exode* (Paris: Cerf, 1989), 2:171–72. LXX's repeated use of the verb *doxazō* in verses 1, 2, 6, and 11 takes on significance when it is noted that these verses represent the first occurrences of the expression in LXX; and it is not used again until Exod 34:29, 30, and 35, where it translates Hebrew *qrn* denoting the radiance of Moses's face following his experience of the Divine Presence. For a study of the whole song in the LXX version, see Deborah Gera, "Translating Hebrew Poetry into Greek Poetry: The Case of Exodus 15," *BIOSCS* 40 (2007): 107–20.

9. The *Mekhilta of R. Ishmael* on this verse offers a variety of interpretations of the word, one of which, "I will enshrine him," Sarna incorporates into his English translation of the poem: see his *The JPS Torah Commentary*, 77, thereby signaling the importance of the "sanctuary language" which we encounter in Exod 15:13, 17.

the LXX begins the song with the first person plural form "let us sing" against the singular "I will sing" of the Hebrew, suggesting perhaps some kind of (future?) congregational participation.[10] It would be hazardous to draw any conclusions from this evidence, although it is reasonable to point out that the Greek translation at least "opens the doors" to thoughts about how this song might be appropriated by future generations of readers or singers.[11] In this respect, it is worthwhile to recall that manuscripts of the LXX books have been found at Qumran, suggesting that the LXX's reading of the song could have been known to Jews in the homeland.

BEYOND THE SEPTUAGINT:
THE SONG IN JUDAISM AND EARLY CHRISTIANITY

Mention of the sanctuary in the song, and the business of "glory" in the LXX, require further consideration, since Philo of Alexandria, whose writings were preserved by Christians, describes a Jewish ascetical group called Therapeutae whose fame has spread far and wide.[12] These men and women, Philo tells us, modelled their liturgical practices on aspects of the temple service, the high-point of their celebrations (almost certainly on the Feast of Weeks, which "closes" the season of Passover) being focused on the Song at the Sea, when the men and women of the group united to sing like the two choirs led by Moses and Miriam at the Sea of Reeds. Philo describes their experiences in somewhat hyperbolic fashion; but he leaves us in no doubt that these ascetics have overcome their passions, casting aside the restraints which the physical body imposes on the soul,

---

10. Likewise, the LXX's version of the Song of Miriam (Exod 15:21) begins in the same way. The idea that it was sung antiphonally, at least, is ancient: see Sarna, *The JPS Torah Commentary*, 76; Kugel, *Traditions of the Bible*, 593–95; and below.

11. This remains the case whether or not one accepts the view of Henry St. J. Thackeray, *The Septuagint and Jewish Worship: A Study in Origins*, 2nd ed. (London: Oxford University Press, 1923) that the origins of LXX are to be sought in the liturgical needs of Egyptian Jews. While most students no longer accept Thackeray's particular argumentation and the evidence he employed to support it, the notion that the Greek translators of Scripture may well have been motivated by liturgical factors (*inter alia*) is quite widely held: see, e.g., Dines, *The Septuagint*, 47–50.

12. On the Therapeutae, see Emil Schürer, *The History of the Jewish People in the Age of Jesus Christ*, 3 volumes, rev. and ed. by Geza Vermes, Fergus Millar, and Matthew Black (Edinburgh: T&T Clark, 1979), 2:591–97; Joan E. Taylor, *Jewish Women Philosophers of First Century Alexandria: Philo's 'Therapeutae' Reconsidered* (Oxford: Oxford University Press, 2003); Timothy H. Lim, *The Holy Books of the Essenes and Therapeutae* (New Haven: Yale University Press, 2013).

and have achieved at the moment when they sing the song that union with the heavenly world towards which all their spiritual efforts have been directed. For them, the redemption of Israel once realized in ages past at the exodus from Egypt is made present in their own lives, as they take part in the great song.[13] The chanting of the song is the goal, the high point of their liturgical celebrations: they have arrived at their destination, which might be described as lying outside time itself.

Elsewhere in his writings, Philo talks of the song as a hymn of victory sung by those who have overcome the passions and the sinful mind which accompanies them, the four-footed horse mentioned in the song representing symbolically the four passions (folly, cowardice, intemperance, and injustice) yoked to the mind mounted upon them.[14] Such persons are equipped to sing the Song at the Sea in the Lord's sanctuary, as indeed they do according to the Christian apocalypse of John 15:3, where the seer views singers in the heavenly world chanting the Song of Moses, as he calls it.[15] Not long after the composition of that Christian document, we encounter in the Mishnah a dispute among Rabbinic authorities about the song which strongly suggests that it was sung publicly in some kind of formal worship. Thus, R. Akiba states that it was recited in the same fashion as Hallel, whereas R. Nehemiah declares that it was recited in the same manner as the Shema.[16] This is the only reference in the Mishnah to the song; but some centuries later we learn from the Babylonian Talmud

---

13. See especially Taylor, *Jewish Women Philosophers*, 322–34, noting (326) Reuven Kimelman's comments on the redemption from Egypt as a foreshadowing, if not an actual paradigm, of future redemption: "Therefore, [j]oining in the chorus of past redemption ... the worshipper finds him/herself praying for, if not actually announcing, the future redemption." Taylor is quoting Kimelman's article "The Shema' and its Rhetoric: The Case for the Shema' being more than Creation, Revelation and Redemption," *Jewish Thought and Philosophy* 2 (1992), 111–56.

14. See, for example, Philo, *Leg.* II.102; *Agr.* 80–83; *Ebr.* 11; *Sobr.* 13.

15. For reasons which will become apparent presently, we might here record the observations made nearly a century ago by Robert H. Charles, *A Critical and Exegetical Commentary on the Revelation of St. John*, 2 vols (Edinburgh: T&T Clark, 1920), 1:xcix–c, cii, concerning knowledge and use of this apocalypse by the Roman Church. He also briefly noted (*A Critical and Exegetical Commentary*, 2:36) the song's possible use in the temple service, and its appearance in the synagogue liturgy, and in some of Philo's writings. Revelation's reference to the Song of Moses in a liturgical setting is significant in the light of the esoteric and mystical character of the apocalypse delineated by Peter Schäfer, *The Origins of Jewish Mysticism* (Princeton: Princeton University Press, 2009), 103–11.

16. See *Soṭah* 5:4.

that it was sung in the temple at the time of the Sabbath afternoon sacrifice.[17] It is almost impossible to establish whether the Talmud is conveying historical information on this point, but, for our purposes, it matters little; what is of significance is the fact that some Jews, by the fifth or sixth centuries CE at the latest, believed that the song had been a part of the temple service.

Returning briefly to the Christians, we may record that Eusebius of Caesarea, who lived c. 260 to 340 CE, in other words, not long after the redaction of the Mishnah, identified Philo's Therapeutae precisely with Christians, and in so doing brings their liturgical and ascetic practices into prominence, possibly as a primitive template for worship which Christians (particularly ascetics and contemplatives) of his own day might emulate.[18] Certainly the Song at the Sea eventually became the first of nine "odes" or "canticles" which were regularly included as a group of texts collected at the end of the Psalter in complete LXX Bibles. This seems to be well established by the sixth century CE at the latest;[19] and the liturgical use of some of the odes continues to this day amongst the eastern churches.[20] With these somewhat disparate pieces of information in mind, let us now consider the place of the song in the liturgical texts as they have come down to us in traditional usage.

---

17. See b. Roš Haš. 31a, describing how the text was divided into portions for recitation separately on succeeding sabbaths: what precisely was sung, and when, is disputed.
18. See Eusebius, Hist. Eccles. II.16-17, and Epiphanius of Salamis, Haer. 29.4, 9-10; Jerome, Adv. Jovinianum 2.14. Valuable also are the insightful comments of Jean Daniélou, Théologie du Judéo-Christianisme (Tournai: Desclée, 1958), 408-9. Taylor, Jewish Women Philosophers, 279-82, rightly notes the chronological gap between Therapeutae and early Christians; but the influence of Eusebius was such that his linking of the two groups would not have passed unnoticed in Christian thinking.
19. See Sidney Jellicoe, The Septuagint and Modern Study (Oxford: Clarendon, 1968), 202-3. Detailed discussion of the manuscripts which record the Odes, their dates, and their provenance is provided by James Mearns, The Canticles of the Christian Church Eastern and Western in Early Mediaeval Times (Cambridge: Cambridge University Press, 1914): see 7-14 for Greek manuscripts; and for the evidence from the Roman Church (which principally concerns us) see 51-53. See also Heinrich Schneider, Die altlateinischen biblischen Cantica (Beuron: Hohenzollern, 1938).
20. For details and discussion, see Heinrich Schneider, "Die biblischen Oden in Jerusalem und Konstantinopel," Bib 30 (1949): 433-52.

THE SONG AT THE SEA AND THE PSALTER

The LXX Bibles are not alone in placing *Shirat Ha-Yam* in association with the Psalter. In rather different ways, both the service of the synagogue and the Catholic breviary make a similar move. The latter allotted the song as the proper canticle for Lauds of Thursday, and the canticle was invariably followed by the chanting of Psalms 148, 149, and 150, concluding the Psalter. Indeed, it was these three, final poems of the Psalter which led to the designation of the whole service as "lauds," as is evident already from the *Rule of St Benedict* 13.[21] In the synagogue morning service, the section known as P^esuqei de Zimra has at its core Psalms 145 (in reality Ps 144:15)–150, preceded and followed by a designated blessing: this arrangement is attested by the Babylonian Talmud as followed by some pious individuals, but apparently had yet to become a statutory part of the service.[22] These psalms achieved that distinction universally, and to them were eventually added 1 Chronicles 29:10–13; Nehemiah 6:9–11; and *Shirat Ha-Yam*. Apparently at first the recital of the song was confined to Sabbaths; but the evidence suggests that it was very popular amongst Roman Jews, who extended its use to weekdays—when, precisely, this happened, is unknown, but the eleventh century *Mahzor Vitry* records and approves of the practice.[23]

---

21. The Rule is usually dated to around 540 CE. See also Louis Duchesne, *Christian Worship: Its Origins and Evolution*, 5th ed. (London: SPCK, 1919), 446, 452, 454–55, and the comments on the canticles at Lauds in the Rule of St. Benedict by Dom Suitbert Bäumer, *Histoire de Bréviaire*, trans. Reginald Biron (Paris: Letouzey et Ané, 1905), 248–49. For the history of the Office of Lauds, its relationship to Matins, and the place of Psalms 148–150 in these services, see Robert Taft, *The Liturgy of the Hours in East and West: The Origins of the Divine Office and Its Meaning for Today*, 2nd rev. ed. (Collegeville: Liturgical Press, 1993), 191–209.
22. See *b. Shabbat* 118b; Ismar Elbogen, *Jewish Liturgy: A Comprehensive History*, trans. Raymond P. Scheindlin (Philadelphia: Jewish Publication Society of America, 1993), 72–73, and Abraham Z. Idelsohn, *Jewish Liturgy and Its Development* (New York: Schocken Books, 1972), 82–83, who notes the great reverence accorded to Psalm 145 and its verse 16, "Thou openest Thy hand, and fillest all things living with favour," ensuring that those who recited the Psalm three times each day were assured of a place in the world to come (*b. Ber.* 4b). The blessings associated with these Psalms may date from a later period. The Cairo Geniza documents preserve differing forms of them: attempts to find fixed patterns in the early witnesses for these blessings are critiqued by Joseph Heinemann, *Prayer in the Talmud: Forms and Patterns*, trans. by Richard S. Sarason, SJ 9 (Berlin: de Gruyter, 1977), 9–10, especially n. 15.
23. This is the *Mahzor* of R. Simhah ben Shmuel, who died in 1005. On the Roman provenance of the recital of *Shirat Ha-Yam*, see Elbogen, *Jewish Liturgy*, 75–76.

Its present place in the synagogue service ensures that it stands as the goal and climax of the psalmody which has preceded it. Indeed, there are many verbal links between Psalms 145–150 and the song, of which we may mention here the use of the verb *rûm* "be high" (Exod 15:12; Pss 145:1; 148:14); *niphal* forms of *yārē'* "to fear" (Exod 15:11; Ps 145:6); and references to "the deeps" (Exod 15:5, 8; Ps 148:7), the Divine Name (Exod 15:2; Ps 148:13), and dancing (Exod 15:20; Ps 149:3). The element of joyful praise and thanksgiving which pervades Psalm 150 is present also in the song. It is God's Kingship, however, his divine sovereignty, which binds the song to Psalms 145–150: as the liturgy stands today, the final assertion of the song, "the Lord shall reign as King for ever and ever," takes up the opening declaration of Ps 145:1, "I shall exalt You, O my God the King," providing a frame for all that is recited in between.[24]

The song itself leads up to affirmation of God's kingship with pervasive references to movement: the movement of the elements of the created order in carrying out the divine plan (Exod 15:4–8); the movement of the Egyptians intent on destroying Israel (Exod 15:9–10); and the movement under divine guidance of Israel into the promised land (Exod 15:13–17). The Song can be read as describing a solemn procession of God's redeemed people, the people of Israel, from pharaoh's forces through the waters of the sea and beyond: the goal of that procession is the Lord's sanctuary, the mountain of his inheritance, the place where he abides, the sanctuary which his hands had established (vv. 13, 17). From the standpoint of the "narrative" set out in the song, that goal lies in the future, and leaves open for the worshiper the question whether the song is to be read historically, referring to Israel's eventual sojourn at Mount Sinai to receive the Torah; or to the more immediate future when she will settle in the land of Israel and build the temple on Mount Zion; or to a more distant future, when the Lord shall restore His Shekhinah to Zion once and for all. The liturgical goal of the Song at the Sea, however, might equally be the service of the synagogue in which the worshiper is now participating, with *Pᵉsuqei de Zimra* preparing the way for the formal recital of Shema with its resounding affirmation of the Lord's unity and kingship.[25] Indeed,

24. For further references to the divine kingship within this section, see Pss 146:10; 148:1; 149:2.
25. Note especially the response "Blessed be the Name of the Glory of His Kingdom forever," which immediately follows the recitation of the first verse of *Shema'*. According to the Mishnah (*Yoma* 3:8; 6:2), this was proclaimed in the temple by the worshipers when they heard the high priest pronounce the Divine Name on the Day of Atonement.

the prayer *'ezrat 'aboteinu*, which follows the recital of Shema, leads up to explicit quotation of verses 11 and 18 of the song, "Who is like unto Thee, O Lord, among the gods? Who is like unto Thee, renowned in holiness, fearful in praises, performing wondrous deeds?" and "The Lord shall reign as King for ever and ever."[26]

The Catholic use of this song at Lauds also ensures its close association with the final poems of the Psalter, highlighting the elements of praise and thanksgiving for the decisive acts of the Almighty in redeeming Israel. What is immediately noticeable, however, is that the song does not represent the final word of the psalms chanted at Lauds: Psalms 148–150 follow it, and it will have been preceded by the recitation of four other psalms, so that it stands embedded in the midst of the psalmody allotted to Thursday.[27] It is sung once a week, not every day; and it is one of six other Old Testament canticles used at Lauds throughout the weeks of the liturgical year.[28] Five of these other canticles appear in the collection of the Septuagint's "Odes," which we mentioned earlier: these appear to have been so significant for Christian readers and worshipers that the scribes from early times collected and wrote them out in a convenient "supplement" to the Psalms. The sixth canticle is the Song of King Hezekiah (Isa 38:10–20), which the Church understood as expressing a prefiguring of Christ's resurrection. In this scheme of things, the Song at the Sea is but one of an admittedly small number of solemn canticles extracted from the Books of Moses and the Prophets (Daniel being included in their number by the Christians) which focus on deliverance and redemption, and the thanksgiving and praise which that deliverance should elicit.

---

26. On the place of these verses in the prayer, which he describes as a "vigorous hymn," see Elbogen, *Jewish Liturgy*, 21–22. Note also that in Exod 15:11, the word *qōdeš* translated above as "holiness" can also be rendered as "sanctuary."

27. In the traditional Office of Lauds on weekdays, the *Miserere*, Psalm 51 (Psalm 50 LXX), is regularly recited in first place. On Thursdays, this is followed by Psalms 90, 63, and 67 (LXX 91, 62, 66), then the canticle *Cantemus Domino*, and the final three psalms of the Psalter.

28. The canticles are arranged as follows: on Sunday, the Song of the Three Young Men (Dan 3:52–88 LXX) is recited; on Monday, a canticle from Isaiah 12:1–6; on Tuesday, the Prayer of Hezekiah (Isa 38:10–20); on Wednesday, the Song of Hannah (1 Sam 2:1–10); on Friday, the Song of Habakkuk (3:2–19); and on Saturday, the final Song of Moses (Deut 32:1–43).

THE SONG AT THE SEA AND THE PASCHAL CELEBRATIONS

With the Easter Vigil, however, the song takes on a very specific role. The traditional liturgy for Holy Saturday (*Sabbato Sancto*) includes the reading of Israel's safe passage through the sea (Exod 14:24–31), followed at once by the first three verses of the Song at the Sea in the Old Latin version: "Let us sing to the Lord, for gloriously He has been covered with honors: horse and mounted rider He has thrown forward into the sea: helper and protector He has become for me, for salvation. This is my God, and I shall honor Him: my father's God, and I shall exalt him. The Lord destroys wars: the Lord is His Name."[29] What governs the liturgy on this night is the sacrament of baptism. In Christian thought, the crossing of the waters of the sea is one of the most ancient and significant pre-figurations (or types) of the sacrament, noted as such already in the New Testament.[30] Those who had been preparing for baptism in the weeks leading up to Easter would know that their forthcoming passage through the baptismal waters re-presents Christ's passion and death, and their coming out of the waters a re-birth into a new status as Christians, a status which (as we shall see presently) this liturgy defines; and that those baptismal waters draw their significance from Israel's earlier passing through waters at the sea from slavery and death to freedom and light. On this occasion, the *Cantemus Domino* is chanted at night, just as the going out of Egypt took place at night. "This night," for the Catholic liturgy, has an immediate and powerful significance, since the proclamation of Easter, which has preceded the scriptural readings, has made repeated reference to "this night." Prominent among these is the declaration, "This is the night, in which first You made our fathers, the children of Israel led forth out of Egypt, to cross over the Red Sea on a dry path."[31] The proclamation is made by a deacon, who has earlier identified himself as one privileged to be gathered among "the number of the Levites," a phrase evoking the

---

29. *Cantemus Domino gloriose enim honorificatus est: equum et ascensorem projecit in mare: adjutor et protector factus est mihi in salutem. Hic Deus meus et honorabo eum: Deus patris mei, et exaltabo eum. Dominus conterens bella: Dominus nomen est illi.*

30. See especially 1 Cor 10:1–4. It should be noted that St. Paul, writing to gentile converts at Corinth, does not set out to explain the language he uses here; and it is reasonable to assume that the links between baptism and the crossing of the sea had been made by Christians before his time.

31. *Haec nox est, in qua primum patres nostros, filios Israel eductos de Aegypto, Mare Rubrum sicco vestigio transire fecisti.*

world of the temple service.[32] He will continue to speak of "this night" on which the Egyptians were despoiled, the Hebrews made rich, "the night on which heavenly things are joined to those earthly, divine things to human."[33] The Latin translation of the segment of the Song at the Sea has as its centerpiece, thanks to the LXX, the assertion that the Lord is the worshiper's helper, protector, and salvation, the last a key word in the Christian economy of redemption. All this is pointing forward to that moment in the liturgy when the candidates will be baptized; but not before a prayer, which immediately follows the final words of the chant *Cantemus Domino*, has summed up what has been said.

> O God, whose ancient miracles we observe to shine forth brilliantly also in our own times: who by the water of regeneration art occupied with the salvation of the nations, as Thou didst deliver one people from Egyptian persecution by the power of Thy right hand: grant that the fulness of the whole world may cross over into the children of Abraham and into the dignity of Israel: through our Lord Jesus Christ ...[34]

Whether this prayer presents the exodus from Egypt and the Song at the Sea simply as a "pre-figuration" or a "type" of what is believed to be happening in this liturgy may, perhaps, be questioned. Are these traditional Christian theological terms strong enough to bear the extraordinary weight of what is being claimed here?[35] "The children of Abraham" and "the dignity of Israel" are already existing realms—perhaps ideal or utopian realms, but realms nonetheless—into which the newly baptized are to cross over; without the continuing reality of the original events

---

32. The identification of Christian deacons with the Levites is already attested in *Apostolic Constitutions* II.25, and taken as traditional by St Jerome, *Epistle* 146 *Ad Evangelum*, noting that bishops, presbyters, and deacons hold in the church the same corresponding positions as those occupied in the temple by Aaron, his sons the priests, and the Levites, respectively.

33. *O vere beata nox, quae exspoliavit Aegyptios, ditavit Hebraeos! Nox, in qua terrenis caelestia, humanis divina junguntur.*

34. *Deus, cujus antiqua miracula etiam nostris saeculis sentimus: dum, quod uni populo, a persecutione Aegyptiaca liberando, dexterae tuae potentia contulisti, id in salute gentium per aquam regenerationis operaris: praesta; ut in Abrahae filios et in Israeliticam dignitatem, totius mundi transeat plenitudo. Per Dominum.*

35. For the classic treatment of Christian typology, see Jean Daniélou, *Sacramentum Futuri: Études sur les Origines de la Typologie Biblique* (Paris: Beauchesne, 1950), and the insights of Robert Murray, *Symbols of Church and Kingdom: A Study in Early Syriac Tradition* (London: T&T Clark, 2006), especially 290-94.

at the sea, and the song which celebrates them, the prayer loses much of its point. The "ancient miracles" can be understood as a present reality and, while the "one people" is contrasted with the many nations, it is a fact that Scripture explicitly (1 Chron 17:21) speaks of Israel precisely as "one people," a unique people serving the only God. The Song at the Sea, as represented by its segment here, points the way forward to the world of Abraham's children and the dignity of Israel, which will be further illustrated in the remaining, lengthy readings (all from the Septuagint), culminating in the baptism of the catechumens and their entry into what some patristic sources describe as the land of milk and honey.[36] They have experienced the Lord as a helper and protector who has become for them "salvation"; and their first celebration of the Eucharist following baptism brings them into the temple, the sanctuary where they receive the body and blood of the one who spoke of his body as a temple.

CONCLUDING REMARKS

The journey from Hebrew Bible to liturgical use by Jews and Christians of the Song at the Sea is lengthy and poorly mapped; but some things stand out, and point to ways in which it has been, and still is appropriated by believers of both religious traditions. The "lyrical outpouring" of emotions of those who first experienced the going out from Egypt, as we have seen, has sufficient references to an undefined future to evoke application of this song to future generations: by the time of the Septuagint, it appears that the song is a great communal anthem, with its invitation "Let us sing!" calling to all Israel. Between the Hebrew Bible and its ancient versions on the one hand, and the liturgical texts of Jews and Christians on the other, lies a "tunnel period" not exactly replete with information; but enough has survived for us to permit certain observations.

First is the association of this song with the temple service. Sometimes this association is faintly delineated, as perhaps in the case of the LXX translation; sometimes it is rather more pronounced, as in the case of the Therapeutae; later, it is explicit, as we know from the Babylonian Talmud. Second is the public chanting of the song, on the Jewish side strongly implied by the Mishnah, on the Christian side strongly implied

---

36. In some churches it was the custom to give milk and honey to the newly baptized: see Tertullian, *Cor.* 3; *Res.* 16; and Hippolytus, *Ap. Trad.* 21–34, the last possibly providing evidence for practice in the Roman Church of the early third century.

by its inclusion among the LXX "odes" which form a supplement to the Psalter. Perhaps not surprisingly, this issues ultimately in the direct juxtaposition of the song with the triumphal, concluding praise-poems of the Psalter in both Jewish and Christian liturgy. One can only speculate whether the singing of the Song at the Sea along with those psalms at Lauds by Roman Christians "spilled over" into Jewish liturgical custom. It was at Rome, most probably, that the song became part of daily *Pesuqei de Zimra*, and since the work of Daniel Stökl Ben Ezra and others on the inter-relatedness of Jewish and Christian liturgical customs, such speculation may not be entirely idle.[37] Third, the song in a manner of speaking describes a journey in several stages, with the goal of the Lord's sanctuary set clearly before it. That the sanctuary might be construed by both Jews and Christians as the heavenly temple, such that the song sets out a "mystical" destination for those who take part in it.[38] Certainly as matters now stand, it prepares the Jewish worshiper for the recital of Shema, and is indeed briefly reprised in the following prayer *'ezrat 'aboteinu*. Its appearance in the Easter liturgy for Christians underscores its fundamental importance for any understanding of baptism, anciently referred to as *phōtismos*, "illumination" of mind, soul, and spirit.[39] Perhaps some such "enlightenment" befell the Therapeutae as they sang the song at the climax of their Pentecostal celebrations, as dawn was breaking.

Finally, for the individual worshiper, or the individual reader of this poem, *Shirat Ha-Yam* may come to mean many things; and those who have undergone trials and tribulations in their lives, only to experience divine help in their sorrows, can reflect on this ancient text with thanksgiving and reverence. For it does indeed speak of a "crossing over," and that may incline some to discern mystical possibilities as a text which speaks of the world to come as much as of this world. Traditional Jewish exegesis of Exodus 15:1 from early times understood the introductory statement *'āz yāšîr mōšeh* as meaning not only "then Moses sang," but also as "then Moses shall sing," indicating that the Song at the Sea will be the great

---

37. See above, n. 19, and Daniel Stökl Ben Ezra, *The Impact of Yom Kippur on Christianity*, WUNT 163 (Tübingen: Mohr Siebeck, 2003), 290–321.

38. For some Jews, this may have been under consideration before the turn of the eras: see the remarks of Peter Schäfer, *The Origins of Jewish Mysticism*, 147–148 concerning Exod 15:11 and the Songs of the Sabbath Sacrifice found at Qumran.

39. See Justin, *Dialogue* 61; Clement of Alexandria, *Paidagogos* I.6.26:2. The New Testament background for such thinking may be encountered at Hebrews 6:4; see also *Odes of Solomon* 11:14.

victory hymn of those who experience the Messianic redemption at the end of days.[40] Although St. Ambrose was writing for Christians, his words about the exodus and its victory hymn are patient of a much wider application and are worth quoting as a finale to this essay.

> Those who pass through this fountain, that is to say, from earthly things to heavenly—which is indeed the *transitus*, the Passover, the passing over from sin to light—those who pass through this fountain will not die but rise again.[41]

---

40. See *Mekhilta de R. Ishmael, Shirta* 1:8–10 (Rabbi, with reference to the Resurrection); *b.Sanh.* 91b. It should also be noted that *Shirat Ha-Yam* was almost invariably included in midrashic lists of ten songs said to have been chanted at various points in Israel's history: see the lists set out and discussed by Philip S. Alexander, Appendix A "The Midrash of the Ten Songs (Tg. Cant. 1:1)," *The Targum of Canticles Translated, with a Critical Introduction, Apparatus, and Notes* (Collegeville: Liturgical Press, 2003), 205–9. To Alexander's lists should be added *Tanhuma Beshallah* 10 (middle). Alexander (207) notes that Origen, *Commentary on Canticles* Prologue 4, mentions a list of seven songs, five of which agree with those listed in the various forms of the Midrash of the Ten Songs: in Origen's list, *Shirat Ha-Yam* stands first.
41. Ambrose, *De Sacramentis* I.12.

3

Hannah's Prayer (1 Samuel 2:1-10): On the Interface of Poetics and Ethics in an Embedded Poem

David G. Firth

INTRODUCTION

That Hannah's prayer (1 Sam 2:1-10) stands apart from the material around it in Samuel is obvious to most readers.[1] It is clearly poetic, unlike the rest of the text, which is prose. Although much of the preceding chapter had taken place in the temple at Shiloh,[2] nothing has prepared readers for the clearly elevated language we find here. Indeed, Hannah's earlier prayer, though evidently passionate, was apparently offered silently (1 Sam 1:10–13, cf. 1 Sam 1:26), triggering Eli's misinterpretation of her actions. But here, she not only prays, she speaks, something stressed by the prayer's introduction, which combines verbs for prayer and speech (*watithpalel wat'omer*). Although "prayed and said" might sound clumsy in English, the combination of *pll* (pray) and *'mr* (say) is relatively common in the Hebrew Bible.[3] Nevertheless, within this narrative the combination of

---

1. Silvia Becker-Spörl, *"Und Hanna betete, und sie sprach ..." Literarische Untersuchungen zu 1 Sam 1, 1–10* (Tübingen: Francke, 1992), 16-17, points to shifts in style and chronology around the frame of the prayer as stressing its distinctive character.
2. Conceivably, the phrase *bebeyt YHWH* (1 Sam 1:7) could be construed as a reference to the tabernacle, but that Eli was sitting by the doorposts of the *heykal* (1 Sam 1:9) indicates a more substantial building.
3. It occurs elsewhere in Deut 9:26; 2 Kgs 6:1-18; 19:15; 20:2; Isa 37:15; 38:2-3; 44:17; Jer 32:16; Jonah 2:1-2; 4:2; Dan 9:4; 2 Chron 30:18; and 32:24, occurring when the content of

verbs is given special focus because of the narrator's previous observation that Hannah had prayed silently, meaning that the presence not only of spoken prayer, but a prayer which is in elevated language, is given special prominence. None of this takes away from the fact that the prayer as we currently have it has been placed into the existing narrative, something evident from the fact that were the prayer to be removed, it is doubtful that anyone would miss it. Indeed, although 1 Samuel 2:11 can now be read as what happened after Hannah had prayed, it would follow equally well if it came immediately after 1 Samuel 1:28, closing off the paragraph that reported the family's arrival at the temple in 1 Samuel 1:21. With most scholars, therefore, it is right to recognize the distinctive nature of this poem within its current context.[4]

Yet, it is important in a final form reading of Samuel to give heed to this text, though to do so by noting the effect of the placement of Hannah's prayer within its wider context. That is, to adapt Bailey's approach, we must ask why a compiler would include a piece which clearly does not develop the narrative (in the sense of exploring the plot) at this point.[5] To some extent, an answer to this was already given by Childs, when he argued that this poem (along with those in the Samuel Conclusion) provide

---

the prayer is to be reported directly. By contrast, in 1 Sam 8:6, Samuel is said to have prayed, but there we only have פלל because the content of the prayer is not reported. Of these parallels, the most similar is Jonah 2:1-2 in which a poetic prayer is included, showing the same pattern of shifts within the text as we see here. This makes the suggestion of Theodore J. Lewis, "The Textual History of the Song of Hannah: 1 Samuel ii 1-10," VT 44 (1994), 25 (followed by David Toshio Tsumura, The First Book of Samuel NICOT [Grand Rapids: Eerdmans, 2007], 136) that "prayed" be omitted on the grounds of lectio brevior less persuasive, especially as his one LXX exemplar can be explained in other ways.

4. E.g., Hans Joachim Stoebe, Das erste Buch Samuelis KAT (Gütersloh: Gerd Mohn, 1973), 106, Ralph W. Klein, 1 Samuel WBC (Waco: Word, 1983), 14. The separation of the poem from the surrounding narrative is a different issue from whether or not Hannah might herself have uttered this prayer. Andrew E. Steinmann, 1 Samuel CC (St Louis: Concordia, 2016), 76-77, thus argues there is nothing in the poem that could not have been prayed by Hannah. This cannot be ruled out (not least because she could have used an existing prayer), but does not of itself alter the distinctive literary form here. Likewise, the date at which the prayer was added, whether relatively early, or late in the post exilic period (e.g., Walter Dietrich, "Stefan Heyms Ethan ben Hoshaja und der Hauptverfasser der Samuelbücher," in The Books of Samuel: Stories—History—Reception History, ed. Walter Dietrich [Leuven: Peeters, 2016], 23), does not affect this point.

5. See Randall C. Bailey, "The Redemption of Yahweh: A Literary Critical Function of the Songs of Hannah and David," BibInt 3 (1995), 215.

a hermeneutical key by which we are to read Samuel from a theocentric perspective.[6] This points to the fact that Hannah's prayer is intentionally placed in the text at this point,[7] and that, though it might be separate on literary-critical grounds as coming from a different source to the main narrative, it is not to be set aside as "secondary." Rather, as will be argued here, it is only when we understand Hannah's prayer as a poem that is embedded in its narrative context, and not simply added to it, that we can fully appreciate its function within the book. To demonstrate this, it will first be necessary to consider the poem as a work in its own right (since the narrative actually highlights this feature) and second, to reflect on its function within the book of Samuel in which it establishes the motif of the reversal of fortunes, a motif that runs through the whole book. Approached this way, it will be possible to see how the poem's embedded nature impacts the book as a whole and is generative for the ethic it develops.[8]

READING HANNAH'S PRAYER AS A DISTINCT POEM

As a first step in this reading process, we need to read the prayer as a discrete text.[9] This properly recognizes that it is, in literary terms, a work that is distinctive from the context in which it is now found. As a complex piece of poetry, this text also poses numerous questions, only some of which can be addressed in this paper. Indeed, even the surrounding text's own designation of this poem as a "prayer" might be questioned if we operate on a narrow definition of this as something spoken by a human to God since much of the poem is clearly addressed to a listening audience, with only a small portion addressed directly to God. This,

---

6. Brevard S. Childs, *Introduction to the Old Testament as Scripture* (London: SCM, 1979), 273.

7. See James W. Watts, *Psalms and Story: Inset Hymns in Hebrew Narrative* (Sheffield: JSOT, 1992), 19–40, and idem, "'This Song': Conspicuous Poetry in Hebrew Prose," in *Verse in Ancient Near Eastern Prose*, eds. Johannes C. de Moor and Wilfred G.E. Watson (Neukirchen-Vluyn: Neukirchener Verlag, 1993), 345–58, for markers of inset poetry.

8. This approach also takes seriously the suggestion of H.H. Klement, *2 Samuel 21–24: Context, Structure and Meaning in the Samuel Conclusion* (Bern: Peter Lang, 2000), 112–13, that Hannah's prayer be seen as a point of prophetic insight within the book.

9. Note Walter Dietrich, *Samuel: Teilband I. 1 Sam 1–12* BKAT (Neukirchner-Vluyn: Neukirchner Verlag, 2011), 65–107, who separates the poem out from the surrounding context to treat it in its own right. Dietrich believes the poem itself contains an initial stratum from pre exilic Judah which has been supplemented substantially by a post exilic reworking (*1 Samuel 1–12*, 77–81), but for our purposes the text will be considered as a whole.

perhaps, is why the poem is often referred to as "Hannah's Song" in the secondary literature, even though at no point is she said to have sung. The task of treating the poem as a discrete text needs to begin, however, by noting precisely that the poem itself does not self-define any genre (and, of course, the categories of song and prayer are not necessarily contradictory), and that therefore any genre label we give is something that emerges from the process of reading it. Both of these designations ("song" and "prayer")[10] can be supported to some extent from within the text—the elements of rejoicing which mark the poem's opening (note the verbs *'lts, rmh,* and *smch* in verse 1) are consistent with a song, even if they do not require it. But Yahweh is addressed directly only at two points in the poem, in the last word of verse 1 and the middle of verse 2—and then only by a pronominal suffix. The rest of the poem speaks about Yahweh, naming him nine times (vv. 1 [x2], 2, 3, 6, 7, 8, 10 [x2]), but it does not address him.[11]

Should we therefore speak of this poem as a prayer or a song or something else? We have already observed that prayer and song are not necessarily to be set in opposition to one another, but it is also the case that the genre we assign to a text shapes our reading of it. The simplest option is simply to describe this text as a poem since its poetic features are easily

---

10. The *Gattung* of the poem is also much disputed; see Dietrich, *1 Samuel 1-12,* 70, for the options, though they are all in some way variants on the two main options noted above.

11. Many manuscripts read *be'elohey* for *beYHWH* in verse 1aβ. The variant does not affect the argument here because even if this variant is adopted, it still speaks about God, not addressing him. The situation in 2aβ is more complex because of the significant variants in the textual tradition (helpfully outlined by P. Kyle McCarter Jr., *1 Samuel: A New Translation with Introduction and Commentary* AB 8 (Garden City: Doubleday, 1980), 68-69, and Anneli Aejmelaeus, "Hannah's Psalm in 4QSamᵃ," in *Archaeology of the Books of Samuel: The Entangling of Textual and Literary History,* eds. Philippe Hugo and Adrian Schenker (Leiden: Brill, 2010), 27-31. In LXX, this second address to God is absent, though has a different line at this point, and McCarter omits it from his reconstruction, as also does Lewis, "Textual History," 28. There is enough preserved here of 4QSamᵃ to suggest that it may have included both the lines we have in MT and the additional line in LXX. This suggests that 4QSamᵃ was here aware of both textual traditions, perhaps hinting at its occasionally midrashic character; see Alexander Rofé, "Midrashic Traits in 4Q51 (so-called 4QSamᵃ)," in *Archaeology,* eds. Hugo and Schenker, 75-88. However, as I have argued previously (David G. Firth, *1 & 2 Samuel,* AOTC (Nottingham: Apollos, 2009), 52, the awkwardness of MT at this point would more likely indicate that it is the original text. Becker-Spörl, *"Und Hanna betete,"* 6, does not consider this verse problematic for interpreting the poem in terms of the final coherence of MT.

recognized, especially the concentration of parallel units here.[12] This has the benefit of staying with elements that the text presents in its form. But this does not take us very far since poems can be of varying types, something known to all students of Psalms. That Yahweh is addressed at only two points does not prevent it from being a prayer, as an interchange between addressees is not uncommon in Psalms.[13] For example, Psalm 30 shifts between addressing Yahweh (vv. 2–4, 11–13) and a congregation of some sort (vv. 5–10), so the interchange seen in this poem can be seen elsewhere. What separates this poem from others is the extent to which this feature occurs, since elsewhere the various audiences tend to receive a more equal amount of attention. However, that Yahweh is addressed directly at two points would still permit the designation of "prayer," even if it is more one that Yahweh overhears rather than being the primary point of address. In particular, it is that these points of direct address to Yahweh occur near the beginning of the poem which leads to its designation as a prayer.

But that we can consider it as a prayer does not mean it is not a song. Here, the evidence is even more inferential than for labelling it as a prayer. This is because none of the words associated with songs in Hebrew occur within the poem. But again, comparison with various psalms shows that this would not prevent the poem from being considered a song. To take only one example, Psalm 4 likewise contains no vocabulary that would lead us to suppose it is a song. However, its superscription includes the note *lamnatseach*, and this is most commonly interpreted as referring to some form of musical leadership,[14] something that in this instance would seem to be confirmed by the additional notes that it was *bigniyoth* ("with stringed instruments") and also a *mizmor* ("a psalm"), both of which make explicit the musical associations. As such, the absence of any vocabulary to associate the poem with singing here cannot rule out the traditional designation. Moreover, as noted, the exuberant language with which the poem opens is not inconsistent with this being a song. Nevertheless, a first

---

12. Samuel T.S. Goh, *The Basics of Hebrew Poetry: Theory and Practice* (Eugene: Cascade, 2017), 58, notes that there are other important features in Hebrew poetry, especially to do with aspects of sound. However, the density of the parallelism here clearly marks this text as poetry.

13. See further, David G. Firth, "Psalms of Testimony," *OTE* 12 (1999), 440–54. Other examples of this bifurcation of address occur in Psalms 40, 116 and 138.

14. The parallel in 1 Chron 15:21 suggests the terminology is associated with musical leadership.

reading of the poem may need a clearer designation of how it presents itself than this traditional label might suggest.

Given that there has been no settled designation for the poem in the history of research, we will not resolve the issue here. But rather than focusing directly on the normal form critical categories, we might do better to focus on how the poem communicates. Most notably, attention needs to be focused on something central to the poem, but which has not been as prominent in its discussion. That is, the bulk of the poem is making statements about Yahweh, even if some opening comments are directed to him. The poem thus presents itself as (primarily) a series of declarations about Yahweh that are directed to an audience rather than as speech to Yahweh. That there is some bifurcation of address means that this is the language of worship in that Yahweh is addressed, but that also a wider group is meant to hear and thus to learn about Yahweh.[15] We might therefore describe this as a didactic praise poem that integrates testimony with declarations about Yahweh.

The language about Yahweh is predominantly expressed as praise, but it moves through first, second, and third person in sequence in order to refine its didactic goals. We can trace this movement through the poem. Thus, in verses 1–2 the poet speaks in the first person, providing reasons for exultation. This still involves some third person declarations about Yahweh, but this is because the testimonial element needs to recount why the poet can offer praise while also addressing Yahweh. This shifts grammatically in verse 3, which employs the second person plural in a pair of negated admonitions. Use of the plural here thus distinguishes it from the second person singular in the preceding verses, and makes clear that another audience is presupposed. Although the balance of the psalm is expressed in the third person, describing Yahweh's acts, all of these elements flow from the negated admonitions of verse 3.[16] Hence, although the opening verses can assume that Yahweh is (in effect) over-hearing the balance of the poem, verses 3–10 are primarily spoken to an audience who is present and who need to know about Yahweh's acts, and through them come to an understanding of his character.

---

15. On the significance of shift in grammatical person for the didactic mode of Old Testament poetry, see David G. Firth, "The Teaching of the Psalms," in *Interpreting the Psalms: Issues and Approaches*, eds. Philip S. Johnston and David G. Firth (Leicester: Apollos, 2005), 164–70.

16. Following many manuscripts in verse 3bβ, and reading with *qere lo* for *lo'*, the initial *'al* in this verse can be assumed by ellipsis in verse 3aβ.

This audience is not to multiply haughty speech, and the reasons for this are found in both the testimony of the poet and also, more thoroughly, in the summary of the ways in which Yahweh acts. These elements are tied together by repetition of the word "horn" (*qeren*) in verses 1 and 10. The poet's experience is thus consistent with the wider actions of Yahweh which the bulk of the poem describes. In particular, the consistent emphasis of the poem is that Yahweh brings down the powerful while raising up the weak, the so-called reversal of fortunes motif. This provides a particular focus on the keyword *gebohah* in verse 3.[17] The warning is given to those who would regard themselves as "high" or "exalted," making clear that a proper understanding of Yahweh requires awareness of the fact that he is the one who raises up, something already said of the poet (v. 1), and which is characteristically done for the lowly in the balance of the poem. Just as the poem is also careful to progress from first to third person, so also its language is careful in its use of spatial language of raising up and bringing low, with this providing a frame of reference for understanding Yahweh's work of sustaining the weak and defeating the powerful. The *gebohah* might be "exalted" or "powerful," but the balance of the poem explains that whichever sense is given to this word, those who place themselves in this position set themselves in opposition to Yahweh.

None of this would necessarily prepare a reader of the poem for the introduction of the king in verse 10.[18] Indeed, that Yahweh judges (*yadiyn*) the ends of the earth might suggest that he has no need of any human figure to achieve his purposes. Yet this is surely the rhetorical surprise that is sprung by the poem—at no point has it indicated how Yahweh brings down the powerful. We know that Yahweh has acted for the poet, and we know that Yahweh has characteristic ways of dealing with the world. But now we know that he acts through his king. Yahweh has a way of conducting politics, and that politics is to be representative of Yahweh's character. The audience addressed by the poem now know at least one means by which this is to happen. And any king who hears this poem is thus reminded of how they are to conduct themselves.

---

17. The centrality of the word remains, even if we omit one occurrence of it, as seen in a number of manuscripts.

18. In LXX, "our king" rather than MT, "his king." Although mention of the king is unexpected, Dietrich, *1 Samuel 1–12*, 78, includes it in his old preexilic layer.

THE POEM WITHIN THE CONTEXT OF THE BOOK OF SAMUEL

Consideration of (at least some of) the poetics of this poem enables us to read it as a discrete text. Nevertheless, we only have it as an embedded text, and our next concern is to consider its place within Samuel. With Watts, we can consider it to be an example of "inset poetry," a poem which stands out from the prose which surrounds it.[19] As he notes, inset poems usually occur at the end of a plot item within a narrative though they may also flag up larger narrative concerns.[20] Our concern here is to trace some of the ways in which the placement of this poem here in Samuel achieves this goal, though without overwriting the original rhetorical functions of the poem. That is, these elements are taken seriously[21] but now given an extended reference through interaction with the text into which it is now placed. It is this interaction that we now trace.

Curiously, although designated as a "song" even though there is no contextual material which requires this, other inset poems within Samuel are provided with such markers—when David returns from the killing of Goliath, the women sing, dance, and play musical instruments (1 Sam 18:6-7).[22] David is said to have chanted (*wayeqonen*) his lament over Saul and Jonathan (2 Sam 1:17-27) and also over Abner (2 Sam 3:33-34), and uttered the words of a song (2 Sam 22:1-51) in the Samuel conclusion. Even David's last words (2 Sam 23:1-7) characterize him in musical terms, even if the exact sense of the line (2 Sam 23:1) is not altogether clear. Indeed, the only inset poem in Samuel lacking any explicit musical notation is Hannah's, though it may be that David's last words are likewise spoken rather than sung. Instead, this poem is presented simply as one that Hannah "prayed and said" (1 Sam 2:1).

This introduction to the poem is thus careful to characterize it primarily as prayer. More particularly, as we have already noted, that Hannah speaks here means that we go from her earlier silence in prayer to an abundance of words. This switch prepares for a similar pattern in 1 Samuel 3:1-4:1a. In Samuel's initiation report[23] we are initially told of the scarcity of Yahweh's word (1 Sam 3:1), but as the chapter progresses

---

19. See Watts, "Conspicuous Poetry."

20. Watts, "Conspicuous Poetry," 352.

21. Even the reference to the barren bearing seven (2 Sam 2:5) can be read with reference to Hannah, albeit as hyperbole.

22. Even subsequent reflections on this poem do so with reference to music; 1 Sam 21:11 [MT 21:12], 29:5.

23. See Firth, *1 & 2 Samuel*, 75.

and Samuel encounters Yahweh this situation changes. After 1 Samuel 3:1, we do not come across the lexeme "word" (*dabar*) until 1 Samuel 3:7, but after this it occurs some fourteen times in this narrative, moving us from a scarcity of Yahweh's word to an abundance.[24] Hannah moves from silence in addressing Yahweh to an abundance of words following Samuel's birth. After Samuel's initiation as a prophet, Israel moves from a scarcity of words from Yahweh to an abundance. This suggests that even though the phrasing of "she prayed and said" might be customary, it is still used to embed this prayer within the larger narrative, both reflecting back on Hannah's previous experience and preparing readers for other issues that arise in Samuel.

That Hannah's prayer shows signs of being carefully embedded at this point indicates that there are good reasons for exploring the other poems of Samuel as embedded texts.[25] We cannot examine this issue in detail here, but this would support Klement's observation on the structure of Samuel in which the principal poems (1 Sam 2:1–10; 2 Sam 1:17–29; 22:1–51; 23:1–7) are all structurally significant for the book.[26] Nevertheless, we can note that these poems share certain formal features,[27] while the means by which each is embedded in its context helps shape the ways in which we read them. That Samuel provides clues to the embedding of each of these poems in their context while also linking them suggests that these poems have been intentionally placed within the larger narrative to interpret that particular context while also interacting with each other to provide clues to the overall interpretation of Samuel.

Perhaps the most important element of Hannah's prayer that is developed in the subsequent narrative is the reversal of fortunes motif, though this is also tied to the emergence of the monarchy, something also hinted at within the poem. We can briefly note the linkage of these two intertwined themes across the book and their climax in the Samuel Conclusion (2 Sam 21–24).[28]

---

24. See Donald J. Wicke, "The Structure of 1 Samuel 3: Another View," *BZ* 30 (1986): 256–58.

25. Firth, *1 & 2 Samuel*, 29–30, and David G. Firth, *1 & 2 Samuel: A Kingdom Comes* (London: Bloomsbury, 2017), 49–50.

26. Klement, *2 Samuel 21–24*, 157.

27. Firth, *A Kingdom Comes*, 49–50.

28. On the importance of these chapters for the rhetoric of the book as a whole, see David G. Firth, "Shining the Lamp: The Rhetoric of 2 Samuel 5–24," *TynBul* 52 (2001): 214–20.

The theme of the reversal of fortunes, where the powerful are brought down and the weak raised up, is an important one for Samuel. The first glimpse of it is already seen in Hannah's own story. Although she is seemingly Elkanah's first wife, she suffers because of her lack of children, something for which she is vexed by his other wife (and her rival) Peninnah. This vexation had pushed her to the point of "thundering" (*harr 'imah*, 1 Sam 1:6).[29] The noun here is an unusual one, but is capable of being understood in context. Nevertheless, it also anticipates the declaration of Hannah's prayer that Yahweh would "thunder" (*r 'm*) in the heavens, something that contributes to him judging the ends of the earth.[30] Within Hannah's story, we see how Yahweh provides her with children, so that she eventually has six (1 Sam 2:21), so that the lowly one is raised up. But the connections with thunder noted in the conflict with Peninnah and which then echo in Hannah's prayer are themselves picked up twice elsewhere within Samuel, each time in a setting where Yahweh brings down the powerful, showing himself to be judge of the ends of the earth.

The first example of Yahweh thundering occurs in 1 Samuel 7:10. In this instance, Israel had gathered at Mizpah where they engaged in a water ceremony (1 Sam 7:5–6). When the Philistines heard that Israel had gathered, they prepared to attack as Samuel was offering up the burnt offering (1 Sam 7:7–10). But it was at this point that Yahweh thundered, causing confusion among the Philistines so they were defeated before Israel. The language of the victory here is careful to note that it was Yahweh who brought confusion onto the Philistines, while the use of the *niphal* (*wayinnagpu*) also avoids claiming any contribution to the victory by Israel. Israel here was at a point of weakness, whereas the Philistines came from a position of power, but it is Yahweh who has reversed their fortunes, including a direct allusion to Hannah's prayer through the thunder motif.[31]

---

29. Note the unusual dagesh in the *resh* here. Usually, this phrasing is understood as an idiom pointing to grievous vexation, and though this is probably true, it represents another point where the surrounding narrative prepares for the poem by including unusual vocabulary.

30. Within the poem, there is also a play on the closely similar sounding verb *rmh* ("lifted up") in vv. 1 and 10.

31. Although Samuel requests Yahweh to send thunder in the dry season in 1 Sam 12:17–18, the vocabulary is different, separating those events from the background of Hannah's prayer.

The thunder motif's other occurrence is in David's song in 2 Samuel 22, providing another link between Hannah's prayer and the other poems of the book. Here, (2 Sam 22:14), David affirms that Yahweh "thunders from the heavens" (*yar 'em min shamayim*), a close echo of the statement in Hannah's prayer (1 Sam 2:10). David's song poses many interpretative issues of its own, but this verse occurs in a section which describes Yahweh's power relative to the creation as a whole (2 Sam 22:8-16). Immediately following this section, David[32] reflects on how Yahweh sent from on high and drew him from many waters, rescuing him from enemies who were too powerful for him (2 Sam 22:17-20). David's own experience within this song can then be generalized in the observation of 2 Samuel 22:28 that Yahweh saves a humble people, but brings down the haughty. In this instance, the verbal root used (*hiphil* of *shpl*) is the same as in Hannah's song (1 Sam 2:7), providing another link between them. This verbal correlation demonstrates the link between the thunder motif and the theme of the reversal of fortunes. Indeed, these are the only two occurrences of this verb in Samuel.

David's Song is said to have been spoken on the day Yahweh delivered him from all his enemies and from Saul. Within the book, it is thus a reflection on how the reversal of fortunes motif has been experienced by David, acknowledging that David came to reign as king only because of Yahweh's work on his behalf. But David's rise to power is itself part of a repeating pattern within Samuel where the powerful are brought down. This pattern is, as noted, already present in Hannah's own story relative to Peninnah, but it also continues through a series of changes of power. Thus, Eli's family is brought down and loses the priesthood at Shiloh, with Samuel initially becoming the reliable priest announced by the man of God (1 Sam 2:34). But Samuel's family will not succeed him, and the failings of his sons are presented as a trigger for the request for a king (1 Sam 8:1-5). Saul then becomes king, even though he described himself in lowly terms (1 Sam 9:21).[33] Yet in the end, Saul was brought down, and David was raised up to become king. David thus discovers that Hannah's declaration that there is no "rock (*tsur*) like our God" (1 Sam 2:2) is also

---

32. David's actual relationship to this poem is not considered here, but within the book of Samuel, David has become the "I" who speaks at this point.

33. Saul's language here is probably largely conventional given that his father could be described as a man of substance (*chayil*) in 1 Sam 9:1. Nevertheless, the narrative presents him as someone who did not initially grasp for power.

true in his own experience as the song four times refers to Yahweh as "rock" (2 Sam 22:3, 32, 47 (x2)). Indeed, this link is carried forward into David's "Last Words" (2 Sam 23:1-7) where Yahweh is referred to as "the rock of Israel" (2 Sam 23:3). In this final poem, David reflects on the importance of rulers acting justly. Within the narrative structure of Samuel, this effectively means acknowledging that since he was "raised high" (2 Sam 23:1) then all subsequent rulers need to acknowledge that they can also be brought low if their rule is not consistent with Yahweh's purposes. In her prayer, Hannah had noted that Yahweh was the one who "raised" people up (1 Sam 2:8), so when we read that David has been raised up (2 Sam 23:1, both times using *hiphil* of *qwm*) we know from the background of Hannah's prayer that he can also be brought low.

Hannah's prayer had declared that Yahweh had raised her "horn" (a symbol of strength) and that he would do so for his king. Outside of the main songs, the word "horn" (*qeren*) occurs elsewhere only in the account of David's anointing (1 Sam 16:1, 13). These occurrences are surely significant since it is here that David becomes Yahweh's anointed, the references to anointing providing another link to Hannah's prayer. Otherwise, it occurs only in Hannah's prayer (1 Sam 2:1, 10) and in David's song (2 Sam 22:3) where David refers to Yahweh as "the horn of my salvation." Since it was Yahweh who had raised Hannah's horn, it is clear from the wider narrative that there too he is regarded as a horn of salvation. In his song, David has discovered that what Hannah had announced, that Yahweh would "raise the horn of his anointed."

HANNAH'S PRAYER AND THE ETHICS OF SAMUEL

The discussion so far has shown that Hannah's prayer provides an important grid for reading much of the books of Samuel. In particular, we have noted that when considered in its own right, the poem functions to address an audience who hear the praise of one who gives thanks to Yahweh. But through this praise, the poem also instructs an undefined audience about the need to avoid arrogance because Yahweh is one who measures actions. This process of measuring actions leads to him bringing down the powerful and raising up the weak, including the barren like Hannah. Hannah's own story thus becomes one example of Yahweh acting this way. However, as we have noted, the ways in which this poem is embedded within Samuel go far beyond Hannah's own story. As such, the poem now functions both to conclude Hannah's story to that point and

also to introduce the wider themes of the bringing down of the powerful
and raising up of the weak. Indeed, we can see that although Hannah's
own story continues beyond this point (1 Sam 2:18–21), her prayer needed
to be recorded at the point it is (before she has had other children) because
the key element is established after her dedication of Samuel, not after
she has had six children in total. Beyond that, the careful range of verbal
links established across the book through *Leitworte* means that readers
are continually brought back to the prayer as a means of evaluating events
within it.

The possibilities of reading the narrative texts of the Old Testament
ethically has received some attention from Gordon Wenham.[34] Narrative
texts do pose certain difficulties for readers if we are to discern their
ethics precisely because the narrators of the Old Testament so seldom
express their moral standpoint directly.[35] Wenham thus develops a model
that looks for those things that a narrator commends, though since the
narrators of the Old Testament so seldom provide exact guidance on this
we are still left needing wider awareness.[36] From the perspective of the
wider canon, this can come from the legal, prophetic, and wisdom traditions, and these could indeed contribute to our understanding of the
ethics of Samuel.[37] Such an ethic might be generalizable, though it will
always remain in the particulars of that narrative.[38] However, reading
Hannah's prayer in the context of the book as a whole suggests that one
of its key functions is to provide readers with an ethical framework with
which to read the rest of the book, one that allows readers to see the particulars of each narrative while also seeing that the narrator of the fin-
ished book continues to commend certain ethical stances through Hannah.

As is well known, the Old Testament's narrators generally prefer to
show rather than tell—that is, they do not often make explicit ethical

---

34. Gordon J. Wenham, *Story as Torah: Reading the Old Testament Ethically* (Grand
Rapids: Baker Academic, 2000).
35. Wenham, *Story as Torah*, 2.
36. Following his model, he is concerned with the implied author (Wenham, *Story
as Torah*, 8). However, within the Old Testament the implied author is usually the
narrator, except for embedded narration which is usually reported within dialogue.
37. In terms of a wider reflection on biblical ethics, for a Christian reader this would
also mean drawing on the New Testament, but since my concern is with Samuel's
ethics, it seems wisest only to refer to those texts and traditions which might have
been formative for it.
38. Cf. Robin Parry, *Old Testament Story and Christian Ethics: The Rape of Dinah as a Case
Study* (Milton Keynes: Paternoster, 2004), 46–47.

comment, even when modern readers often wish they would. But within Samuel, Hannah's prayer is given this role, and this goes well beyond its function of providing a first mention of kingship. As is typical of embedded poems, the narrator allows this one to be voiced by a character.[39] This allows readers to see and feel the resolution of Hannah's pain from being childless through her own prayer and praise. But it now leaves open the question of who is addressed by the bulk of the prayer. If this was a pre-existing poem (as seems likely) then within the temple those addressed would have been worshipers who were there. They are reminded of Yahweh's acts in the reversal of fortunes and also his provision for his king. But within Samuel, that is no longer the audience addressed. Hannah's prayer still addresses Yahweh, but the secondary audience addressed directly from 1 Samuel 2:3 is no longer a worshiping congregation encountering the poem alone. Instead, it is those who now encounter the books of Samuel who are addressed directly. They have encountered Hannah's story, and, in the prayer, they are now the ones addressed, told not to speak arrogantly. They need to learn this because of how Yahweh acts, bringing down the powerful and raising the weak.

At first, this might be thought to mean something like avoiding the sort of vexatious speech previously used by Peninnah. This conclusion would allow for the particularity of this story, while also seeing that there is something generalizable from this story. But the use of *Leitworte* which continually connect parts of the larger narrative of Samuel (which includes its main poems, each of which is also an embedded poem, but each of which now functions differently because of its place within the story) pushes readers to realize that Hannah's prayer has provided the narrator with a mechanism for commenting on almost all aspects of the larger story. It is this which makes this poem so unusual within the Old Testament, for no other embedded poem is given the importance of Hannah's prayer. That the narrator then uses two embedded poems from David to provide a closing reflection on the themes established by Hannah's prayer points to the importance given to this poem. Readers

---

39. See Watts, "Conspicuous Poetry," 348. This is why Wenham, *Psalms as Torah*, is less relevant for our purposes. In this work, Wenham emphasizes the self-involving nature of the Psalms, showing how they shape those who recite them, since this act involves those using them making these their own prayers. But Hannah's prayer remains a poem voiced by someone else so that readers are addressed by it rather than it becoming their own prayer.

have been assured that this is how Yahweh acts, and Hannah's own story has demonstrated this. But the wider narrative also consistently shows that when the powerful forget that Yahweh brings down the powerful, then Yahweh does give strength to the weak. Moreover, when anyone forgets that power is by definition not something to be grasped, then it is Yahweh who brings them down. This is true for Penninah, for Eli and his family, for Samuel and his family, and for Saul and his family as each of them looks to hold power for themselves. David may emerge as the one who can claim an "enduring covenant" with Yahweh (2 Sam 23:5), but the narrative has shown him going perilously close to making the same mistake. David, let us be clear, is far from a saint across Samuel, but at the point where he seems likely to make the same mistakes as his predecessors, he repents (2 Sam 12:13–14). Without this, David's claims in 2 Samuel 22:22–25 might seem ridiculous, since he has hardly kept his hands clean (2 Sam 22:21). But since a claim like this is elsewhere associated with innocence of a particular charge,[40] it is likely in light of the song's introduction that the reference is to David not seizing power when the chance presented itself in 1 Samuel 24 and 26. Moreover, David's observations on how a monarch should rule in his Last Words (2 Sam 23:3b–4) indicate that he has now learned the truth of Hannah's declaration, in spite of his manifest failings. As Yahweh's anointed within Samuel, David has indeed received strength from Yahweh (1 Sam 2:10). In his sin, he was brought low, but his confession put him in a position where Yahweh would again raise him up.

In the end, for Samuel, David is the king introduced in Hannah's prayer, the one brought from a relatively lowly position to a place of power while others are brought down. Readers addressed through Hannah's prayer are thus reminded not to try to exalt themselves but rather to humble themselves. However, they do not humble themselves under the king, they humble themselves under Yahweh, because a king only has power if Yahweh gives it. This is as true of David as anyone else, and indeed this continues to provide an ethical framework for modern readers of Samuel.

---

40. Firth, *1 & 2 Samuel*, 539.

4

Bending the Silence: Psalms through the Arts

Ellen F. Davis

PART I: PSALM 38

In an extended essay on the indispensability of the active, creative imagination, George Steiner begins with a parable of radical social change. He imagines a society in which all academic and journalistic reviews of the arts, analytic talk *about* painting, sculpture, dance, music, and literature, is illegal. "What would be banned is the thousandth article or book on the true meaning of *Hamlet* and the article immediately following in rebuttal, qualification or augment."[1] Despite the ban, such a society would not lack critical engagement with the arts, because all serious art is *itself* a critical act; "the focused light of both interpretation (the hermeneutic) and valuation (the critical normative) lies in the work itself."[2] Therefore the best interpreters of a work are sometimes its original creator(s), and often those who recreate it through performance, professional or amateur, and even aficionados who might commit to memory a piece of music or literature. Such direct engagement stands in some contrast to modes of criticism motivated by professional concerns but not necessarily by a sense of personal obligation to the work, of being "answerable" to it in such a way as "to give it intelligible life."[3]

---

1. George Steiner, *Real Presences* (Chicago: University of Chicago Press, 1989), 5.
2. Steiner, *Real Presences*, 17.
3. Steiner, *Real Presences*, 7–8.

Steiner's vision of a society in which the meaning of artistic creations is judged and communicated exclusively by those who are themselves in some sense artists is much more radical than this current essay, but they share an underlying premise: "The best readings of art are art."[4] In what follows, I treat a small suite of lament psalms, Psalms 38 and 42–43,[5] reading them through the work of several poets (one of whom is also a preacher), a visual artist, a choreographer, and a dancer. My aim is to explore through these later artists how the ancient poems engage their audience in a way that remains vital to this day. I start from the understanding that the lament psalms display at the highest level the quality that characterizes Hebrew poetry throughout the Prophets, Psalms, and wisdom literature, namely a sustained capacity for eliciting a response, for generating the personal involvement of those who repeat or pray them, and thus potentially changing the conversation from the abstract and technocratic to something that is profoundly human.

If these particular psalms can do that, it is because they are really good lyric poems, a genre that in the Bible (and often elsewhere) consistently demonstrates a dialogical form, emotional depth and intensity, metaphorical richness, rhythmic concision, and because of all those, memorability and quotability. In other words, biblical lyric lends itself to *re-expression* in various modes; it is, as F.W. Dobbs-Allsopp observes, "uniquely reutterable."[6] Surely the scholarly rediscovery of the poetry of lament is one of the most theologically and pastorally significant developments within biblical studies in recent decades.[7] (It is also potentially liturgically significant, although that potential remains underdeveloped in most contexts known to me—monastic communities being the exception.) Here I begin

---

4. Steiner, *Real Presences*, 17.
5. I offer my own translations of these Psalms in appendix 1 at the end of this chapter.
6. F.W. Dobbs-Allsopp, *On Biblical Poetry* (New York: Oxford University Press, 2015), 206. Dobbs-Allsopp's study gives an excellent overview of the characteristics of biblical poetry. For a fine recent study of Isaiah as an instance of lyric poetry, and the characteristics that mark that genre, see Katie M. Heffelfinger, *I Am Large, I Contain Multitudes: Lyric Cohesion and Conflict in Second Isaiah*, BIS 105 (Leiden: Brill, 2011).
7. Several benchmark studies by Claus Westermann and Walter Brueggemann gave strong impetus to the reawakening of interest in lament. I would note especially volume 28 of *Interpretation: A Journal of Bible and Theology*, published in January 1974, which was devoted to lament. It included both Brueggemann's "From Hurt to Joy, from Death to Life" (3–19) and Westermann's "The Role of the Lament in the Theology of the Old Testament" (20–38). Both essays have been subsequently republished and have exercised wide influence.

to read Psalm 38 through its reutterances, first by the seventeenth-century poet John Donne, quite possibly the greatest preacher of the psalms in the English language, and second through a piece of choreographed lament from Ekklesia Contemporary Ballet.

Implicit in my title is a certain perspective on laments and on poetry altogether. Walter Brueggemann has recently written of poetry as "the art of breaking the silence" born of uncertainty and fear.[8] Without a doubt this psalm is one of many that indicate it is often not safe or wise to speak: "I am ... like the mute, who does not open his mouth" (Ps 38:14). Nonetheless, I am not completely satisfied with Brueggemann's image of *breaking* silence. Rather, it seems to me that good poetry *bends* silence, yet without rupturing it. Indeed, the rhythm that is constitutive of poetry is itself a delicate balance between utterance and silence. In psalms recitation, the importance of silence is observed in the monastic practice, followed by some church traditions, of pausing for a beat or two after the first colon of each verse. The poet-preacher and the dancer whom I treat in the first half of this essay must in their artistic performances reckon regularly with the ineffable power of silence. Therefore they may be more likely than most biblical scholars to intuit how this lament, precisely in its poetic form, may conduce to human healing and wholeness.

John Donne implies the importance of silence in explaining his own special love for the psalms as preaching texts and for devotion. He relishes their "cheerfull forms, ... where all the words are numbered, and measured, and weighed ... God speaks to us *in oratione strictâ*, in a limited, in a diligent form."[9] The crafted, deliberate form of the psalms is for Donne a mark of divine solicitousness, that we humans might take pleasure in the artful communication of God's word to us. "Religion is a serious thing,

---

8. Brueggemann cites Seamus Heaney as the source of this notion, although the article to which he refers does not use that metaphor nor clearly imply it. See Walter Brueggemann, *Preaching from the Old Testament* (Minneapolis: Fortress, 2019), 74. He cites Francis X. Clines, "Seamus Heaney, Poet of 'the Silent Things,' " *The New York Times*, August 30, 2013, accessed at https://www.nytimes.com/2013/08/31/opinion/seamus-heaney-poet-of-the-silent-things.html. See also Francis X. Clines, "Poet of the Bogs," *The New York Times Magazine*, March 13, 1983, accessed at https://www.nytimes.com/1983/03/13/magazine/poet-of-the-bogs.html.

9. John Donne, *The Sermons of John Donne*, eds. George R. Potter and Evelyn M. Simpson (Berkeley: University of California Press, 1955), 2:49–50. Here, all citations that refer directly to Donne's treatment of the psalm follow the seventeenth-century orthography from Potter and Simpson's edition.

but not a sullen."[10] The silence inherent to poetry is the chief quality whereby the psalms of lament invite our engagement as readers, reciters, and re-articulators of their message. In its formal restraint, its refusal to "disturb // the silence from which it came," a good poem expresses regard both for those whom it addresses and for the mystery of life it seeks to illumine.[11] Religious lyric treats the mystery of living in conscious relationship to the Divine, and so God is the first addressee in most psalms and all the biblical laments.

As ordered, probing verbal expressions, formulated in the first person, keenly attuned to a mixed audience composed of God and humans, and suggestive of multiple possibilities for meaning, the lament psalms foster the existential expression of an authentic self. The "I" of the lament psalms is not an insistent, self-absorbed ego but rather a true self, born of a crisis of the spirit—the generative condition for all personal lyric, as the contemporary American poet Gregory Orr observes.[12] It is self-discovered and developed in community, reaching out to its audience through the highly flexible rhetorical strategy of dialogue. W.R. Johnson's argument about Greek lyric poetry may apply equally to the psalms: the speaker discovers himself through speaking to and for another. "The act of discourse clarifies the speaker's personality, he learns who and what he is by yielding himself wholly to the act of discourse; ... by discoursing, describing, deliberating, he becomes himself."[13]

Further, a work of traditional art such as a psalm can never be a solo composition and performance; "any poem worth the name is the product of a convocation."[14] A good poem exists, in Wendell Berry's words, "at the center of a complex reminding, to which it relates as both cause and effect."[15] It marks a certain point in a long conversation, and every re-articulation that is not merely rote—even that qualification may not signify much, as rote repetition shapes memory—every re-articulation marks another moment in the conversation, which assumes new forms through countless generations.

10. Donne, *The Sermons of John Donne*, 2:170.
11. Wendell Berry, "How to Be a Poet," *Poetry* (January 2001), 270.
12. Gregory Orr, *Poetry as Survival* (Athens: The University of Georgia Press, 2002), 39.
13. W. R. Johnson, *The Idea of Lyric: Lyric Modes in Ancient and Modern Poetry* (Berkeley: University of California Press, 1982), 31.
14. Wendell Berry, "The Responsibility of the Poet," in *What Are People For?* (New York: North Point Press, 1990), 89.
15. Berry, "The Responsibility of the Poet," 88.

Memory

The psalm itself begins with memory: *mizmor leDavid lehazkir*, "A David psalm, for reminding." Who knows what that exceptional superscription means?[16] *Lehazkir*—maybe this is a reference to an ancient melody to which the psalm was once sung, or possibly it was associated with a token sacrifice (*'azkarah*, Lev 2:2, 6:8, etc.), a portion that is burnt as a "reminder," in lieu of turning an entire grain offering into smoke.[17] Those suggestions may be historically plausible, but there is no particular evidence for either. More exegetically grounded and theologically promising is the suggestion of Artur Weiser and Robert Alter that the phrase carries a connotation of confession, calling sin to mind (cf. Gen 41:9; 1 Kgs 17:18).[18] That is the direction that Donne moved several centuries before, in a series of seven or more sermons preached on this "Psalm for Remembrance" at Lincoln's Inn, probably during the summer of 1618.[19] Following Saint Bernard and earlier Christian theologians, Donne recognizes memory as one of three faculties of the soul that are indispensable for our knowledge of God, and it possibly takes precedence even over understanding and will: "The art of salvation, is but the art of memory. ... All instruction, which we can give you to day, is but the remembering you of the mercies of God. ..."[20] When the psalmist (David) is "lock'd up in a close prison, of multiplied calamities, this turns the key, this opens the door, this restores him to liberty, if he can remember."[21]

What the psalmist remembers is himself, "but sometimes that's the hardest of all; many times we are farthest off from our selves; most forgetfull of our selves."[22] Remembering my self accurately means seeing (in the Authorized Version of 1611) "There is no soundnesse in my flesh, because of thine anger, neither is there any rest in my bones, because of my sinne"

---

16. Psalm 70 is the only other psalm that begins with the superscription להזכיר, "for reminding."

17. On possible meanings of the superscription, see Amos Hakham, *The Bible, Psalms with the Jerusalem Commentary* (Jerusalem: Mosad Harav Kook, 2003), 1:297. On the token offering, see Jacob Milgrom, *Leviticus 1–16* (New York: Doubleday, 1991), 182.

18. See Artur Weiser, *The Psalms: A Commentary* (Philadelphia: Westminster, 1962), 323; Robert Alter, *The Book of Psalms* (New York: Norton, 2007), 134.

19. Six of Donne's sermons on Psalm 38 are extant, and in these he makes reference to one or more sermons that have not been preserved. See Evelyn Simpson's Introduction to *The Sermons of John Donne*, 2:16.

20. Donne, *Sermons of John Donne*, 2:73–74; spelling original.

21. Donne, *Sermons of John Donne*, 2:74.

22. Donne, *Sermons of John Donne*, 2:74; spelling original.

(Ps 38:3 AV, Heb 38:4). Donne's persistent emphasis on the realities of our sin and the multiple ways it hurts us sounds distinctly unfashionable to our generation of preachers and biblical interpreters. We even have biblical warrant for avoiding it: the psalmists rarely acknowledge guilt, let alone dwell upon it (Psalm 51 excepted). But sometimes that is what we must do in order to remember ourselves and reclaim a relationship with God, as the psalmist does: "For you, O Yнwн, I wait-in-hope. It is you who will answer, my Lord, my God" (38:16).[23]

I recently offered a meditation on Psalm 38 at a gathering of health-care professionals assembled to consider the currently acute opioid crisis in the U.S. The day began, predictably, with PowerPoint, maps, and statistics showing the depressing metrics of the crisis; in contrast to Donne's description of religion, the mood was serious and sullen both. Then we turned to a reading of the psalm, and something changed in the room. Through the twenty-two lines of that quasi-alphabetic poem, we could hear human voices. Nurses, doctors, and medical social workers heard the voices of their patients, their clients, their neighbors, crying out the guilt and alienation from God that often attend addiction, crying out the unremitting psychic, physical, and social pain that now defines their existence:

> For my iniquities have mounted over my head; they are like a
>   heavy burden, too heavy for me.
> My sores stink, they fester because of my folly;
> I am bent, bowed very low; all day long I go about in mourning.
> For my loins are filled with burning; there is no health in my body.
> I am numb and utterly crushed; I roar, from the growling of
>   my heart.
> My Lord, all my longing is before you; and my groaning is not
>   hidden from you.
> My heart palpitates; my strength forsakes me, and the light of
>   my eyes—that too is absent from me.
> My intimates and companions stand distant from my plague,
>   and my own kin stand far away.
> They strike, those who seek my life, and they who wish me
>   harm speak violence;
> deceit they mutter all day long. (Ps 38:5-13)

---

23. Author's translation (see appendix 1 at the end of this chapter). All translations are mine, unless otherwise noted.

In our society, the pretensions of technocracy and professionalism may discourage us from using language adequate to the enormity of suffering.[24] We seek to "manage pain" and "contain damage"; the very terms in which we speak may beguile us into denying how much is beyond our comprehension and control. However, the intellectualization of pain is not a purely modern phenomenon; it may be the temptation of the highly educated in every age. Donne cautions the barristers and the law students of Lincoln's Inn against learning patience in affliction "from the stupidity of Philosophers, who are but their own statues, men of stone, without sense, without affections, ... that no pain should make them say they were in pain. ..."[25]

By contrast, the Bible in both Testaments does not shy away from the persistent realities of pain, human weakness, and sin; nor do liturgical and literary traditions that are well shaped by the biblical witness. Accordingly, Wendell Berry considers how Donald Davie's poem "Advent" is shaped within a "pattern of reminding," which he identifies as the "Judeo-Christian tradition," that facilitates the expression of authentic feeling, even if its message is not innovative.[26] Likewise the preacher Donne consistently and in varied ways traces a pattern of reminding that stretches through the story of salvation from Adam to Christ. Thus he directs his congregation in applying that pattern to their own personal histories:

> Study all the history, and write all the progres of the Holy Ghost in thy selfe. ... Hide nothinge from God, neyther the diseases thou wast in, nor the degrees of health that thou are come to, nor the ways of thy fallinge or rising; for *Dominus fecit, et erit mirabile* [The Lord made (it), and it will be marvelous"; cf. Ps 118:23]. If I mistake not the measure of thy conscience, thou wilt find an infinite comfort in this particular tracing of the Holy Ghost, and his working in thy soule.[27]

---

24. Walter Brueggemann identifies one ready temptation in our technological culture: a propensity toward "control, explanation, and solution that eventually leads to denial of the inescapably unsettled quality of human life" (*Preaching from the Old Testament*, 113).

25. Donne, *Sermons of John Donne*, 2:53.

26. Berry, "The Responsibility of the Poet," 91.

27. Donne, *Sermons of John Donne*, 2:159.

COMFORT

How, then, does lament lead to comfort, at least in some measure? In a suggestive study, *Poetry as Survival*, Gregory Orr identifies the "survival function" of the personal lyric as "help[ing] us express and regulate our emotional lives, which are confusing and sometimes opaque to us."[28] Awareness of the chaotic in ourselves and in the world generates "a spontaneous ordering response," an innate faculty possessed by everyone: "Why not call it 'imagination' and recognize it as a fundamentally human cognitive capacity?"[29] The story of Orr's own discovery of poetry as a lifeline offers insight into the kind of crisis that might generate a lyric poem, including a lament:

> When I was twelve years old I was responsible for a hunting accident in which my younger brother died. ... At the time ... a friend of the family counseled me that my brother's death was all part of God's plan, which was necessarily inscrutable to us on earth. This notion of a divine order that had the power to subsume such violent disorder didn't seem believable to me and failed to help me live through the traumatic crisis that had become my life.
>
> ... At the time of my brother's death, no one proposed philosophical attitudes to me, but had they done so I doubt I would have gained any consolation or understanding from them.
>
> ... I lived for about four years after my brother's death without any hope at all. Nothing that I found in my culture sustained me. ... Then, thanks to Mrs. Irving, the librarian [and teacher of the small "honors English" class] in my small public school, I discovered poetry. ... I wrote a poem one day, and it changed my life. I had a sudden sense that the language in poetry was "magical," ... that it could create or transform reality rather than simply describe it. That first poem ... liberated the enormous energy of my despair and oppression as nothing before had ever done. I felt simultaneously revealed to myself and free of my self by the images and actions of the poem. ... I knew that if I was to survive in this life, it would only be through the help of poetry.[30]

---

28. Orr, *Poetry as Survival*, 5.
29. Orr, *Poetry as Survival*, 16–17.
30. Orr, *Poetry as Survival*, 6–8.

Orr is describing a mystery, the revelatory experience of hope and plea-sure[31] that derives from the patterned language of the personal lyric poem. In its fidelity to "embodied being," the personal lyric is distinct from both philosophy and religion, viewed as abstractions. "The personal lyric says to the self in its suffering: 'I will not abandon you. Nor will I ask you to abandon yourself and the felt truth and particulars of your experience.' "[32] It is no small part of the mystery that the poem does not need to include explicitly "comfortable words" in order to gesture toward hope.[33] Witness César Vallejo's prose-poem, an unrelieved lament that concludes with the words, "Today I suffer come what may. Today I simply suffer" (*Hoy sufro suceda lo que suceda. Hoy sufro solamente*)." The title of Vallejo's poem is, "I Am Going to Speak of Hope" (*Voy a hablar de la esperanza*).[34]

If Psalm 38 speaks of hope, it does not do so overtly. Indeed, it lacks the two most hope-filled elements of typical Israelite lament psalms: the expression of confidence that God has heard the prayer and will act, and the vow to offer praise when God has wrought deliverance. Yet Donne reads the psalm toward salvation, as a model for the healing of the self in relation to God, and the experience of judgment is the correction neces-sary for our soul's health. The key to his reading is the thoroughly theo-centric and dialogical character of the psalm; every word—of petition, complaint, and accusation—is directed straight to God. "Your arrows have descended on me," says the psalmist, "and upon me your hand has descended" (Ps 38:3). Far from a reason to despair of God, Donne reads that accusation as the warrant certifying God's presence:

> Consider all the arrows of tribulation, even of tentation [tempta-tion], to be directed by the hand of God, and never doubt to fight it out with God, to lay violent hands upon heaven, to wrastle with God for a blessing, to charge and presse God upon his contracts and promises, for *in umbra pugnabis* ["you will fight in the shade"], though the clouds of these arrows may hide all suns of worldly

---

31. Orr, *Poetry as Survival*, 8.
32. Orr, *Poetry as Survival*, 29.
33. In the traditional service of holy communion in the Book of Common Prayer, the confession and absolution of sin is immediately followed by these words: "Hear what comfortable words our Saviour Christ saith unto all who truly turn to him. ..."
34. Spanish and English versions of the poem may be found at https://spanishpoems. blogspot.com/2004/05/csar-vallejo-voy-hablar-de-la-esperanza.html and in César Vallejo, *The Complete Poetry* (Berkeley: University of California Press, 2007), 342–43.

comforts from thee, yet thou art still under the shadow of his wings
[cf. Ps 63:8].[35]

Further, Donne reads Psalm 38 around Christ; in the final sermon in the
series he hears it as Jesus' own prayer, in Gethsemane and on the cross.[36]
The psalmist's confession of guilt—"Yes, I declare my iniquity" (Ps 38:19)—
is no hindrance to that Christological reading, for Christ assumed every
element of our humanity. "As my mortality, and my hunger, and thirst,
and wearinesse, and all my natural infirmities are his, so my sins are his
sins."[37] Christ assumes the burden of our sin, but he does not thereby
leave us unburdened. On the contrary, he lays on "two for one," imposing
the double burden of repentance—"that sin which was forgotten with
pleasure, must now be remembered with Contrition"—and thankfulness
to God.[38] This is a source of "endlesse comfort," that "all my sins shall no
more hinder my ascending into heaven, nor my sitting at the right hand
of God, in mine own person, then they hindered him, who bore them all
in his person, mine onely Lord and Saviour Christ Jesus, blessed for ever."[39]

DANCE

The most powerful contemporary interpretation of Psalm 38 known to me
is a solo dance choreographed by Elisa Schroth of Ekklesia Contemporary
Ballet in Connecticut. Several years ago, Ekklesia initiated its Psalm
Projects, with the goal of allowing these lyric poems to speak directly
to dimensions of individual and social experience in our contemporary
world. Being nonverbal, dance does not lend itself to close exegesis, but
in our shared work we are discovering that it can foster rich theological
interpretation. The intense physicality and visuality of dance capture
the poem's sensuality and imagery; its resonant silence is suggestive
of multiple dimensions of meaning, multiple occasions of application.
The three-minute piece *Lament* was initially created as part of a full-
length narrative ballet that follows the biblical story from creation to
new creation; in that context, it depicts Jesus's agony in Gethsemane.
However, *Lament* also functions as a freestanding piece, one that is well
suited to represent the agonized address to God in Psalm 38. If John Donne

---

35. Donne, *Sermons of John Donne*, 2:69.
36. Donne, *Sermons of John Donne*, 2:161.
37. Donne, *Sermons of John Donne*, 2:138.
38. Donne, *Sermons of John Donne*, 2:142.
39. Donne, *Sermons of John Donne*, 2:142–43.

hears Jesus's prayer in Gethsemane through Psalm 38, I propose that the reverse movement is equally valid: a dance choreographed to represent Gethsemane can lead us into Psalm 38.

Lament is set to Max Richter's A Blessing, plaintive music for strings.[40] The dancer begins standing, back turned to the audience, both hands raised—perhaps in a gesture of supplication. Then he begins a slow backward descent, a "hinge," bending only at the knees in a seemingly impossible movement, ending in a sudden collapse that leaves him prone on the floor; "upon me your hand has descended" (Ps 38:3). The movements throughout are alternately taut and fluid; the dancer leaps up, light and spinning, and then repeatedly returns to the floor. At one moment his arms are splayed out and behind, apparently under duress, even torture: my enemies … grow strong, and many are those who hate me for a lie" (38:20). His hands press in on his head and torso, as though wounded: "There is no health in my body because of your indignation" (38:4). At other times, the dancer reaches up and out with clear direction, in both appeal and offering of self: "For you, O Yнwн, I wait-in-hope. It is you who will answer, my Lord, my God!" (38:16). The piece ends with a near-echo of the beginning: standing with back to the audience, one arm raised in a gesture of acknowledgement, he descends in slow, painful submission to God—but this time the final move that brings him all the way to the floor is controlled, deliberate. Thus the dance concludes, as does the psalm, without full resolution. The absence of any external resolution, typical even of laments that make a stronger move in the direction of praise than does Psalm 38, is apt both to Jesus's prayer in Gethsemane and too much of our own experience. When Donne applies that psalm to Jesus's agony, in the final sermon of his series, he observes, "The Father was allwayes with him, and is with us, but our deliverance is in his time, and not in ours. …"[41]

---

40. Max Richter, A Blessing, from the album The Leftovers (HBO): Season One Soundtrack, released 4 August 2015. The dance I am describing is performed by Paiter van Yperen. At the time of my writing, Elisa Schroth has choreographed a second version of Lament, set to different music, for another dancer.

41. Donne, Sermons of John Donne, 2:161; spelling original.

PART II: PSALM 42–43

The second lament in my suite is unique in the Psalter: a single psalm in two movements, each of them distinct enough to have been assigned a different psalm number at some point in the editing process. Located at an important juncture, at the head of the second canonical division in the Psalter (Psalms 42–72), Psalm 42–43 is unique in content as well as form. In both its parts, the psalmist conducts a persistent examination of self alongside a vigorous dialogue with God. The refrain, thrice-repeated with variations, is without parallel in its self-interrogatory character:

> How bent down, my self, and wrought you are;
> hope to God, for still I acclaim him,
> his saving Presence—my God! (42:6, cf. 42:12, 43:5)

The peculiar mode of self-address—*nafshi*, "my self"—is retained throughout; the refrain appears as the final verse of the psalm. Nonetheless there is a change in tone from one movement to the next. In the first (Ps 42), depression is reinforced by doubt of God: "Why have you forgotten me?" (42:10). In the second (Ps 43), the psalmist takes a bolder stance, beginning with a demand for divine vindication before his opponents:

> Execute judgment for me ... ; defend my case from a people
>   of bad-faith!
> For you are my stronghold God—why have you ignored me?
>   (43:1-2)

Now the psalmist expresses confidence that hope will indeed be satisfied; he will again experience God as a source of joy:

> Send out your light and your truth; *they* will lead me.
> They will bring me to your holy hill and to your dwelling-place.
> Let me come to God's altar, to the God of my utmost joy,
> and I will acclaim you on the lyre, O God, my God! (43:3-4)

The progression between the two parts of the psalm shows depression gradually yielding to the remembrance and anticipation of joy. (It is intriguing in this regard that the superscription for the whole psalm is designated a *maskil*, which may be a genre marker for a song of joy.[42]) But how does that shift in mood happen? In order to explore that question, I

---

42. Robert Alter derives this suggestion about the function of the *maskil* from Amos 5:13 (*Book of Psalms*, 110).

read the psalm through insights offered by three modern and contemporary American artists: a visual artist and two poets. Printmaker and papercut-artist Diane Palley "reutters" Psalms 42–43 in two images, one created for each major movement. Her original papercuts were then recreated in the form of two silkscreened and sandblasted glass panels that now frame the entrance to the Chapel at Duke Divinity School.[43] By contrast to her explicit visual commentary, whatever reflections of the psalm I find in the work of the two poets is indirect; neither Theodore Roethke (1908–1963) nor Mary Oliver (1935–2019) seems to have written in conscious response to this particular psalm. Nonetheless Roethke had some interest in the Christian mystical tradition, and Oliver may well have known the psalm from long experience worshiping in the Episcopal Church in Provincetown, Massachusetts.[44] Regardless of their specific intentions, the work of these modern poets illumines certain aspects of Psalms 42–43, because they share with the ancient poet several interrelated characteristics:

First, the psalmist and the modern poets are dialogical to an unusual degree; they pursue a running conversation among self, God, and the audience, namely us. All of them write persistently in the first person; this poem eschews "objectivity" and frankly presents a personal perspective, albeit one that is widely shared. Further, in no sense is it a monologue. The psalmist and Theodore Roethke struggle visibly with different voices within themselves, including, for the psalmist, the remembered taunts of enemies. Oliver very often speaks explicitly to her reader; the frequent use of "you" in her poems draws us in directly.

Second, these poets share an abiding concern with discovering and holding onto a stable self in the face of severe challenge. The specific nature or source of the challenge may not be spelled out, but what is clear is that the poet is on a journey, "determined to save // the only life you could save" (Oliver).[45] We know enough about Oliver and Roethke to recognize that each of them writes as a survivor—respectively, of childhood sexual abuse and of bipolar disorder, long misdiagnosed and

---

43. Her images are reproduced in appendix 2 at the end of this chapter.

44. Neal Bowers argues that Roethke's struggle with bipolar disorder contributed to his interest in mysticism; see his *Theodore Roethke: The Journey from I to Otherwise* (Columbia: University of Missouri Press, 1982).

45. Mary Oliver, "The Journey," in *New and Selected Poems* (Boston: Beacon, 1992), 1:115.

mistreated.[46] Although it would be foolish to speculate on what trauma the psalmist may have experienced, the complaint indicates that it was public and devastating:

> With bone-shattering attacks (literally: "With murder in my bones") my opponents revile me. (Ps 42:11)

Third, each poet shows a deep sensitivity to the nonhuman world—animals, water, rocks, and so forth—and further, treats the inner, spiritual landscape as inseparable from the outer, physical landscape. The geographic images of the psalm are enigmatic within the context of that singular and relatively brief poem, but they stand out more clearly against the countless references to water, woods, plants, and animals in Oliver and Roethke's extended *oeuvres*. Fourth and finally, all these poets write honestly about despair and express an intense desire to overcome the distance between self and God—"From me to Thee's a long and terrible way" (Roethke)[47]—and further, they succeed to some degree. All of them lay at least a tentative claim on what they do not hesitate to name as happiness.

THIRST AND TRANSFORMATION

Beginning with the first lines of the psalm, the translator wrestles with the psalmist's peculiarly intensive form of self-reference: *nafshi*, "my self, my whole-being" in its full physicality:

> As a deer yearns toward streambeds,
>   so my whole-self (*nafshi*) yearns for you, O God.
> I (*nafshi*) thirst for God, for the living God.
> When will I come and [see[48]] the face of God? (Ps 42:2–3)

Repeated seven times, the word *nafshi* punctuates both movements of the poem (42:2, 3, 5, 6, 7, 12; 43:5); it is one of the two words most often repeated.[49] This density of occurrence suggests that to render it consistently

---

46. Mary Oliver writes about the abuse of a child in "Rage" (*New and Selected Poems*, 1:108–9). Among Roethke's poems that seem to refer directly to his illness, see especially "The Waking" and "In a Dark Time," in *The Collected Poems of Theodore Roethke* (Garden City: Doubleday, 1966), 108 and 239.

47. Roethke, "The Marrow," in *Collected Poems*, 246.

48. The Hebrew reads "be seen," which is commonly taken to be a late scribal emendation to avoid anthropomorphizing the deity—something that does not bother many or most biblical writers (e.g., Num 12:8; Job 42:5)!

49. The most frequent word in the psalm is *El/Elohim*, "God," which appears twenty times: Ps 42:2, 3 (3x), 4, 5, 6, 7, 9, 10, 11, 12 (2x); 43:1, 2, 4 (3x), 5 (2x).

as the personal pronoun "I" (as I do in 42:3) would be under-transla-
tion. However, the once-conventional translation "my soul" is problematic, for it hides the implied physicality of the word. In this metaphor of
insatiable thirst, the rare literal meaning of *nafshi*, "my throat," cannot
be entirely elided. My translation "whole-self" in the first line may be
heuristically useful, but it is only barely idiomatic in English, and using
it seven times would ruin the poem. In the second line, then, I render it
with the first-person pronoun, which is often the sense of this seminal
Hebrew word. Elsewhere I use simply "self," following Roethke's own
usage of the word "self," which appears periodically in his later works.
In these "sometimes metaphysical" poems, he describes his attempt "to
break from the bondage of self, from the barriers of the 'real' world, to
come as close to God as possible."[50] Roethke writes variously of "the long
journey out of the self" ("Journey to the Interior"), "the self [that] per-
sists like a dying star" ("Meditation at Oyster River"), how "the lost self
changes" ("The Far Field"), and "death of the self in a long, tearless night"
("In a Dark Time").[51] For him, as for this psalmist, "self," as both term and
concept, is poetically indispensable.

It is tempting to romanticize longing for God, at least from the outside,
but the psalm immediately opposes that temptation with the metaphor of
a deer suffering extreme thirst. Elsewhere in Hebrew poetry, a deer may
represent attractive qualities that humans wish to claim for themselves:
speed, grace, physical prowess (e.g., 2 Sam 2:18; Isa 35:6; Ps 18:34; Song
2:9, 17). Here, it displays an unenviable vulnerability; thirst in the semi-
arid land of Israel is an imminently life-threatening condition. Similarly,
Roethke expresses the searing pain of longing and doubt evoked by God's
felt absence:

> Brooding on God, I may become a man.
> Pain wanders through my bones like a lost fire;
> What burns me now? Desire, desire, desire.
> Godhead above my God, are you there still?[52]

---

50. Theodore Roethke, "On 'In a Dark Time,'" in *The Contemporary Poet as Artist and Critic: Eight Symposia*, ed. Anthony Ostroff (Boston: Little, Brown, 1965), 49; cited in Richard Allen Blessing, *Theodore Roethke's Dynamic Vision* (Bloomington: Indiana University Press, 1974), 199.
51. See Roethke, *Collected Poems*, 190, 193, 201, and 239.
52. Roethke, "The Marrow," in *Collected Poems*, 246. The poem was first published in *The New Yorker*, May 19, 1962, fifteen months before Roethke's sudden death.

"Godhead above my God"—Roethke's imagination stretches beyond his earlier, presumably more contained conception of the divine, as agonizing desire drives him to become more fully human: "I may become a man." Another (posthumously published) poem "The Longing" suggests something more of how pain enables transformation. He longs for what does not change with time, "the imperishable quiet at the heart of form; I would be a stream ..." Such transformation requires that he rid himself of ordinary human pettiness,

> ... unlearn all the lingo of exasperation, all the distortions of
>   malice and hatred;
> I would believe my pain. ...[53]

The psalm's opening metaphor of discomforting thirst is followed by a second metaphor whose meaning is more ambiguous:

> My tears have been food for me day and night,
> when they say to me all the time,
> "So where is your God?" (Ps 42:4)

There is a connection between the two metaphors: if the psalmist is swallowing tears, then his physiological *nefesh*, his throat, is parched. However, Diane Palley, in what she sometimes calls "visual midrash," develops the metaphor of tears as food in a surprising and hope-filled direction. In a schematic representation of ancient Israel's rain-fed agriculture, she shows rain in the shape of teardrops falling upon the hill country. The terraced landscape is decked with the traditional "seven species," the crops that constitute the essential wealth of the land of Israel: wheat, barley, grape, fig, pomegranate, olive, and date (see Deut 8:8). Palley, who works with Jewish traditions of iconography and spirituality, has created an image of sorrow that leads to healing. As far as I know, her reading is wholly original, but it is consonant with the teaching of the great Hasidic master and mystic Reb Nachman of Bratslav (1772–1810), who famously understood Psalm 42 as a psalm of healing. This is one of ten psalms (16, 32, 41, 42, 59, 77, 90, 105, 137, and 150) that constitute what he called the *Tikkun HaKlali*, "the General Rectification," prescribing their recitation as a remedy for moral and spiritual failings.

---

53. Roethke, "The Longing," in *Collected Poems*, 188.

LANDSCAPES OF HEALING

"The art of salvation, is but the art of memory" (Donne). Remembering is the most important activity of this psalmist's self: "These things I remember, and I pour out my self (*nafshi*)"; he recalls the festal procession to God's house, "a pilgrim throng" (Ps 42:5). But then immediately the psalmist's imagination is transported to another landscape, one that is also symbolically rich:

> My self is bent down within me; therefore I remember you
>   from the land of Jordan and the Hermon Range, from Mount
>   Mizar. (42:7)

These are the holy mountains of ancient Canaanite religion, the abundantly watered region on the southern end of the Lebanon Range, near where the Jordan has its source. The poet's memory fuses that remote, numinous landscape with the familiar, more modest heights of the Judean hill country, as does another psalmist who imaginatively redescribes Mount Zion as "beautiful in elevation ..., the far reaches of the north" (48:3).

For our poet, the precipitous northern landscape is productive of the psalm's most memorable image:

> Deep to deep calls out at the sound of your waterfalls.
> All your breakers and waves sweep over me. (42:8)

"Deep to deep calls out"—the phrase is resonant at many levels: outer landscape calling to inner landscape, body to spirit, human heart to the heart of God, pain calling forth the potential for new life. Indeed, the divine water for which the thirsty psalmist longed is now revealed to be both overwhelming and refreshing; the drenching breakers leave in their wake a fresh perception of God's *ḥesed*, covenant-love:

> By day YHWH commands his covenant-love,
> and by night his song is with me, a prayer to the God of my
>   life. (42:9)

Is the resonant landscape itself guiding the psalmist in prayer? That is one possible reading of the conjunction of these two verses, an inference that might be correlated with Roethke's description of the emergence of his own mature and more whole self. For him, healing is fostered by contemplation of "the advancing and retreating waters" of his inner landscape and likewise of the Pacific Northwest, where he spent his later years:

I, who came back from the depths laughing too loudly,
Become another thing;
My eyes extend beyond the farthest bloom of the waves;
I lose and find myself in the long waters;
I am gathered together once more;
I embrace the world.[54]

Mary Oliver, too, in any number of her poems, affirms that the nonhuman world not only guides us to realize our selves more fully, but even instructs us in spiritual realities. In "Five A.M. in the Pinewoods," which she identifies as "a poem about the world // that is ours, or could be," she writes of an intimate, fearless encounter with two deer:

I was thinking:
so this is how you swim inward,
so this is how you flow outward,
so this is how you pray.[55]

Like the psalmist, Oliver registers a moment of new perception about how we may sense the reality of divine presence and attention by directing our imaginative and loving attention to the God-marked world.

In another poem, Oliver follows the psalmist (consciously or not) in detecting the numinous in a waterfall. She sees the water

unspooling
like ribbons made of snow
or god's white hair.

...

light-hearted to be
flying at last.[56]

Oliver's image of "The white, scrolled // wings of the tumbling water" finds a remarkable visual echo in Diane Palley's interpretation of the boisterous waters of Psalm 42. In Palley's first image, the curling waves do indeed seem to be flying, rising out of a stream that teems with piscine

54. Roethke, "The Long Waters," in *Collected Poems*, 198. The poem as originally published in *The New Yorker* (June 2, 1962), 34 reads, "long waters" in the antepenultimate line. In *Collected Poems*, the line reads "the long water" (singular). I have adopted the original reading, which is identical with the poem's title.
55. Oliver, "Five A.M. in the Pinewoods," in *New and Selected Poems*, 1:83–84.
56. Oliver, "The Waterfall," in *New and Selected Poems*, 1:19.

life. Its eighteen fish are an allusion to the Eighteen Benedictions of the *Amidah*, the "Standing Prayer" that constitutes the core of the Jewish daily prayer liturgy. Eighteen is also the numerical value of the letters that make up the Hebrew word *ḥai*, "living" (see Ps 42:3).

The Eighteen Benedictions is a litany of blessings, naming God's essential attributes and acts of faithfulness to Israel and humankind: "the Shield of Abraham," "the One who revives the dead," "the holy God," etc. In naming God thus, the *Amidah* bears a resemblance to Psalm 42 itself, which stands out among the psalms for the way it multiplies divine appellations, some of them unique to this poem. Maybe no other psalm of this length names God so variously: "living God" (42:3), "my God" (42:7, 12, 43:4), "God of my life" (42:9), "God my Rock" (42:10), "my stronghold God" (43:2), "God of my utmost joy" (43:4). For this exploration of how psalms both bespeak and elicit religious engagement, it is important that this highly introspective psalmist never lapses into self-absorption. Rather, naming God repeatedly and creatively, the poet maintains an insistent dialogue with God throughout.

Diane Palley uses the stream to follow the flow of the prayer through her two images. In the second, treating Psalm 43, the scrolled waters have become subdued; they rise on smaller wings. Now just three fish—a nod to the Trinity, in an image created for a Christian worship space—make their way in a stream that seems to be illumined by the rising sun: "Send out your light and your truth; *they* will lead me." "So this is how you flow outward," Oliver might say in response: from inner tumult to petition addressed to God, from being mired in depression to actively seeking grace, from a focus on my desperate need to anticipation of intimate encounter with the longed-for Other: "I will come to God's altar, to the God of my utmost joy."

That anticipation is clear in this psalm, but it is not the final word. Rather the poem ends with the self-questioning refrain:

How bent down, my self, and how wrought you are;
hope to God. ... (Ps 43:5)

The journey of the self is not complete in this psalm, and that is a key element of its realism. The psalmist's achievement is not to close the "long and terrible" distance between the self and God, but rather to keep hoping, with a clear direction for that hope. Thus the psalm evidences, in Roethke's words, "one of the ways man [sic] at least approaches the divine—in this comprehensive human act, the really good poem."[57]

---

57. Theodore Roethke, "On Identity," in *On Poetry and Craft: Selected Prose of Theodore Roethke* (Port Townsend: Copper Canyon Press, 2001), 42.

Appendix 1

Translations of Psalms 38 and 42–43

Ellen F. Davis

PSALM 38

1. A David psalm, for calling to mind.

2. O YHWH, do not rebuke me in your rage nor chastise me in your wrath!

3. For your arrows have descended on me, and upon me your hand has descended.

4. There is no health in my body because of your indignation, no soundness in my bones because of my offense.

5. For my iniquities have mounted over my head; they are like a heavy burden, too heavy for me.

6. My sores stink, they fester because of my folly;

7. I am bent, bowed very low; all day long I go about in mourning.

8. For my loins are filled with burning; there is no health in my body.

9. I am numb and utterly crushed; I roar, from the growling of my heart.

10. My Lord, all my longing is before you; and my groaning is not hidden from you.

11. My heart palpitates; my strength forsakes me, and the light
    of my eyes—that too is absent from me.

12. My intimates and companions stand distant from my plague,
    and my own kin stand far away.

13. They strike, those who seek my life, and they who wish me
    harm speak violence; deceit they mutter all day long.

14. But I, like the deaf I do not hear; and like the mute who don't
    open their mouth,

15. I have become like a person who does not hear and has no
    rebuke in his mouth.

16. Yet for you, O Lord, I wait-in-hope. It is you who will answer,
    my Lord, my God!

17. For I said, "What if they rejoice over me … ?!" When my foot
    slips, they vaunt themselves over me."

18. Indeed I am ready to stumble, and my agonies are ever
    before me.

19. Yes, I declare my iniquity; I am in dread because of my offense.

20. But my enemies are alive, they grow strong, and many are
    those who hate me for a lie—

21. those who return me evil for good, who oppose me because
    of my pursuing the good.

22. Do not forsake me, O Yhwh; my God, do not be far from me!

23. Hurry to my aid, my Lord, my deliverance!

PSALM 42

1. Of the leader, a maskil of the Korahites

2. As a deer yearns toward streambeds,
    so my whole-self[1] yearns for you, O God.

3. I (nafshi) thirst for God, for the living God.
    When will I come and [see[2]] the face of God?

4. My tears have been food for me day and night,
    when they say to me all the time, "So where is your God?"

5. These things I remember, and I pour out my self:
    how I made procession in the crowd, making my way to the
    house of God,
    to the sound of jubilation and thanksgiving—a pilgrim throng.

6. How bent down, my self, and wrought you are;
    hope to God, for still I acclaim him, his saving Presence—
    my God!

7. My self is bent down within me; therefore I remember you
    from the land of Jordan and the Hermon Range, from
    Mount Mizar.

8. Deep to deep calls out at the sound of your waterfalls.
    All your breakers and waves sweep over me.

9. By day YHWH commands his covenant-love,
    and by night his song is with me, a prayer to the God of my life.

10. I say to God my Rock, "Why have you forgotten me?
    Why do I go about in gloom under hostile pressure?"

11. With bone-shattering attacks my opponents revile me,
    while they say to me all the time, "So where is your God?"

12. How bent down, my self, and how wrought you are;
    hope to God, for still I acclaim him, my saving Presence and
    my God!

---

1. Hebrew: *nafshi* (literally, "throat, neck"), connoting the totality of the living person,
including the physical self.
2. Hebrew reads: "be seen."

PSALM 43

1. Execute judgment for me, God; defend my case from a
   people of bad faith!

2. For you are my stronghold God—why have you ignored me?
   Why do I continue to go about under pressure of
   the enemy?

3. Send out your light and your truth; *they* will lead me.
   They will bring me to your holy hill and to
   your dwelling-place.

4. Let me come to God's altar, to the God of my highest joy,
   and I will acclaim you with the lyre, O God, my God!

5. How bent down, my self, and how wrought you are;
   hope to God, for still I acclaim him, my saving Presence
   and my God!

Appendix 2

Diane Palley's Images of Psalms 42–43

These images are described on pages 69–75, and are reproduced here by permission of the artist, Diane Palley.

AS A
DEER LONGS
FOR STREAMS OF
WATER, SO MY SOUL
LONGS FOR YOU, O GOD

MY SOUL THIRSTS FOR GOD, FOR THE LIVING GOD

MY TEARS HAVE BEEN FOOD FOR ME DAY AND NIGHT

HOPE IN GOD FOR I SHALL YET PRAISE HIM
MY EVER PRESENT HELP AND MY GOD
Psalm Forty-Two

SEND OUT
YOUR LIGHT
AND YOUR TRUTH
THEY WILL LEAD ME
THEY WILL BRING ME TO YOUR HOLY MOUNTAIN AND TO YOUR DWELLING PLACE

ושלח אורך
ואמתך המה
ינחוני

הוחילי לאלהים כי עוד אודנו
ישועת פני ואלהי
Psalm Forty Three

5

Psalms "Translated" for
Life in the 21st Century:
A South African Perspective

June F. Dickie

INTRODUCTION

Before considering some ways in which the psalms are taking on a new life for contemporary South Africans, an abbreviated history of approaches to Bible translation is given. Thereafter the changing definition of "translation" is discussed, and reception theory, which provides a framework for how a reader interprets a text, is reviewed.

APPROACHES TO BIBLE TRANSLATION IN THE MODERN ERA

Over the last hundred years, the Bible has been translated into many languages and cultures.[1] Initially translators sought to retain not only the message of the original but also its form. As Nida and Taber note, "The older focus in translating was the form of the message, and translators took particular delight in being able to reproduce stylistic specialities, e.g., rhythms, rhymes, plays on words, chiasm, parallelism, and unusual

---

1. As of 2018, 683 languages have a complete Bible, another 1,534 have a New Testament, and portions are available in a further 1,133 languages. There are currently 2,659 active translation projects and work may be needed in another 2,163 languages (Wycliffe Bible Translators: https://www.wycliffe.org.uk/about/our-impact/).

grammatical structures."[2] However, they continue, "The new focus has shifted from the form of the message to the response of the receptor ... This response must then be compared with the way in which the original receptors presumably reacted to the message when it was given in its original setting."[3] This notion of "dynamic equivalence" was later refined by de Waard and Nida to "functional equivalence" in which the goal is to use forms in the receptor language which achieve the same functionality as that achieved by the source text.[4] This requires a careful analysis of the source text, including the performative, emotive, and aesthetic functions, which are so critical in poetry (the focus of this paper).

Through the 1990s, an emphasis on linguistics persisted in translation theory. One of the notions promoted was that when translating a dynamic source text[5] (for example, a literary or poetic text), a literal approach is not possible.[6] Wendland makes a similar observation, arguing that a literal approach is not suitable when translating a literary text which has artistic and rhetorical force. In his words, "The compositional procedure must be loosened up in order to allow gifted translators the freedom to more fully access and creatively utilize the stylistic and expressive resources of the receptor language."[7]

The next development in translation theory was a focus on the aesthetic features of the text. Although Nida and Taber had noted the importance of "rhythmic features of poetry," not much attention had been given to the poetic, literary, and rhetorical effects of texts.[8] The person to lead the field in this area has been Ernst Wendland, and in 2006, he developed his LiFE approach (Literary Functional Equivalence).[9] Closely related to a focus on the literary features of a text are its oral characteristics. Poetry should always be sounded aloud, and thus the poet-translator

---

2. Eugene A. Nida and Charles R. Taber, *The Theory and Practice of Translation*, Helps for Translators 8 (Leiden: Brill, 1969), 1.

3. Nida and Taber, *The Theory and Practice of Translation*, 1.

4. Jan de Waard and Eugene A. Nida, *From One Language to Another: Functional Equivalence in Bible Translating* (Nashville: Thomas Nelson, 1986), 36.

5. A dynamic text has elements which are "expectation-defying." See, Basil Hatim and Ian Mason, *The Translator as Communicator* (London: Routledge, 1997), 28.

6. Basil Hatim and Ian Mason, *Discourse and the Translator* (London: Longman, 1990).

7. Ernst R. Wendland, "Towards a 'Literary' Translation of the Scriptures: With Special Reference to a 'Poetic Rendition,'" *AcT* 22 (2002): 179.

8. Nida and Taber, *The Theory and Practice of Translation*, 148.

9. See Ernst R. Wendland, *LiFE-Style Translating*, SIL International Publications in Translation and Textlinguistics 2 (Dallas: SIL International, 2006).

must understand the features of oral communication. This is not simply giving sound to printed text. As Fry notes, oral discourse is very different from written discourse.[10] The text must be completely restructured using features of aurality (e.g., mnemonic cues) so that it can be received by the ear and not the eye.[11]

Foley extended the notion of "orality" to that of "performance."[12] Performance of a biblical text introduces many new issues, both positive and challenging. On the positive side, they highlight the rhetorical function of a text. As Foley notes, they can "restore at least some of the original dynamism that stories have in oral performance."[13] But they also raise new questions, for example, how to evaluate the accuracy of the text. As Rowe observes, "The translation theory that supports printed modern language versions of ancient texts may prove inadequate for the requirements of new media forms."[14] Indeed, embodied performances of texts require us to stretch our ideas of what translation is.[15]

Changing Concepts of the Notion of "Translation"

Interest in "new media" translation has been growing recently, beyond that of audio in the 1990s to film and other multi-media performance,

10. Euan McG. Fry, "Faithfulness: A Wider Perspective," in *Fidelity and Translation: Communicating the Bible in New Media*, ed. Paul A. Soukup and Robert Hodgson (Franklin: Sheed & Ward; New York: American Bible Society, 1999), 14.

11. Luther sought to produce a German translation "for the ear," to be read aloud in public worship. "He constantly read his sentences aloud, testing ... for their melodic flow." Paul Wendland, "Bible Translations for the 21st Century" (Lecture given at Bethany Lutheran College as part of the The Bjarne Wollan Teigen Reformation Lectures, Mankato, MN, October 25–26, 2012), 19.

12. John Miles Foley, *The Singer of Tales in Performance* (Bloomington: Indiana University Press, 1995).

13. John Miles Foley, *Oral Tradition and the Internet: Pathways of the Mind* (Urbana: University of Illinois Press, 2012). See www.oraltradition.org.

14. Gary R. Rowe, "Fidelity and Access: Reclaiming the Bible with Personal Media," in *Fidelity and Translation: Communicating the Bible in New Media*, eds. Paul A. Soukup and Robert Hodgson (Franklin: Sheed & Ward; New York: American Bible Society, 1999), 51.

15. Susan Bassnett, *Translation* (London and New York: Routledge, 2014), 153–57.

as well as virtual translations.[16] Foley asserts that cyber-techniques (an "e-edition") can recover more of what the page fails to capture.[17]

The product of translation is also no longer necessarily restricted to words on a page. Cronin claims that "we need an expanded understanding of what language is."[18] If language is the code or form used to communicate a message, then language can include the performance arts and the visual arts, among others. In that case, text language may be translated into forms such as song, rap, spoken poetry, drama, dance, mosaic, drawing, or painting. But Cronin goes even further than this and extends the notion of translation to other "forms of transference," for example those linked with ecology, travel, and the sustainability of food. Gentzler refers to "post-translation," where translation is viewed as "transdisciplinary, mobile, and open-ended."[19] He asserts, "New definitions of translation and rewriting are needed for the twentieth-first century, those that include ideas of rewriting, reinvention, transformation, and trans-adaptation."

Pym asserts that "localization" is replacing "translation," and "the goal of localization is to get a maximum amount of information to a maximum amount of people."[20] This suggests that oral communication, and the inclusion of as many members of the community as possible in the translation effort are relevant. This idea is central to the empirical study: including community members in the translation process and using oral communication. This is also in line with the thinking of Shirky.[21] He contends that the millennial generation is no longer content to simply receive a final product (a Bible in their language) but they want to be involved in the *process* that brings that product into being.

---

16. The business sector are calling this era the "digitoral" era (digital + oral). The oral/aural dimension is being "catalyzed with the technology that tethers social networks together." Samuel E. Chiang, Editorial. *Orality Journal*, 2 (2013), 8.

17. See Foley, *Oral Tradition and the Internet*. See also his website www.oraltradition.org.

18. Michael Cronin, "Translation Lecture 2" (Paper given at Nida School of Translation Studies, Misano, Italy, 2016).

19. Edwin Gentzler, "Rethinking Translation and Rewriting *Hamlet* in China" (Paper given at Nida School of Translation Studies, Misano, Italy, 2016).

20. Anthony Pym, *The Moving Text: Localization, Translation, and Distribution* (Philadelphia: John Benjamins, 2004).

21. Clay Shirky, *Cognitive Surplus: Creativity and Generosity in a Connected Age* (New York: Penguin, 2010).

The past decade has also seen a greater focus on power relations and ethics as being central to Bible translation.[22] This has come out of a challenge to the goal of "equivalence" in translation, as have the criteria used for evaluating a translation.[23] Equivalence has been seen as unattainable;[24] rather, translation is conceived of as "manipulation" or "re-writing," a creative act.[25] This shifts the perspective from "faithfulness to the past" to "acceptability in the present," with the needs of the receptor community being uppermost. This notion of fidelity as "the relevance of a translation to its specific time and audience"[26] has long been the standard in India, and is currently the accepted *modus operandi* in China when it comes to non-sacred literature.[27]

Within Bible translation, this concept has been strengthened by the growing interest in performance translation. The presence of an audience and its particular needs and interests motivates the translator to create or re-create something new. Maxey argues that this is not to imply the (Bible) translator does not respect the source text or value the Bible's historicity, but recuperating the written text may no longer be the primary goal of Bible translation.[28]

Other long-held notions of Bible translation have also been challenged in recent years. The goal of a "clear" translation has been criticized as

22. As Michaela Wolf argues: "Translation ... always involves—voluntarily or not—asymmetrical power relations." See her "The Third Space in Postcolonial Representation," in *Changing the Terms: Translating in the Postcolonial Era*, eds. Sherry Simon and Paul St-Pierre Simon (Ottawa: University of Ottawa Press, 2000), 127.
23. Theo Hermans claims that equivalence between texts is not achieved, but rather is imposed, in "Translation, Equivalence and Intertextuality," *Wasafiri* 18 (2003): 39–41.
24. Bella Brodzki claims that "The difficulty of translation derives ... from the inherent non-equivalence of languages. See her "History, Cultural Memory, and the Tasks of Translation," in T. Obinkaram Echewa's *I Saw the Sky Catch Fire*, PMLA 114 (1999): 218.
25. E.g., André Lefevere, *Translation, Rewriting, and the Manipulation of the Literary Fame* (London: Routledge, 1992). Sherry Simon defines translation as "an expanded writing that is inspired by the encounter with other tongues, including the effects of creative interference." See her *Translating Montreal: Episodes in the Life of a Divided City* (Montreal: McGill-Queen's University Press, 2006), 17.
26. Shantha Ramakrishna, "Cultural Transmission through Translation: An Indian Perspective," in *Changing the Terms: Translating in the Postcolonial Era*, eds. Sherry Simon and Paul St-Pierre Simon (Ottawa: University of Ottawa Press, 2000), 90.
27. Gentzler, "Rethinking Translation."
28. James A. Maxey, "Alternative Evaluative Concepts to the Trinity of Bible Translation," in *Translating Values: Evaluative Concepts in Translation*, eds. Piotr Blumczynski and John Gillespie (New York: Palgrave Macmillan, 2016).

showing an erroneous idea of monovalent meaning (with a singular authorial intention). Ambiguity is an important concept, particularly in the case of poetry.[29] The current notion of reception theory allows for gaps of indeterminacy to be interpreted by readers or audiences. This is discussed next.

RECEPTION THEORY

Reception theory states that readers bring their own context to the way they interpret a text. The reader has a creative role and participates fully in the determination of the meaning of the text.[30] The need for the reader to perform such an active role arises from the "gaps" in the text. These gaps may be the result of translation ambiguities or arise from the use of metaphors.[31] Indeed, metaphors are "aids to reflection" and so invite the readers to participate.[32] Consequently the interpreting of poetic (or literary) text is a "creative activity [bringing together] text and imagination."[33]

The reader generally fills the "gaps" in the text based on his/her experience. As Fretheim notes, "What we bring to the text will inevitably affect what we see in the text."[34] Soukup adds the idea of the reader's "needs" and "background" which also play a role in the way meaning is negotiated (within the range of possible meanings).[35] This is in line with relevance theory: people exert minimal effort for maximum benefit, and thus the first "meaning" that makes sense to one's experience will be the view that

---

29. For example, Andrei S. Desnitsky notes, "Deliberate ambiguity is a common feature of highly creative writing such as poetry." See his "Thread and Tracery, or Prose and Poetry in the Bible," *BT* 57 (2006): 89. Also see Terence E. Fretheim, "The Authority of the Bible and the Imaging of God," in *Engaging Biblical Authority*, ed. William P. Brown (Louisville: Westminster John Knox, 2007), 45–52.
30. John A. Darr, *Herod the Fox: Audience Criticism and Lukan Characterization*, JSNTSup 163 (Sheffield: Sheffield Academic, 1998), 29.
31. Fretheim, "The Authority of the Bible," 51.
32. Ruth apRoberts, "The Multiplication of Similitudes," in *Approaches to Teaching the Hebrew Bible as Literature in Translation*, eds. Barry N. Olshen and Yael S. Feldman (New York: Modern Language Association of America, 1989), 69.
33. Wolfgang Iser, *The Implied Reader: Patterns of Communication in Prose Fiction from Bunyan to Beckett* (Baltimore: John Hopkins University Press, 1974), 279.
34. Fretheim, "The Authority of the Bible," 52.
35. Paul A. Soukup, "Understanding Audience Understanding," in *From One Medium to Another: Communicating the Bible through Multimedia*, eds. Paul A. Soukup and Robert Hodgson (Kansas City, MO: Sheed & Ward, 1997), 103–4 and 107.

is taken.[36] As the "gaps" provide hermeneutical possibilities for readers to apply the text in ways that are meaningful to their personal situations, there could be several valid readings for a particular text.[37] Meaning for the individual arises where the horizons of the reader and the text fuse.[38]

There are other criteria that may be applied to determine the validity of a reader's interpretation. Foley[39] asserts that the way gaps are filled should harmonize with the context of the complete text. This includes the literary context (what Iser refers to as "consistency building") as well as the historical and sociological context of the text.[40] This suggests that only a limited number of interpretations are possible for a given text, and some will be more true to the author's intent than others.[41] Indeed, Hirsch believes that the ultimate determiner of meaning should be authorial intent as the meaning assigned by the audience is simply "derived."[42] However, in the empirical translations, personal interpretation (in line with reception theory) triumphed over the traditional determiners of the meaning of the text. Although attention was given to the historical and social context of the particular psalm, and to maintaining consistency within the psalm (taking cognizance of the literary context), the main factor in determining meaning was "the needs and experience of the reader."

EMPIRICAL STUDY

In this study, three sub-genres of psalms are studied with the goal to translate them in a way that is meaningful for different communities. Those who compose the translations are not professional Bible translators

---

36. See Ernst-August Gutt, *Relevance Theory: A Guide to Successful Communication in Translation* (Dallas: Summer Institute of Linguistics; New York: United Bible Societies, 1992).

37. Wayne C. Booth, "'Preserving the Exemplar': Or, How Not to Dig Our Own Graves," *CI* 3 (1977): 407–23.

38. Hans-Georg Gadamer, *Truth and Method*, 2nd ed.; trans. J. Weinsheimer and Donald G. Marshall (Berkeley: University of California Press, 1991).

39. John Miles Foley, *Immanent Art: From Structure to Meaning in Traditional Oral Epic* (Bloomington: Indiana University Press, 1991), 41.

40. Iser, *The Implied Reader*.

41. Susan Rubin Suleiman, "Introduction: Varieties of Audience-Oriented Criticism," in *The Reader in the Text: Essays on Audience and Interpretation*, eds. Susan Rubin Suleiman and Inge Crosman (Princeton: Princeton University Press, 1980), 23–24.

42. E.D. Hirsch Jr., *The Aims of Interpretation* (Chicago: University of Chicago Press, 1976).

but community members who bring a particular gift—either a poetic sensitivity or capacity in a creative art—and after studying the psalm, apply their gift to compose or perform "a translation." This new creative product carries the same message and rhetorical force as the original but with a beauty that is appropriate and sensitive to the audience.

The first part of the empirical study considers two praise psalms, viz. Psalms 134 and 93. The second part includes two lament psalms, viz. Psalms 3 and 13, as models for those in pain to compose their own laments. And the third part focuses on a wisdom psalm, viz. Psalm 133, and invites various artists to study the message of the psalm and find new ways to convey its message using various media (music, dance, song, and spoken poetry). Each of these "translation styles" is described and evaluated in the sections below.

EMPIRICAL STUDY: TRANSLATING PRAISE PSALMS INTO
ANOTHER LANGUAGE

The first part of the empirical study involves translating praise psalms into Zulu. Thus it is necessary to understand a little about the current Zulu Bible. The version used in almost all of the Zulu churches was translated in 1959, during the era of "literal translations," following the structure of the Hebrew text. Consequently the translation often sounds unnatural or stilted. In particular, the Zulu psalms do not include the features of Zulu oral art, and so do not sound like Zulu poems. This aggravated a particular Zulu poet to the extent that he requested Eugene Nida, then secretary of the United Bible Societies, if he could recompose the Zulu psalms using the features of Zulu praise poetry (*izibongo*). He did so, and according to Nida, was very successful.[43] However, unfortunately his efforts were never incorporated into an official Zulu translation.

A second problem with the current Zulu Bible is that it is not written in the language spoken by Zulu youth. Most of them are now in English-medium schools and so no longer read or write the difficult consonantal clusters and clicks which are prevalent in "deep Zulu" (spoken by the older population). Rather they speak "light Zulu." And a third problem with the current situation is that Psalms are very rarely read, either in the church or privately. Consequently most Zulu youth are unaware that the Bible contains poetry, full of emotion and lyrically beautiful, like their traditional poetry.

---

43. Eugene A. Nida, *Fascinated by Languages* (Amsterdam: John Benjamins, 2003), 82.

Four groups were invited to participate in psalms workshops, one group at a time. The first consisted of a youth group from AmaOti township near Durban; the second was a collection of Anglican youth and choir members from various congregations in Pietermaritzburg (PMB); the third comprised students at the Lutheran Theological Institute in PMB; and the fourth group were "poetry fans" from the PMB poets' group, Tree of Life. A workshop consisted of four days (preferably, although in some cases, only three days were available). Participants were given basic training in Bible translation, poetics (Hebrew and Zulu), and Zulu music / rhythm. Then each day they focused on one short psalm: first Psalm 134, then Psalm 93, and finally Ps 145:1–8.⁴⁴ The background to each psalm was discussed as well as key terms. Attention was also given to the poetic devices used in the Hebrew text and the functions they achieved. Then participants were encouraged to use features of Zulu oral art to achieve the same functionality, and they made a translation of the psalm (individually or in groups). This was checked by the researcher for general accuracy, and then they (in groups) converted the written psalm into a performance (rap, spoken poetry, song, or a combination of these).

A few examples follow, showing how the Zulu youth translated the Hebrew into their own context. In the first example, the poet gave an interesting interpretation to the colon 'stand by night' in Ps 134:1. Most commentators and translations indicate that this refers to those who were serving at night-time. However the Hebrew terms הָעֹמְדִים ('the ones standing before YHWH)' and בַּלֵּילוֹת ('at night') can also be understood as 'the ones persevering' and 'a time of trial' respectively.⁴⁵ Thus the poet in Example 1, who was going through a time of great personal difficulty, read his context into the Hebrew text, and gave the translation of 'persevering through difficulties.'

<hr>

44. Examples from translations of Psalm 145 are not included for lack of space, and as they showed similar features to those in Psalm 134 and Psalm 93. A full set of the poets' translations can be seen in June F. Dickie, "Zulu Song, Oral Art, Performing the Psalms to Stir the Heart: Applying Indigenous Form to the Translation and Performance of Some Praise Psalms" (PhD diss., University of KwaZulu-Natal, 2017).
45. See "עמד" BDB, 764 and "לַיְלָה ,לַיִל" BDB, 539.

Example 1[46]

| Mdumiseni nina eniqiniselayo | [with] the LORD through difficulties |
| kuSimakade nase binzimeni | (And) praise him you who persevere |

In the third verse of Psalm 134, some poets expressed 'heaven and earth' using different picture-language. In Example 2 below the poet used two parallel cola to translate the concept. The imagery refers to the creation, as does that in the original Hebrew text. The extended expression (using two poetic lines, 3c and 3d, instead of the one found in the Hebrew) contributes to the rhythm of the poem, and the repetition/parallelism has a mnemonic function.

Example 2

3a. Engathi Inkosi yamakhosi inganibusisa eyaseSiyoni,	May the Lord of lords may he bless-you from Zion,
3b. engathi anganibusisa	may he bless you
3c. lo owahlukanisa ubumnyama nokukhanya	this one who separates darkness and light
3d. owahlukanisa amanzi nolwandle.	who separates water and sea.

The central section of Psalm 93 (vv. 3–4) refers to "floods," "many waters," and "waves of the sea" (ESV). Both verses show threefold repetition which "gave the psalmist an opportunity to build a thought or an emotion to a climax."[47] The imagery of "overwhelming water" was not particularly relevant to the Zulu poets, and so most changed this, usually remaining with imagery of natural phenomena (such as wind, fire, a mountain, or a lion). In Example 3, the poet has interpreted "waves" as an enemy, and added the simile of a lion, to convey the idea of increasing attack.

---

46. These examples are listed in full in Dickie, "Zulu Song," Appendix 2a: "Audio Recordings from Workshops."
47. John T. Willis, "The Juxtaposition of Synonymous and Chiastic Parallelism in Tricola in Old Testament Hebrew Psalm Poetry," VT 29 (1979): 479–80.

Example 3

3a. Noma isitha singahlasela,   Even if the enemy
    Jehova,   attacks, LORD,
3b. sihlasele nhlangothi zombili,   they attack both ways,
3c. sihlasela kuhle kwebhubesi,   they attack strongly like
                                         a lion

The next poet changed the imagery of water to that of wind, growing in
intensity. He also introduced personification (4b in Example 4) which is
typical of Zulu poetry, ascribing personal attributes to natural phenomena.

Example 4

3a. Umoya uyavunguza ke   The wind is blowing (filler)
3b. izivungu-vungu   gales they are
    ziyavunguza, Mdali,   blowing, Creator,
3c. kuvunguza sansunami.   blowing a tsunami.
4a. Ungophezu kwezivungu-vungu,   You are above the
                                         strong gales,
4b. izivungu-vungu ziyakulalela,   the gales will listen to you,
4c. unamandla okumisa insunami.   you have power to stop
                                         a tsunami.

The next example is interesting in that the poet maintains the original
metaphor of overwhelming water until the last line, when he introduces
an image of a mountain. For the Zulu, this is the biggest, strongest image
they could imagine, and so it serves as the ultimate superlative.

Example 5

4a. Unamandla ngaphezu   You are powerful above the
    kwenhlokomo yemifula!   big sound of the rivers!
4b. Unamandla ngaphezu   You are powerful above the
    kwemidumo   roar of the waves of the sea!
    yamagagas'olwandle!
4c. Unamandla,   You are powerful, you are
    unamandl', uSimakad'   powerful, LORD,
4d. ongaphezu   above the highest mountain!
    kwezicongco zezintaba!

The next poem (Example 6) mixes metaphors, which is typical of Zulu poetry, but the poet maintains the threefold parallelism in both verses 3 and 4, and repeats the imagery from verse 3 in verse 4, thereby indicating that the LORD is stronger than all the problems mentioned. This is important, to convey the message of the Hebrew, and to retain the rhetorical force (retaining the tricola structure, with increasing intensity, e.g., in v. 3, from a "roar" to an "attack" of wind with one intensifier, to "blowing" with two intensifiers).

Example 6

3a. Nakuba isitha sibhodla okwebhubesi,	Even tho' enemy it is roaring like a lion,
3b. Nakuba izivunga-vunga zisihlasela ngamandla,	Even tho' strong winds attack strongly,
3c. Nakuba umoya uvunguza ngamandla,	Even tho' wind is blowing strongly with power,
4a. inamandla Nkosi ngaphezu kwebhubesi,	LORD is more powerful than the lion,
4b. inamandla Nkosi ngaphezu kwezivungu-vungu,	LORD is more powerful than the storm
4c. inamandla Nkosi ngaphezukwezivungu-vungu ezivunguza ngamandla.	LORD is more powerful than the storm blowing with power.

The outer verses of Psalm 93 (vv. 1–2 and 5, forming an inclusio frame) were also given interesting interpretations by some of the Zulu poets. For example, ESV translates verse 1 as "he has put on strength as his belt," but in Example 7 below, the poet translated the notion of strength through introducing the image of a lion. However, he did maintain the idea of wearing/being clothed which appears twice in the Hebrew text. (Although "belt" is used in the ESV, it is not in the Hebrew):

Example 7

1a. Simakade uyingonyama, ugqoke amandla,	LORD you are a lion (king), you are wearing strength/power,

Apart from these interesting translations using a thought-provoking choice of words, the performances of the Zulu poets also served to convey part of the meaning of the text using nonverbal means. For example, one poet chose to adjust the tempo of his song before the final line of Psalm 134, making it more up-beat.[48] This break in the established rhythm served to indicate that this was the high point, or main message, of the psalm. He then sang the final line of Psalm 134, the blessing, very slowly, giving it significant focus.

Another group, when singing Psalm 93, began with the central verses (3–4) which carry the main message of the psalm, and used this as a chorus sung after verses incorporating the other ideas. In this way, they enabled the audience to join in with the chorus and take it away with them in their memories, thereby holding on to the main point of the psalm.

Another performance began with drums and a chorus singing a catchy rhythm with the words "Hee mama, hee baba" repeated for a minute and a half, calling mothers and fathers to come and give attention.[49] During this period, the audience members joined in, singing or snapping fingers. Then, while the singers hummed the tune in the background, a poet spoke his translation of the psalm. The initial drumming and repetitive singing served to draw in the audience and was much appreciated by many of them. Then, once they were all fully "connected," the main message was given through spoken poetry. The different media added texture and interest, highlighting the element in focus.

EMPIRICAL STUDY: "IMITATING" LAMENT PSALMS IN ANOTHER CONTEXT

Lament differs from praise in that it tends to be more personal and specific. A person in pain is often not able to find the words to express what he/she is feeling, and in such cases, reading psalms of lament can be very helpful. The language of the lament psalms is of a *general* nature allowing a person to be able to identify with that expressed. However, at times there is a need to give a more specific account of one's pain, and to compose one's own lament. In such cases, it is very helpful to follow the *structure* of biblical laments. As Brueggemann notes, it is the form and structure of biblical lament that facilitates the grieving process. He lists

48. Dickie, "Zulu Song," 137.
49. Dickie, "Zulu Song," Item 5, Appendix 2b: "Video Recordings from Workshops."

the features of such laments as including an address to God, complaint, affirmation of trust, petition, words of assurance, and a vow of praise.[50]

For this empirical study, eight Zulu women from an AIDS-support group near PMB were invited to participate in a lament workshop of two hours. First, we studied together two short psalms of lament, to distinguish the typical characteristics of biblical lament. We noted features similar to those listed by Brueggemann: first, the lament is always directed to God. This is important as it is not just a complaint (as is the case when expressed to other people) but being addressed to God, it seeks a response from God. Then the complaint element is also critical, for without complaint or protest, the prayer is not a lament. The complaint may be voiced through rhetorical questions (e.g., "how long will you not listen?") or through statements accusing God of neglect or bemoaning enemy behavior. The next element of a lament is petition, requesting God to relieve the situation or to execute justice against the enemy. Fourth, biblical lament includes the element of remembering God's goodness or faithfulness in the past, through a confession of trust.

Psalms 3 and 13 highlighted these elements: they are addressed to God (Ps 3:1; Ps 13:1), they include complaints (e.g., Ps 3:1b–2; Ps 13:1–2), requests (e.g., Ps 3:7; Ps 13:3), requests for justice against the enemy (Ps 3:7b–c), affirmations of trust (e.g., Ps 3:3–6; Ps 13:5), and sometimes a vow of praise (e.g., Ps 13:6). Participants noted that the biblical lamenter did not hold back in expressing his emotion, even the negative anger and frustration. Clearly God is open to receive such language. They also noted the imagery used (e.g., "shield" in Ps 3:3), and were encouraged to find picture language that reflected their contexts and situations. The empirical compositions (the women's own expressions of pain, rather than translations of psalms) showed great attention to such insightful imagery. For example, one woman wrote:

Example 8

> Lord, till when will I suffer?
> For how long will people play me?
> They make me like a car that won't start, a useless one.
> Till when?

---

50. Walter Brueggemann, *The Message of the Psalms: A Theological Commentary* (Minneapolis: Augsburg, 1984), 54.

Another ended her lament with the words:

Example 9

> Lord, answer me in my cry,
> Sweep my soul.

The next lament was composed by a group of five women in the AIDS-support group:

Example 10

> My God, listen to our prayer.
>> Don't hide when we need you. I'm confused and tired.
>> We only need you, Lord.
> My God, listen to our prayer.
>> When bad people talk bad about us, they spit on our backs.
>> If we had wings, we would fly to a better place.
> My God, listen to our prayer.
>> God, make them talk nonsense. Make them go mad.
>> Because they have done bad to our community.

Before composing this lament, the women had also studied Psalm 55, and their use of "if we had wings" is clearly a reference to Psalm 55:6, as they imagine how they would escape, if possible. They also introduce an interesting metaphor when describing their enemies, saying "they spit on our backs." Their study of Psalms 3 and 13 had also given them confidence to ask God to execute revenge on their enemies. Thus they ask God to "make them go mad." In their community, the worst position to be in is to be labelled as "mad," as this leads to being ostracized from the community, and without access to the basics of life (food and shelter).

Although these compositions of lament prayers by Zulu women cannot be called "translations" in the strict sense of the word, the *structure* of biblical laments is apparent in their compositions. In the wider understanding of what a translation is, giving priority to "the needs of the receptor community in the present" rather than being faithful to a message in the past, means that such usage of psalms is quite acceptable.[51] Perhaps one would prefer to call them "rewritings," or examples of "Scripture use," but what is important is that the biblical psalms are providing a form

---

51. Ramakrishna, "Cultural Transmission," 90.

that is helpful to sufferers, and so provide another way in which psalms are being interpreted in the twenty-first century.

The third kind of "translation" examined in this paper is that from one medium to another, *viz.*, from written text to a combination of dance/movement, instrumentation, song, and spoken poetry. This is discussed next.

EMPIRICAL STUDY: TRANSLATING A WISDOM PSALM INTO OTHER MEDIA

Psalm 133, a short wisdom psalm, was selected to be studied together by a group of creative artists (a dancer, musicians, singers, and a poet), and for them to each then formulate a way of using their creative gift to communicate the message of the poem. Clearly it was necessary for them to first understand well the main message, and how the imagery supported this theme. Thus together we studied the Hebrew text, noting word repetitions and the structure. This is represented below:

הִנֵּה מַה־טּוֹב וּמַה־נָּעִים שֶׁבֶת אַחִים גַּם־יָחַד׃ 1

behold how-good and-how-pleasant to-dwell brothers even-together

כַּשֶּׁמֶן הַטּוֹב‪|‬ עַל־הָרֹאשׁ יֹרֵד עַל־הַזָּקָן 2a

like-oil the-good over-the-head fall-down over-the-beard

זְקַן־אַהֲרֹן שֶׁיֹּרֵד עַל־פִּי מִדּוֹתָיו׃ 2b

beard-of-Aaron which-falls over-mouth-of garments-his

כְּטַל־חֶרְמוֹן שֶׁיֹּרֵד עַל־הַרְרֵי צִיּוֹן 3a

Like-dew Hermon which-falls over-mountains-of Zion

כִּי שָׁם‪|‬ צִוָּה יְהוָה אֶת־הַבְּרָכָה חַיִּים עַד־הָעוֹלָם׃ 3b

indeed there he-commands YHWH the-blessing life until-forever

Poetic features in the Hebrew text (e.g., sound patterns) as well as the content of the psalm help delineate the three sections of the poem. There is a frame consisting of verses 1 and 3b, with supporting imagery in the middle section (vv. 2–3a).[52] The frame is held together with the middle

___
52. F.W. Dobbs-Allsopp notes how the opening couplet is linked to the closing triplet, and resolve into a frame. See his "Psalm 133: A (Close) Reading," *JHS* 8 (2008): 23. Also, Brian Doyle refers to the phonetic parallelism between cola 1 and 3b, constituting

section through repetition (e.g., טוב "good" in verses 1 and 2a), wordplay between verses 2 and 3 (כשמן "like oil" and כי שם "indeed there") and assonance in verses 1 and 3b. The outer frame comprises strong declarative statements, presenting the main message. The middle section provides supportive figurative language, adding texture and color, thus making the message more memorable.

Another way in which one can describe the poem is as a staircase, leading up to the highest point of the psalm. In every line, except verse 3b, a word or phrase is repeated from the previous line. But no part of verse 3a is repeated in verse 3b. This suggests that verse 3b is the apex of the poem, the high point, the main message: there (where people are living in unity) is where God commands a blessing of abundant life.[53]

The middle section of the poem (vv. 2–3a) is comprised of three couplets with vivid imagery, giving two pictures of the nature of "brothers living in unity." The first picture is of good-quality oil, pouring down on to the head, and then the beard, of the high priest (Aaron). The second picture is of refreshing dew, coming from the snowy mountain of Hermon to the dry hillocks of Zion. Space precludes a detailed analysis in this paper of the imagery, but what is important for translation is to try and determine what insight they provide as to the nature of "brothers living in unity."[54] Oil for the hair and beard was to nourish and strengthen; thus people living in harmony brings strength to the community.[55] Similarly, dew speaks of life-giving refreshment, which those living in unity give to their community.

The artists were encouraged to represent the main message of the psalm in their media, maintaining or adapting elements of the imagery to strengthen the message. An important aspect of the oil imagery (thrice

an inclusio. See his "Metaphora Interrupta: Psalm 133," *Ephemerides Theologicae Lovanienses* 77 (2001): 14.

53. Dobbs-Allsopp ("Psalm 133," 21–22) notes that "This is not eternal life, but finite existence (i.e., life and not death) ... life, good and whole and abundant, for as long into the future as possible." J. Clinton McCann Jr. also asserts that this refers to "the fullness of enjoying life in the presence of God as his gift." See his "Psalms" in *The New Interpreter's Bible*, eds. Leander E. Keck, et al. (Nashville: Abingdon, 1996), 4:1, 214.

54. For further analysis see June F. Dickie, "Psalm 133: Sacred Wisdom Interpreted by Contemporary South Africans," *Journal for Semitics* 29 (2020): 1–16.

55. The nourishing qualities of good oil help form an understanding of harmonious living. Dew implies a life-giving gift of a generous God. Both imply necessary aspects of life. Doyle, "Metaphora Interrupta," 19.

repeated) is its downward movement (יֵרֵד). This signifies the blessing which YHWH will give and suggests a tactile experience of blessings flowing down upon the covenant people. The other important factor is the abundance of the oil—not just rubbed into the hair and the beard, as would normally be the case when conditioning the hair, but poured over the head and cascading on to the beard and continuing to fall even further. The second image, of dew descending from a place of much water (Hermon) to the arid hills of Jerusalem, signals the blessing of refreshment that only God can give. Although the physical movement of dew between these two locations is unlikely, Dobbs-Allsopp calls it a "fabulous image" highlighting the idea of superfluity and contributing to the high rhetoric.[56]

With regard to the final verse, and in particular the sense of שָׁם ('there'), several commentators assert that it refers to the phenomenon of living in harmony rather than to a precise location, Zion.[57] Thus the artists sought to represent the message that when people live together in unity (as a result of God's blessing), God continues to give God's blessing of abundant life. That living together in unity is strengthening and refreshing to the whole community: God's blessing flows down to those in unity, and on to others.

The artistic representation of this message began with a guitar quietly playing, and a singer bringing the words (his translation of the psalm):[58]

Verse 1:	Like a cascade, an overflow	Verse 2:	Like living water,
	Of precious oil, poured out.		Like early morning dew
	Like a cascade, an overflow		A flowing river
	Of precious oil falling down.		These dry and weary bones made new.
	Chorus:		Come look and see how good,

---

56. Dobbs-Allsopp, "Psalm 133," 16.
57. Brian Doyle, "Metaphora Interrupta," 6.
58. The composer and singer is Jonathan Crowther, Church of the Holy Spirit, Cape Town.

Come look and see how beautiful,

Come look and see how good,

Come look and see how wonderful!

Bridge: This is his blessing, abundance
of life

His people together, until forever.

In terms of exegetical accuracy of the song,[59] one notes the following:

Hebrew	Song
Behold	Come look and see (x4 in chorus)
people living in unity	his people together
(blessing) falling down (x3)	poured out, an overflow, falling down, flowing
oil and dew	precious oil, water, dew, river
(blessing)	living water, dry and weary bones made new, his blessing
'life abundant'	living (water), abundance of life, until forever

The guitar music glided into a melody played by a violinist, seated high. Progressively she was joined by other instruments, first a quiet drum, then another drum, then various other instruments. As the music began to swell in harmony, movement began: initially one dancer did a distinctive head roll, and then reached out in a very strong, controlled movement to touch two others in front. They then also began to do the head roll, the three moving in synchrony. Then all of them repeated the movements, reaching out and each touching another one. Thus, progressively the number of those moving in harmony increased, with very distinctive movements (suggesting the intentionality of the head-decision to be in harmony).[60]

The dancers were arranged in a pyramid, so movement was seen to be downward, from the top to the bottom. Then the dancers began to do a sideways step, with those in a higher position doing gentle bends

---

59. My only concern with the exegetical accuracy is that the connection between "living together in unity" and "God giving the blessing of abundant life" may not come through strongly.

60. Artur Weiser notes that the message of the psalm is that there is a need to "*strive to accommodate one another in love and with a conciliatory spirit.*" See his *The Psalms: A Commentary* (Philadelphia: Westminster, 1962), *ad loc*; (emphasis added).

and those lower down doing deeper "squats" all in synchrony, with one another and with the beat of the music. Again the idea suggested was of harmony and downward movement. Their hands reached up and flowed down and out, suggesting the direction of God's blessings. At the end they all stopped, pointing in different directions as they gave out the blessing they had received. They then drew their hands in and stood still, as the singer-guitarist read the following poem (another translation of Psalm 133, complementing and interpreting the movement):

> Oil silent, seeping, softening,
> > rain refreshing, resonating:
> > > one hears Your song and starts to play
> Strings plucked — sweet sounds,
> > another hears, the river grOWS
> Heads act, in harmony, intentionally,
> > the river runs, opens new ways, swells to a surge
> > cascading
> > > L
> > > I
> > > F
> > > > E
> > to those outside

When the poem ended, the musicians and dancers all moved outside, disappearing through the three exits to take the blessing to those in the wider community. After they had left, someone in the audience (planted by the arranger) stood up and cried out loudly, "Yes, unity." From the other side of the room, another person stood up and called out "Unity in community." Some children in the audience then picked up flags on which were written comm-UNITY (written in the form of a cross, spelling the letters horizontally and vertically). As they waved them, the band began to sing the song, and the audience joined in.

In terms of the connection between the Hebrew text and the symbolism of the movement and the music, the following is noted:

Hebrew	Symbolism of Movement/Music
Behold	Calling attention, quiet, then single instrument
people living in unity	synchronized movement, in harmony with one another and with rhythm of instruments
(blessing) falling down (x3)	visual downward, hands reaching up, and then down and out, receiving blessings and passing them out to others
oil and dew	bringing life progressively to more and more, as dancers touch more people and music swells with more instruments
commands a blessing	strong movements of head-rolls, touching others, arms reaching out
life abundant	dancers coming *alive* as they are touched by those above

The original motivation behind the psalm may have been one of "to strengthen the ancient family norm at a time of its decline,"[61] or to "promote the concept of reunification between the northern and southern tribes of Israel."[62] The message portrayed by the dance/music, poem, and song are certainly in line with this theme of "God's blessing arising from (and enabling) people who are living in unity." However, the contribution of the artistic translations is perhaps more to draw people to the written text than to replace it. To get the full message and emphasis of God's word, one does need the written word, but the artistic translations are the language of many people and will certainly draw in many that would perhaps not initially be interested.

CONCLUSIONS

The language of the psalms is fairly open and adaptable to the various contexts of its hearers.[63] As Dobbs-Allsopp points out, the interpretation given will depend largely on the specific context in which it is heard.[64] In the contemporary situation, there is a need for people to be able to read their own contexts into the meaning of a psalm, and this paper has shown various ways in which this can be done. Not only does involving the community in Bible translation ensure that the language is contemporary, but it also builds commitment to, and sense of ownership of, the biblical

---

61. Weiser, *The Psalms*, 783.

62. Adele Berlin, "On the Interpretation of Psalm 133," in *Directions in Biblical Hebrew Poetry*, ed. Elaine R. Follis (Sheffield: Sheffield Academic, 1987), 142.

63. Patrick D. Miller, *Interpreting the Psalms* (Philadelphia: Fortress, 1986), 50–51.

64. F.W. Dobbs-Allsopp, "Psalm 133," 7.

message. With the millennial generation crying out for "involvement in the process," it is worth exploring new ways of translating God's message.

6

Prosody and Preaching: Poetic Form and Religious Function in Biblical Verse

Benjamin D. Sommer

> *"the scandal of it,*
> *the refusal to deliver a denouement."*
>
> —Michael Symmons Roberts[1]

Scholars have long discussed the nature of biblical poetic parallelism. But the relationship between our understanding of the biblical poetic line and the function of biblical poems as Scripture has not received the attention it deserves.[2] In this essay, I discuss how theories of prosody help to shape a reading of some sample poems (Psalms 27 and 114, and, more briefly, Psalm 19). In particular, I argue that the religious significance of these poems emerges much more clearly in light of attention to questions of prosody, of what makes a biblical poem a poem at all.

---

1. The last lines of "Manumission," the closing poem of Michael Symmons Roberts' collection, *Mancunia*: Michael Symmons Roberts, *Mancunia*, Cape Poetry (London: Jonathan Cape, 2017), 71.
2. An exception is Patrick D. Miller, "The Theological Significance of Biblical Poetry," in *Language, Theology, and the Bible: Essays in Honor of James Barr*, eds. John Barton and Samuel Balentine (Oxford: Oxford University Press, 1994), 213–30.

STRUCTURE: LINE AND STANZA

In some biblical poems, the structure of the poem as a whole—that is to say, its division into stanzas—recapitulates the structure of a biblical line, and understanding this recapitulation is a key to distilling meaning from the poem. So before we turn to the poem I will use to exemplify this point, it will be helpful to review some information about the nature of the biblical poetic line. Most biblical poems are built from a series of two-part or three-part lines; rarely, one finds four-part lines. The second, third, and fourth parts of a line echo yet go beyond the first part of the line in one way or another. In other words, there is some parallel among various elements of a line. Not infrequently one can note parallels not only within a line but from one line to the next. Now, there are many proposals for how we can refer to lines and their two, three, or four parts; I will follow Benjamin Harshav (Hrushovski) in labeling them *versets*.[3] Thus we can restate what I just said: the versets of a line in biblical poetry parallel each other. There are many types of parallels among these versets. The one most widely noted type, which has been overemphasized in scholarship, involves parallels of meaning. In one type of meaning-based parallelism, words in the first verset correspond to words and phrases with similar meanings in the second; we can call this *lexical parallelism*. For example, see Ps 145:1:

אֲרוֹמִמְךָ אֱ-לוֹהַי הַמֶּלֶךְ / וַאֲבָרְכָה שִׁמְךָ לְעוֹלָם וָעֶד

I extol[4] You, my God and king, / and I bless Your name forever
and ever.[5]

Here, "I extol" in the first verset parallels "I bless" in the second, "You" parallels "Your name." The last element in each verset ("My God and king" and "forever and ever") has no lexical parallels in the other verset. But in the next line of that poem, every element in the first verset parallels and element in the second:

---

3. Benjamin Hrushovski, "Prosody, Hebrew," in *Encyclopaedia Judaica* (Jerusalem: Keter, 1971), 13:1200–1203.

4. Note that in Hebrew, "I extol" is a single word, as is "I bless," so in underlining the correspondences, I treat these as a single unit.

5. All translations in this essay are my own. In this example and in the rest of the essay, I use slashes to indicate the boundaries among the versets within a line. When three-verset or four-verset lines cannot fit on a single line of my prose, I indent all the versets after the first verset instead of separating versets with a slash.

בְּכָל־יוֹם אֲבָרְכֶךָּ / וַאֲהַלְלָה שִׁמְךָ לְעוֹלָם וָעֶד
<u>Each day I bless</u> You / and <u>I acclaim</u> Your name <u>forever and ever.</u>

In another type of meaning-based parallelism, the overall semantic import of one verset is echoed in the second, even if repeated word-for-word parallels do not occur; we can call this *semantic parallelism*, or *whole-verset parallelism*. For example, take Psalm 118:6:

ה' לִי לֹא אִירָא / מַה־יַּעֲשֶׂה לִי אָדָם
Yhwh is with me, I shall not fear; / what can a human do to me?

or Ps 111:5

טֶרֶף נָתַן לִירֵאָיו / יִזְכֹּר לְעוֹלָם בְּרִיתוֹ
He gives provisions to His devotees; / He unfailingly attends to His commitments.

But there are many other sorts of parallel that do not involve lexical or semantic equivalents: these may involve phonological echoes, syntactic structures, or rhythm. (We will consider these sound-based forms of parallelism a bit later in this essay.) Most lines of biblical poetry include several types of parallelism that work in concert, or, even more interestingly, that work at cross purposes.[6]

Several decades ago, both James Kugel and Robert Alter pointed out that the second and third versets of a parallel line in biblical poetry do not merely repeat the information found in the first verset. The second verset of a parallel line in biblical poetry echoes but modifies the first. The structure of the parallel line is not simply a matter of equivalence; rather, it can be summed up with Kugel's phrase, "A, and *what's more,* B." That something more often involves what Alter calls "intensification" of what is found in the first verset. In other cases, the second verset specifies something in the second verset.[7] To cite one example from among many

---

6. Several scholars have turned our attention to the varieties of parallelism in biblical poetry, and especially to phonological parallelism. See Hrushovski, "Prosody, Hebrew"; Alan Cooper, "Biblical Poetics: A Linguistic Approach" (Ph.D. dissertation, Yale University, 1976), *passim*, and, on phonological parallelism, 86–93 (and see esp. the programmatic statements on p. 72 and 80); Stephen Geller, *Parallelism in Early Biblical Poetry*, HSM 20 (Missoula: Scholars Press, 1979); and Adele Berlin, *The Dynamics of Biblical Parallelism*, Revised and expanded (Grand Rapids: Eerdmans, 2008), esp. 103–125.

7. See James Kugel, *The Idea of Biblical Poetry: Parallelism and Its History* (New Haven: Yale University Press, 1981), 1–58 (the phrase I quote comes from the title of ch. 1), and

hundreds, we can look at Ps 29:3–5. The first of the two lines we examine is a three-part line; the second, one of the relatively rare four-part lines.

קוֹל ה' עַל־הַמָּיִם / אֵ־ל־הַכָּבוֹד הִרְעִים / ה' עַל־מַיִם רַבִּים

קוֹל־ה' בַּכֹּחַ / קוֹל ה' בֶּהָדָר / קוֹל ה' שֹׁבֵר אֲרָזִים / וַיְשַׁבֵּר ה' אֶת־אַרְזֵי הַלְּבָנוֹן

Yhwh's voice is over the water;
   The God of glory thunders,
   Yhwh, over the cosmic waters.
Yhwh's thunder—powerfully—
   Yhwh's thunder—majestically—
   Yhwh's thunder breaks the cedars;
   Yhwh shatters the cedars of Lebanon.

For the sake of economy, I have chosen lines that display both specification and intensification. The phrase קוֹל הי at the outset of the first line is ambiguous, since קוֹל can mean "sound," "voice," or "thunder" (as in the phrase, קולות וברקים). The second verset of the first line specifies that Yhwh's קוֹל over the waters is in fact thunder. The third verset both intensifies and specifies, for it speaks not merely of water but of מים רבים—"many waters," or, as Herbert May argued, "cosmic waters," mythological waters associated with creation.[8] The second line also displays both specification and intensification. Yhwh's voice or thunder does something powerfully—but what? It does something majestically—but what? It breaks cedars. Which cedars? Not just any cedars, but, more specifically, the famous cedars of Lebanon. This specification also involves intensification: Lebanon's mountains have more water than most areas in the Near East, and so its cedars were especially tall, strong, and majestic. They were renowned throughout the ancient Near East: kings from as far away as Mesopotamia boasted about sending expeditions to procure cedars of Lebanon for their building projects;[9] similarly, Solomon used them for building the temple in Jerusalem (1 Kgs 5:20–23), and "the cedars

Robert Alter, *The Art of Biblical Poetry* (New York: Basic Books, 1985), 3–26 (the term quoted is from page 11).

8. On the mythological implications of the phrase מים רבים, see Herbert G. May, "Some Cosmic Connotations of *Mayim Rabbîm*, 'Many Waters'," *JBL* 74 (1955): 9–21.

9. See, e.g., the claims about Naram-Sin and Sargon in Benjamin Foster, *Before the Muses. An Anthology of Akkadian Literature* (Bethesda: CDL, 1993), 1:52, 100, as well as the fifth tablet of the Gilgamesh Epic. For an extensive list, see the references in *The Assyrian Dictionary of the Oriental Institute of the University of Chicago*, 21 vols. (Chicago: Oriental Institute of the University of Chicago, 1956–2006), 4:274–275 §a1'.

of Lebanon" are a frequent figure in biblical texts for strength and loft-
iness (e.g., Judg 9:15, Isa 2:13, 10:34, Ps 92:12, 104:16). Any old god might
break a cedar here or there, but it is an impressive deity whose voice
shatters even the mighty cedars of Lebanon.

Having discharged these preliminary duties to discuss poetic
line-structure in the Bible, we can finally move on to the first text I wish
to discuss: Psalm 27, familiar to many Jews as the psalm for the penitential
season. In the Ashkenazic liturgical rite and in the Roman version of the
Italian liturgical rite it is recited daily during the month preceding the
Rosh Hashanah (the New Year's festival) and during the first three weeks
of the new year itself, a period that includes the Ten Days of Return or
Repentance (תשובה) that begin with Rosh Hashanah and end with Yom
Kippur (the Day of Atonement).[10]

In analyzing this text, I would like to model a method of reading in
which we shall first attend to local poetic structures; building on these
local structures, we will move to broader structural elements; finally,
building on the broader structures, we turn to theological interpretation. So it will be worthwhile to take a look at the text as a whole and to
attend to its lineation, because the first thing we need to do when we are
interpreting any biblical poem is to figure out how to divide it into the
lines and versets. In most poetic traditions, that work is done for us. When
one picks up *The Oxford Book of English Verse* or *The Penguin Anthology of
Twentieth-Century American Poetry* or this week's copy of *The New Yorker*,
the conventions of printing tell us how the poet wants the poem to be
divided. Further, in traditions in which poetry scans (that is, in poems

---

10. Psalm 27 was added to Jewish liturgies for the months of Elul and Tishrei (that is,
the months preceding and including Rosh Hashanah and Yom Kippur) in the Middle
Ages. Not all the liturgical rites include it, and variations exist not simply between
the five main rites of the Jewish people (Ashkenazic, Eidot Hamizraḥ/Sephardic,
Italian, Yemenite, and Romani) but within these rites. Thus most Ashkenazic Jews
recite it morning and evening during Elul and Tishrei, but it is recited only in the
morning by German Jews, and it is omitted in the rite of the Vilna Gaon altogether. In
the Italian rite, it is recited each morning during these months in the Roman version
of the rite but not at all in the Milanese version. It is not recited in most versions of
the Yemenite rite. In some Eidot Hamizraḥ rites one recites it morning and evening
all year long, not just in Elul-Tishrei; but Spanish-Portuguese Jews never recite it
as part of their regular liturgy, whether in Elul-Tishrei or the rest of the year. For a
detailed treatment of the recitation of Psalm 27, including variations regarding the
precise days one begins reciting it in Elul and stops in Tishrei, see Moshe Hallamish,
Studies in Kabbalah and Prayer [in Hebrew] (Beer Sheva: Ben Gurion University Press,
2012), 175–85.

that have meter), we know quite precisely where lines begin and end based on the number of syllables they contain and on their patterns of stress or vowel length. But in biblical poetry we have no authoritative editions going back to the time of the poems' composition or evolution.[11] Because biblical poetry is essentially a form of free verse,[12] there is no scansion to determine where lines begin and end. The readers have to figure this out themselves. Usually, the decision of how to lineate is uncontroversial, but sometimes it is open to debate. As we shall see, it is often crucial for interpreting the poem

The poem, as I lineate it, reads:

... ¹

מִמִּי אִירָא   יְ־הוָה | אוֹרִי וְיִשְׁעִי

מִמִּי אֶפְחָד: יְ־הוָה מָעוֹז־חַיַּי

---

11. Most printed editions and manuscripts of the Bible in the original Hebrew do not indicate how to break poems into lines (a few exceptions, such as Exodus 15, Deuteronomy 32, and Judges 5, notwithstanding). A few early manuscripts do suggest lineation, but these manuscripts, both from the Dead Sea Scrolls (e.g., 4QPs[b] and MasPs[a]) and from early medieval Masoretic tradition, were written down many centuries later than the composition of the poems in question. See the extensive discussion of this issue in F.W. Dobbs-Allsopp, *On Biblical Poetry* (New York: Oxford University Press, 2015), 29–38, along with photographs of relevant manuscripts available in the section following p. 232.

12. See Dobbs-Allsopp, *On Biblical Poetry*, 9–10, 95–177, esp. 98–99. Similarly, Hrushovski, "Prosody, Hebrew," 13:1,201, refers to the "free rhythm ... based on a cluster of changing principles" of biblical poetry, which he clearly sees as a type of free verse. On earlier literary critics (esp. Gay Wilson Allen) who rightly recognize biblical poetry as a very early form of free verse, see Dobbs-Allsopp, 95, 393 n. 3, and 396 n. 32. Dobbs-Allsopp points out (177 and 395 n. 13) that Walt Whitman himself already implied a connection between what we now call free verse and biblical poetry in his 1888 essay, "The Bible as Poetry." Whitman cites the claim of Frederick de Sola Mendes (in Mendes' lecture "Hebrew Poets") "that rhyming was not a characteristic of Hebrew poetry at all. Metre was not a necessary mark of poetry. Great poets discarded it; the early Jewish poets knew it not." Mendes, incidentally, was one of the founding members of the Jewish Theological Seminary of America and a graduate of the older JTS in Breslau, Germany. (He is not to be confused with his brother, Henry Pereira Mendes, the American JTS's president from 1897 to 1902.) Whitman's essay is available in Walt Whitman, "The Bible as Poetry," in *Complete Prose Works* (Philadelphia: David McKay, 1892): 379–82. I have not been able to locate Mendes's lecture, which may not exist in print; Dobbs-Allsopp suggested to me the likelihood that Whitman may have heard rather than read the lecture, as he will explain in his forthcoming book on Whitman's relationship to the King James Bible.

2 צָרַ֣י וְאֹיְבַ֣י לִ֑י   בִּקְרֹ֤ב עָלַ֨י ׀ מְרֵעִים֮ לֶאֱכֹ֪ל אֶת־בְּשָׂ֫רִ֥י
הֵ֖מָּה כָשְׁל֣וּ וְנָפָֽלוּ׃

3 אִם־תַּחֲנֶ֬ה עָלַ֨י ׀ מַחֲנֶה֮ לֹא־יִירָ֪א לִ֫בִּ֥י
אִם־תָּק֬וּם עָלַ֨י מִלְחָמָ֑ה בְּ֝זֹ֗את אֲנִ֣י בוֹטֵֽחַ׃

4 אַחַ֤ת ׀ שָׁאַ֣לְתִּי מֵֽאֵת־יְהוָה֮ אוֹתָ֪הּ אֲבַ֫קֵּ֥שׁ
שִׁבְתִּ֣י בְּבֵית־יְ֭הוָה כָּל־יְמֵ֣י חַיַּ֑י
לַחֲז֥וֹת בְּנֹֽעַם־יְ֝הוָ֗ה וּלְבַקֵּ֥ר בְּהֵיכָלֽוֹ׃

5 כִּ֤י יִצְפְּנֵ֨נִי ׀ בְּסֻכֹּה֮ בְּי֪וֹם רָ֫עָ֥ה
יַ֭סְתִּרֵנִי בְּסֵ֣תֶר אָהֳל֑וֹ בְּ֝צ֗וּר יְרוֹמְמֵֽנִי׃

6 וְעַתָּ֨ה יָר֪וּם רֹאשִׁ֡י עַ֤ל אֹֽיְבַ֬י סְבִֽיבוֹתַ֗י
וְאֶזְבְּחָ֣ה בְ֭אָהֳלוֹ זִבְחֵ֣י תְרוּעָ֑ה אָשִׁ֥ירָה וַ֝אֲזַמְּרָ֗ה לַיהוָֽה׃

7 שְׁמַע־יְהוָ֖ה קוֹלִ֥י אֶקְרָ֗א וְחָנֵּ֥נִי וַעֲנֵֽנִי׃

8 לְךָ֤ ׀ אָמַ֣ר לִ֭בִּי בַּקְּשׁ֣וּ פָנָ֑י אֶת־פָּנֶ֖יךָ יְהוָ֣ה אֲבַקֵּֽשׁ׃

9 אַל־תַּסְתֵּ֬ר פָּנֶ֨יךָ ׀ מִמֶּנִּי֮ אַֽל־תַּט־בְּאַ֗ף עַ֫בְדֶּ֥ךָ עֶזְרָתִ֥י הָיִ֑יתָ
אַֽל־תִּטְּשֵׁ֥נִי וְאַל־תַּֽ֝עַזְבֵ֗נִי אֱלֹהֵ֥י יִשְׁעִֽי׃

10 כִּי־אָבִ֣י וְאִמִּ֣י עֲזָב֑וּנִי וַֽיהוָ֣ה יַֽאַסְפֵֽנִי׃

11 ה֤וֹרֵ֥נִי יְהוָ֗ה דַּ֫רְכֶּ֥ךָ וּ֭נְחֵנִי בְּאֹ֣רַח מִישׁ֑וֹר לְ֝מַ֗עַן שׁוֹרְרָֽי׃

12 אַֽל־תִּ֭תְּנֵנִי בְּנֶ֣פֶשׁ צָרָ֑י כִּ֥י קָמוּ־בִ֥י עֵֽדֵי־שֶׁ֝֗קֶר וִיפֵ֥חַ חָמָֽס׃

13 לׅׄוּׅׄלֵׅׄ֗אׅׄ הֶ֭אֱמַנְתִּי לִרְא֥וֹת בְּֽטוּב־יְהוָ֗ה בְּאֶ֣רֶץ חַיִּֽים׃

14 קַוֵּ֗ה אֶל־יְֽה֫וָ֥ה חֲ֭זַק וְיַאֲמֵ֣ץ לִבֶּ֑ךָ וְ֝קַוֵּ֗ה אֶל־יְהוָֽה׃

1 ...[13]

Yhwh is my light and my salvation —	Whom should I fear?
Yhwh is the sure haven of my life —	Whom could I dread?
2 When evil-doers draw near	To slander me,[14]
My enemies and foes —	They're the ones who stumble and fall.

---

13. The first word in this verse (לְדָוִד) is a superscription and not part of the poem itself. Consequently, I need not enter the vexing question of when it was added or why, what it was intended to signify, or how to translate it.

14. *Or:* To devour me *or:* To destroy me.

3	Should an army encamp against me,	My mind will know no fear.
	Should war break out around me,	I will trust in this.
4	One thing I ask of Yhwh,	This do I request:[15]
	To dwell in Yhwh's house	All the days of my life,
	To gaze upon the marvel that is Yhwh,[16]	And to serve in His palace.
5	For He conceals *me*, inviolable, in His shelter,	At times of danger;[17]
	He hides me in His hidden tent,	High on a rock, He lifts me up.
6	So now, I hold my head high	Above my enemies all around.
	I should offer up in His tent	A celebration-meal —
		I should sing and play music to Yhwh!
7	Hear my voice, O Yhwh!	I'm calling! treat me with grace! answer me!
8	On Your behalf my mind speaks:	"Seek *me* out!"
	It is You I seek, Yhwh —	9 Do not hide Yourself from me!
	Don't thrust Your servant away in anger —	You were my help!
	Don't leave me, don't abandon me	O God of my salvation!
10	Indeed, my father and mother abandoned me,	But it is Yhwh who takes me in.
11	Parent me, Yhwh, teaching me Your path,	And lead me on a level road
		While my foes look on.[18]
12	Don't feed me to my enemies!	Yes, lying witnesses rise against me,
		With unfair, violent testimony.
13	Were it not for the fact that I believe	That I shall see Yhwh's own virtue
		While still alive ...
14	Hope that Yhwh will come!	Courage! Let your mind be strong!
		And hope that Yhwh will come.

As is often the case in biblical poetry, there is a variation between two-verset and three-verset lines in Psalm 27. Further, here as elsewhere in biblical poetry there are lines that allow more than one lineation. We need to recall that biblical poetry was made public—that is, published—orally through recitation, though of course scribes used written texts as aids to memorization and for purposes of long-term preservation. Just as two musicians might perform a single piece with different emphases, playing precisely the same notes in somewhat distinctive ways, so too there are places where the scribe or priest or Levite or layperson who performed

15. *Or:* It is what I request.
16. *More literally:* ... upon Yhwh's pleasantness.
17. *More literally:* ... on a day of evil.
18. *More literally:* Because of those who watch me insidiously.

this poem in biblical times might have made different choices than the ones I made above, and some of what I render as two-part lines might have been realized as three-part lines, and vice versa.[19]

In the lineation I have proposed, it is noteworthy that the variation between two-verset lines and three-verset lines is not random. Three-verset lines are used to indicate the end of a stanza (the same phenomenon occurs in many biblical poems; we will encounter it again when we discuss Psalm 19.[20]) Thus our poem has three stanzas, each of which ends with a three-verset line (the last of which simply consists of three-verset lines): verses 6, 12, and 13–14 all conclude a stanza. The stanzas are stylistically distinct in another significant way: in the first (vv. 1–6), the worshiper speaks of God in the third person; in the second (vv. 7–12), the worshiper addresses God in the second person; in the third (vv. 13–14), God is again described in the third person. Each of these stanzas has its own mood: in the first the worshiper is confident; in the second, the worshiper is distressed; in the third, we find expressions of hope along with an implicit acknowledgement that certainty of salvation is not possible.

---

19. Some alternate possibilities for performing certain lines follow. Most would imply a different translation of these lines, which need not detain us here.
Verse 7 could be lineated as a three-verset line:

שְׁמַע־יְ־הוָה 7   קוֹלִי אֶקְרָא   וְחָנֵּנִי וַעֲנֵנִי:

The following lineation for verses 8–9 appears in both Peter Craigie and Marvin Tate, *Psalms 1–50*, 2nd. ed., WBC (N.p.: Thomas Nelson, 2004) and John Goldingay, *Psalms 1–41*, BCOTWP (Grand Rapids: Baker Academic, 2006) (both *ad loc.*):

לְךָ ׀ אָמַר לִבִּי 8   בַּקְּשׁוּ פָנָי   אֶת־פָּנֶיךָ יְ־הוָה אֲבַקֵּשׁ:
אַל־תַּסְתֵּר פָּנֶיךָ ׀ מִמֶּנִּי 9   אַל־תַּט־בְּאַף ׀ עַבְדֶּךָ
עֶזְרָתִי הָיִיתָ   אַל־תִּטְּשֵׁנִי וְאַל־תַּעַזְבֵנִי   אֱ־לֹהֵי יִשְׁעִי:

Verse 13 could be rendered as a two-verset line:

לוּלֵא הֶאֱמַנְתִּי לִרְאוֹת   בְּטוּב־יְ־הוָה בְּאֶרֶץ חַיִּים: 13

Even if we lineate 7 as having three versets and 13 as having two, it remains the case that the boundaries between the stanzas occur where a variation between two- and three-verset lines occurs.
20. As Robert Gordis, "Psalm 9–10: A Textual and Exegetical Study," JQR 48 (1957): 119 n. 32, notes, three-verset lines often are used to end a text or a stanza: "The same stylistic procedure," Gordis points out, "is to be found in Ps 13, 14, 16, 18, 19, 37, 47, 53, 55, 63, 73, 90, 94, 103, 104, 111, 119, 125, 129, 140; Job, chaps. 10, 11, 19, 26." Cf. Wilfred G. E. Watson, *Classical Hebrew Poetry: A Guide to Its Techniques*, JSOTSup (Sheffield: Sheffield Academic Press, 1984), 168–74, who makes the same claim about the stanza-formational role of what he calls the monocolon or orphan line—which is identical to what I am calling the third verset of a three-verset line.

The shift in both mood and grammatical person at the beginning of the second stanza in verse 7 is extremely abrupt. We move suddenly from confidence to need, from believing in God's reliability to worrying about God's absence. How can we account for the stark contrast between the first stanza, in which the worshiper joyously proclaims trust in God, and the second and third stanzas, in which the worshiper betrays the fear that God might be far off?[21]

Hermann Gunkel provides a simple answer to this question by asserting that this chapter contains two separate psalms: the first (vv. 1-6) a song of confidence and the second (vv. 7-14) a classic psalm of complaint and plea.[22] It is not outside the range of possibility that a single chapter in the book of Psalms might contain more than one composition. After all, there are cases in which a single composition takes up more than one chapter of the Psalter: an alphabetic acrostic poem is spread over Psalms 9-10; Psalms 42-43 are also a single composition with a repeated refrain at 42:6, 42:12, and 43:5. Thus the converse—that two separate songs appear in one chapter—is certainly conceivable. But several scholars have successfully defended the unity of Psalm 27. Peter Craigie and Marvin Tate point out shared vocabulary that draws together what Gunkel regards as separate poems: ישע‎ (vv. 1,9), צרי‎ (vv. 2, 12), לב‎ (vv. 3, 8, 14), קום‎ (vv. 3, 12), בק"ש‎ (vv. 4, 8), and חיים‎ (vv. 4, 13), in addition to the theme of seeing God's pleasantness or goodness (vv. 4, 13).[23] Further, it is not quite the

---

21. On this extreme nature of this contrast at verse 7, see Jacob (Gerald) Blidstein, "T'hillim 27," *Yavneh Review*, Spring 1965, 21-23; Ellen Charry, *Psalms 1-50* (Grand Rapids: Brazos, 2015), 139-41. Radaq attempts to minimize the contrast by reading verse 4 as a strictly spiritual request and regarding verse 7 as a reference back to the request in verse 4: the worshiper is confident in God's salvation from physical harm, but asks for the ability to commune with God in the temple or in heaven.

22. See Hermann Gunkel, *Die Psalmen*, Göttinger Handkommentar Zum Alten Testament. Abteilung 2 (Göttingen: Vandenhoeck & Ruprecht, 1968), 112-18. But cf. Hermann Gunkel and Joachim Begrich, *Introduction to Psalms: The Genres of the Religious Lyric of Israel*, trans. James D. Nogalski, Mercer Library of Biblical Studies (Macon, GA: Mercer University Press, 1998), 190-91, where Gunkel emphasizes the connection of the song of confidence in 27:1-6 to the genre of the individual complaint. That is the genre we find in 7-12, a circumstance that seems to move against Gunkel's view that the chapter contains two different songs. Nevertheless, his proposal has been widely accepted.

23. Craigie and Tate, *Psalms 1-50*, 230-31. On literary features that draw poems together in biblical poetry, see Daniel Grossberg, *Centripetal and Centrifugal Structures in Biblical Poetry*, SBLMS 39 (Atlanta: Scholars Press, 1989), 8-13, esp. features 1, 2, 3 are relevant to our text.

case that the first stanza is entirely confident while the second and third
completely lack elements of faith.[24] The first stanza contains intimations
of the darker themes that appear later in the poem. Jacob Blidstein notes
"the progressive deterioration of the roof overhead from 'stronghold (Ma-
oz)' to 'hut (sukkah)' and finally 'tent'—a glimpse into the crisis that is as
yet in the distance."[25] As John Goldingay astutely notes regarding verse
1, the worshiper's statement that he has no reason to fear draws attention to the fact that he apparently is worrying about something.[26] Harris
Birkeland argues for the unity of the psalm by pointing to the presence
of elements of confidence in the second and third stanzas.[27] In the first
versets of the two poetic lines in verse 9, the worshiper begs God not
to abandon the worshiper, but the second versets of both lines confirm
that God is the worshiper's help and salvation. Similarly, in verse 13 the
third stanza at least attempts to restate the confidence of the first stanza,
albeit in a sentence that never reaches completion.[28] These elements of

---

24. Rolf Jacobson captures something crucial about the alleged gulf between the two
parts of the psalm when he notes that the psalm "speaks words of fear. And words of
trust. The two are not as far removed from one another as one might imagine" (Nancy
deClaissé-Walford, Rolf Jacobson, and Beth LaNeel Tanner, *The Book of Psalms*, NICOT
[Grand Rapids: Eerdmans, 2014], 242).

25. Blidstein, "T'hillim 27," 22.

26. Goldingay, *Psalms 1–41*, 392. He further points out (p. 391) that the first stanza's
"appearance of confidence is compromised by the fact that most of its lines have the
short second cola more characteristic of a lament." Indeed, the second verset of the
first five lines of the poem are all quite negative.

27. Harris Birkeland, "Die Einheitlichkeit von Ps 27," ZAW 51 (1933), 218.

28. Gunkel further points out that verse 6 contains a vow, which is a standard way
of ending a complaint song, while verse 7 begins like a classic psalm of complaint
and plea. He argues that all this shows that one poem ends in verse 6 while another
begins in verse 7 (*Die Psalmen*, 114 and 116). See also Gunkel and Begrich, *Introduction*,
177, 184. But Birkeland, "Einheitlichkeit," 219, points out that to define verse 6 as an
ending and verse 7 as a beginning on the basis of this formal criterion puts the cart
before the horse. We can agree that verse 7 can only be a new beginning and cannot be a middle, or that verse 6 must be an ending, only if we put the psalm into a
procrustean form-critical bed. Indeed, Birkeland points out (p. 220), this is not the
only psalm where a vow or a vocative and pleas appear in the middle: in Ps 9:15 we
have a vow in the middle of a psalm, while in Psalm 42–43 (a single song) the plea
begins at 43:1, well into the poem. (Indeed, Gunkel himself noted that the vocative
and plea that typically begin a complaint/plea do occur, albeit "far less frequently in other positions," a circumstance that vitiates his claim in *Die Psalmen*, p. 116;
see Gunkel and Begrich, *Introduction*, 152, and see esp. n. 13 there, in which Gunkel
himself refers to Psalm 42–43. Sigmund Mowinckel, *Psalmenstudien* (Amsterdam:
P. Schippers, 1966), 1:148, points out that at first we can simply regard Psalm 27 as
an individual complaint/plea that has an unusually long statement of trust in its

unity demonstrate that Psalm 27 is a single composition that has to be interpreted as a whole.[29]

We have seen that the first stanza hints at a source of fear even as it speaks of trust in God, and the second betrays worry over the possibility of God's distance while also asserting that God is a source of salvation. The third stanza continues this ambivalence in a particularly intense way. The first word of that stanza, לולא (v. 13), means "if it were not the case that."[30] Thus our verse is the relative clause of a sentence that the speaker

---

first six verses. Such an overdevelopment of that statement of trust is atypical of biblical psalms but hardly impossible, as the similar case of Psalm 42–43 shows. Such a development is quite typical of Akkadian psalms of plea: they often begin with invocations and statements of trust that are, in effect, fairly lengthy psalms of praise. Thus, the first nine lines (out of a total of eighteen) of the plea to Shamash in Alan Lenzi, ed., *Reading Akkadian Prayers and Hymns: An Introduction*, SBL Ancient Near East Monographs (Atlanta: SBL, 2011), 197–216, could have been a self-standing hymn to Shamash, but this does not mean that they are a different prayer from what follows; the hymn is a lengthy first element of the plea, at once acting as an extended vocative and an explanation for why the worshiper turns to Shamash. Similarly, the first nine lines (out of twenty-five) in the prayer to Marduk found in Lenzi, 313–25, are a well-structured hymn to Marduk (as demonstrated by Tzvi Abusch, "The Form and Meaning of a Babylonian Prayer to Marduk," *JAOS* 103 [1983]), but that hymn is but a section of the longer plea psalm into which it is (Abusch shows) very well integrated at a literary-rhetorical level. The same may be said about the hymn of praise that begins the complaint psalm in Ps 89:1–38.

29. It is not outside the realm of possibility that the two sections once existed on their own, and that an editor, noticing the elements that link them, deliberately put them together to form the single composition that is now Psalm 27. Even in that case, however, it behooves us to ask what the editor was attempting to accomplish by putting them together, and especially by putting them together in the order they now have rather than the reverse.

30. Some ancient translations such as the LXX omit this word (Psalm 26 LXX). However, the previous verse in LXX ends with the word ἑαυτῇ, which could be understood to translate the word לה ("to herself, in herself"). No such word appears in the Hebrew of the verse, leading me to wonder if LXX's otherwise superfluous ἑαυτῇ might reflect a Hebrew text that had a (partially erased?) remnant of לולא. Qumran is of limited help here. 4QPsᶜ lacks the beginning of verse 13, but the seven letters in continuation of the verse (the tetragrammaton followed by באר) are just visible, and they appear, to my eye, to have left room for לולא at the beginning of the line (v. 12 seems to have ended at the end of the previous line, though this is not entirely clear from the fragments of 4QPsᶜ.

Similarly, in the MT this word appears with dots above and below it, probably in order to indicate that in late Second Temple times or during the rabbinic era, there were scribes who doubted that the word should be present. (On the use of supralinear dots in the consonantal text underlying MT, see Israel Yeivin, *Introduction to the Tiberian Masorah*, trans. E.J. Revell, MasS 5 [Missoula: Scholars Press, 1980], 44–46, as well as Emanuel Tov, *Textual Criticism of the Hebrew Bible* [Minneapolis: Fortress

does not complete; it is the "if"-clause of a sentence whose "then"-clause never appears.[31] To be sure, the intention of the implied then-clause is clear: what the speaker was thinking was something to the effect of, "If not for my faith that I will see God's goodness, I would be completely lost." But the absence of the then-clause gives the impression that the speaker cannot bring himself to finish his sentence; his utterance brings him perilously close to an emotional place too dangerous to approach. The verse intends to make a statement of confidence, but the speaker cannot quite get the whole thing out. We find in this single verse the back-and-forth of the whole psalm: the confidence of the first stanza and the anxiety of the second are both manifest in this not-quite-complete expression of

---

Press, 1992], 55–57, both of whom discuss all fifteen occurrences of this phenomenon in Scripture. Cf. the discussion of the ten cases in the Torah, specifically in Saul Lieberman, *Hellenism in Jewish Palestine* [New York: Feldheim, 1950], 43–46, who notes that the Rabbis do not always understand them this way. These dots appear not only in vocalized editions of the MT of Psalm 27:13 but also in non-vocalized scrolls of the Psalter; the dots pre-date the work of the Masoretes. See Yeivin [*ibid*]. According to Yeivin, a dot is to be placed above all four Hebrew letters of the word, but below only the first, third, and fourth letters. In fact, various texts differ widely. Aleppo (followed by Breuer editions) have dots above and below all four letters; Leningrad (followed by BHS and Koren) has three dots above and below (and no dots for the letter ו); Seeligman Baer's edition matches Yeivin's description, with three dots above and four below.

The difference between versions with and without this word is substantial. LXX makes our verse into a positive statement: "I believe I shall see the LORD's goodness in the land of the living." But the word לולא was probably called into doubt in some Hebrew texts and left out of LXX (or rendered into the previous verse's ἑαυτῇ) for two reasons. First, the fact that לולא introduces a protasis for which there is no apodosis may have confused scribes. Second, the theological doubt the incomplete protasis reflects may have upset scribes. The text including לולא is to be preferred as *lectio difficilior*, both in terms of syntax and theology.

31. Both Rashi and ibn Ezra see the "then" clause as appearing in the previous verse: "False witnesses would have risen against me if I had not been confident that I would see God's goodness." But this means that the then-clause would begin with כי, which seems unlikely, since כי can mean "if." Granted, we could sensibly translate כי here as "indeed." But beginning a "then" clause with a word that typically introduces an "if" clause would have invited confusion. Further, the clause at the end of the previous verse is the second verset of one poetic line, while our "if" clause in verse 13 is the first verset of a new poetic line. A single compound sentence spread over the last part of one line and the first part of another would be highly irregular for biblical poetry, which by and large shuns strong enjambment of that sort. On the rarity of enjambment in biblical poetry, which overwhelmingly prefers end-stopping, see Dobbs-Allsopp, *On Biblical Poetry*, 44–48, 135–39; Yaakov Kaduri, "Biblical Poetry: How Can It Be?" [in Hebrew] in *The Literature of the Hebrew Bible: Introductions and Studies*, ed. Zipora Talshir (Jerusalem: Yad Ben-Zvi Press, 2011), 297–98; Watson, *Classical*, 332–35.

faith. In the next verse, the psalm closes with imperatives that call on the worshiper (and us) to wait hopefully for God. The fact that these imperatives are deemed necessary points to the existence of doubts that must be overcome. In this one psalm we have a beautiful and brief distillation of the entire Psalter as a book of doubt and faith. As the psalm moves between belief and distress, it "manifests powerful psychological verisimilitude," Robert Alter points out, because its emphasis on trust "does not preclude a feeling of fearful urgency in the speaker's plea to God."[32]

The movement from faith to doubt demands our attention, because the direction of the journey on which this psalm leads us is the opposite of what many readers might have expected of a religious text. Our worshiper does not grow into a more conventional piety over the course of the psalm, casting aside doubts to take up the armor of faith. Rather, the worshiper sets aside a seemingly ideal faith to take on a more realistic one. In fact Blidstein argues that the psalm criticizes the simplistic faith of the first stanza, whose God he labels "an ersatz divinity, a facile projection of [the worshiper] himself."[33] Similarly, Ellen Charry maintains that in the first stanza, the worshiper thinks that "he has God in his pocket."[34] While the faith of that section seems on the surface to be stronger, the truth is that in that section, the worshiper speaks of God (always in the third person!) as something he knows about, but not someone whom he knows. In the second stanza, when the worshiper moves to the second person in order to address God directly, the worshiper at last achieves the experiential contact with God that he yearned for in verse 4 ("One thing I ask ..."). It is precisely when the worshiper speaks directly to God that doubt becomes prominent. God is no longer something the worshiper claims to know all about. In the second stanza, God is a partner in a relationship (though of course the senior partner), and relationships are slippery and unknowable in a way that does not conform to the simplistic faith of the first stanza.

The direction of the psalm's movement is crucial, because it models the maturing of an authentic relationship with God. A simple faith that asks no questions and admits no anxieties is not the most religious faith.

---

32. Robert Alter, *The Book of Psalms: A Translation with Commentary* (New York: Norton, 2007), 91.

33. Blidstein, "T'hillim 27," 23.

34. Charry, *Psalms 1–50*, 139.

A relationship that can articulate anxiety about the beloved's distance is the stronger one. As Charry writes, this psalm tells us that,

> "unpleasant emotions are not to be repressed as untoward but to be healed through models that show how to handle them. Here, the psalmist gives permission to his audience to be emotionally conflicted in relation to God. He does not urge his hearers to 'grin and bear it' or 'put on a happy face,' and he does not disparage honest fear of God-abandonment ..."[35]

A faith that allows no doubt is hubris. When it claims to know for sure what God will and will not do, it denies God's freedom and invests far too much in the believer's impregnable security. Such a faith is the very opposite of true piety. The wavering faith of Psalm 27 is more honest, humbler, and therefore more deeply religious. This faith is neither Pollyannaish nor naive; it is realistic about the fact that God seems absent at times.

The psalm's faith is also, I would like to suggest, quintessentially Jewish. The psalm concludes neither with fear nor with complete confidence but with hope (the last words of the psalm in verse 14 are: וְקַוֵּה אֶל־יְהוָה). The final verse of Psalm 27 recalls the Pentateuch, which does not conclude with entry into the land of Israel and the fulfillment of God's promises. Deuteronomy 34 narrates not the victory of the Pentateuch's central human character but his death. Nonetheless, that chapter leaves us with the expectation that God's promises to Moses and to the patriarchs before him will yet come to fruition with the victory of Moses's assistant, Joshua. Moses's life was a success not because he completed his task but because he did not desist from it—that is, because he lived up to the teaching of his latter-day disciple, Rabbi Ṭarfon in M. Avot 2:16 ("It is not incumbent upon you to complete the task, but you are not free to desist from it"). It is fateful for the Jewish religion that the Torah ends on a note of hope rather than fulfillment.[36] That tendency made it natural that the anthem

---

35. Charry, *Psalms 1–50*, 141.

36. Many scholars have suggested the possibility that in antiquity the Torah was a six-book unit ending with Joshua. Thus it is vital to realize that all the known forms of Judaism (and indeed, of Samaritanism) accept the five-book Torah ending with Deuteronomy. On the fateful nature of Judaism's decision to accord the highest canonical status to the Pentateuch and not to a Hexateuch, see James A. Sanders, *Torah and Canon* (Philadelphia: Fortress, 1972), 27–28, 52, and David Frankel, *The Land of Canaan and the Destiny of Israel: Theologies of Territory in the Hebrew Bible* (Winona Lake: Eisenbrauns, 2011), 25–29. Because the Pentateuch is more sacred and authoritative in the Jewish canon than the rest of scripture, promise takes a central place in the

of the Zionist movement and of the State of Israel is התקוה, "The Hope" (rather than a song with a title like, say, הניצחון, "The Victory"[37]). Hope rather than perfect confidence characterizes the most mature Jewish faith: a readiness to admit one's fears, to look toward God expectantly while renouncing the claim to predict all God's actions. This faith is well displayed by Psalm 27's journey from simple, trusting piety in its first stanza, through doubt in the second, to hope in the third.

It is the dialogue among the two stanzas that is the key to understanding this highly integrated poem. The poem as a whole is structured like a line of biblical poetry. The first stanza introduces the psalm's central theme: ביטחון (to use a later Hebrew theological term) or trust (27:3). The second and third stanzas specify what true ביטחון involves. Insofar as the faith of the last two stanzas is a more mature faith, I think we can contend that the movement from stanza to stanza involves intensification as well, a move from something lower to something higher, from something simplistic to something sophisticated, from theoretical knowledge of God to relationship with God. The movement of the psalm is not one of statement and echo, just as the parallelism of most biblical poetic lines does not involve mere equivalence. Rather, we have a statement, followed by a recasting in more serious terms.[38] (There may, however, be one more turn in Psalm 27; we can arrive there only once we have noted an additional feature of poetry, at the end of this essay.)

Now, everything I said about Psalm 27 in the previous paragraph can also be said about Psalm 19. I have treated that psalm in detail elsewhere,[39] so I will merely summarize the ways that in both psalms, the structure of the whole recapitulates the structure of a poetic line in a

---

shaping of Jewish identity, while fulfillment is secondary. The five-book Torah, the Scroll of Guidance, points towards a goal, but does not bring us all the way there. The Torah leaves us more in the position of Moses, looking towards a promised land, than Joshua, confidently entering it; and it is Moses, not Joshua, who is the prototypical Sage of the Jewish people.

37. Or a song such as שיר בית"ר (the hymn of the Revisionist Zionists), whose tone and lyrics are so contrary to התקוה.

38. We find elsewhere that a whole poem's development from beginning to end involves specification or intensification, so that the poem as a whole behaves like a line of biblical poetry. This is the case, for instance in Exodus 15, which describes the same events over and over in ways that become at once more specific and more metaphorical as the poem progresses.

39. Benjamin D. Sommer, "Nature, Revelation, and Grace in Psalm 19: Towards a Theological Reading of Scripture," *HTR* 108 (2015): 376–401.

theologically interesting way. In Psalm 19, as in Psalm 27, the variation between two-verset and three-verset lines separates the poem into stanzas, and various additional features make this structure clear as well. For example, the types of parallelism in the first stanza are quite varied, while the second stanza begins with a highly regular line structure that repeats itself over four lines, then begins to admit a small degree of variation for two more lines.

As with Psalm 27, Psalm 19 is widely viewed as being split between two utterly separate psalms. One, we are told, deals exclusively with nature, while the other speaks exclusively of revelation. In fact, however, each stanza contains multiple verbal references to the other, and it is at once the tension between them and the strong parallel between them that produce the psalm's theological message. Each stanza describes a way of coming to know God: in the first, one gains knowledge of God through observing God's creation; in the second, one gains this knowledge by coming into a covenantal relationship with Yhwh through Torah and commandment. The first stanza refers to the deity using a regular noun (more specifically, a job title) that occurs but once: אל or God. The second refers to the deity seven times using God's personal name, the tetragrammaton. This difference reflects two different types of connection between humanity and divinity: To refer to a being by the being's job title suggests respect but distance. From observing nature, then, one knows about God. From observing the terms of Yhwh's covenant, however, one begins not just to know about God but to know God. The *knowledge of* God in the first stanza is, at least in principle, universal, while the *relationship with* God in the second is particular.

Various intratextual connections in Psalm 19 make clear that the two ways of knowing God (through creation and covenant, or, if one prefers, through nature and nomos) do not merely complement each other. The knowledge that comes from nature is valid; but it is also limited. It does not draw one into intimacy with God; it does not provide any ethical or moral directive. Thus nomos goes further than nature, supplementing it without superseding it.[40] Knowledge about God in the first stanza

40. This is made explicit in verse 11, which tells us that Torah and commandments are "More desirable than gold, than quantities of platinum; Sweeter than honey, than drippings from the comb." Gold is the color of the sun and an epithet of sun deities, who are also associated with sweetness in the ancient Near East. On gold and sweetness as standard epithets of sun deities, see Nahum Sarna, "Psalm XIX and the Near Eastern Sun-God Literature," in *Fourth World Congress of Jewish Studies Papers* (Jerusalem: World

requires action on humanity's part: we must turn to creation, observe it, think about what we perceive, and come to conclusions. The relationship with God in the second stanza, on the other hand, requires God to turn to humanity. In the first stanza God is object, while in the second God is subject. For this reason the valid but limited knowledge that comes from nature is not rightly termed revelation, if we follow Christopher Seitz in using that term to denote a willful act of disclosure on God's part.[41] This contrast becomes more pointed in the very last verse of the poem, which opens us up to dialogue and redemption, for here the speaker for the first time addresses God directly and refers to the deity as גאלי, redeemer.

The two stanzas of Psalm 19 both deal with theology in the basic sense of the term, but they do not present functional equivalents. Rather, the revelational theology of the second stanza adds something new and valuable to the natural theology of the first stanza. The wording and imagery of the second stanza of Psalm 19 moves us from knowledge of God to relationship with God, from proposition to covenant, from reasoning to deed, from observation to joy, from speculation to law, from detachment to grace.[42] Recall now how Kugel and Alter describe the dynamic nature of the ancient Hebrew poetic line. Intensification and the logic of "A, and *what's more*, B" describe how the second stanza of Psalm 19 relates to the first. In Psalm 19 as in Psalm 27, a simple statement about prosody sums up the core theology of an ancient Hebrew poem.

SEQUENCE VS. CYCLE

I would like to move on to another question of prosody and its connection to theological reading. It has long been recognized that parallelism is the core of biblical poetry; Robert Lowth devoted the most influential chapter in his 18th-century study of biblical poetry to the topic, and the phenomenon was discussed by various medieval Jewish exegetes of the Bible.[43]

Union of Jewish Studies, 1967), 175. Here the second stanza not only compares Torah to sun; it tells us that Torah is better than the sun.

41. Cf. Christopher Seitz, *Word Without End: The Old Testament as Abiding Theological Witness* (Grand Rapids: Eerdmans, 1998), 18–19.

42. For a defense of these readings of each stanza, see the article cited in note 39 above.

43. See Robert Lowth, *Lectures on the Sacred Poetry of the Hebrews*, trans. G. Gregory (New York: Garland, 1971), specifically, Lecture XIX, as well as Robert Lowth, *Isaiah: A New Translation: With a Preliminary Dissertation, and Notes, Critical, Philological, and Explanatory*, 11th ed. (Cambridge: James Munroe & Co., 1834), ix–xli. On the recognition of the principle of meaning-based parallelism in the work of medieval Jewish scholars

More recently the great linguist and literary critic Roman Jakobson has
clarified that *all* poetry is based on the principle of parallelism. According
to Jakobson, verse in languages all around the globe consists of lines—that
is to say, in cultures throughout the world a poem consists of a series of
relatively brief units of discourse, each of which is followed by a pause.
These relatively brief units of discourse will always be parallel to each
other in one way or another.[44] Because of Lowth's long legacy, we biblical
scholars tend to think of parallelism in terms of lexical and semantic
echoing from one verset to the next; this is what I have called "meaning-based parallelism." But parallels among poetic lines can take many
other forms as well. In metrical poetry, lines echo each other because
they share a single pattern of syllables—say, in iambic pentameter, an
unstressed and a stressed syllable repeated five times in each line: "Of
Mans First *Disobedience, and the Fruit* / Of *that* Forbidden *Tree*, whose
mortal *taste* / Brought *Death* into the *World*, and *all* our *woe*." Each of the
10,563 lines that follow these three opening lines from Milton's *Paradise
Lost* is parallel to every other line in the epic, because they all have this
ten-syllable pattern (-/-/-/-/-/) or some small variation of that pattern,
such as an eleventh unstressed syllable at the end of a line.[45] Or each line
of a metrical poem might consist of two groups of four syllables, the first

---

of the northern French school of the eleventh and twelfth centuries, with attention also to the work of the twelfth and thirteenth century Provencal scholar Radak
(c.1160 - c.1235), see Robert Harris, *Discerning Parallelism: A Study in Northern French
Medieval Jewish Biblical Exegesis*, Brown Judaic Studies 341 (Providence, RI: Brown
Judaic Studies, 2004). On the discussions of poetic lines divided into versets in work
of the thirteenth-century scholar Moses ibn Tibbon and the late fifteenth-century
scholar Isaac Abarbanel, see Cooper, "Biblical Poetics," 155 and 158-60 respectively.
On the very important work of the sixteenth-century scholar Azariah dei Rossi, see
Cooper, 17-19; Kugel, *Idea*, 200-204; and Adele Berlin, *Biblical Poetry Through Medieval
Jewish Eyes* (Bloomington: Indiana University Press, 1991), 141-53. Lowth acknowledges
dei Rossi's influence and quotes him at length; see, e.g., Lowth, *Isaiah*, xxxiii-xxxix.
44. See, e.g., Roman Jakobson, "Grammatical Parallelism and Its Russian Facet,"
Language 42 (1966): 399-429; Roman Jakobson, "Linguistics and Poetics," in *Style
in Language*, ed. T. Sebeok (Cambridge: MIT Press, 1968), 350-77; Roman Jakobson,
"Poetry of Grammar and Grammar of Poetry," *Lingua* 21 (1968): 597-609.
45. Though even the variations are often noteworthy: at I:165 note what word provides
the extra, unstressed syllable at the end of the line and thus, by breaking the ten-syllable pattern, introduces discord into an otherwise perfect environment: "And out of
good still to find means of evil." Arguably, the third foot of this line also breaks the
pattern since it most naturally scans as a trochee rather than an iamb. This discordant
line, not surprisingly, is spoken by "th'Archfiend" (I:156), Satan.

employing a short vowel and the next three employing long vowels, as
in Adon Olam:[46] אֲדוֹן עוֹלָם אֲשֶׁר מָלַךְ / בְּטֶרֶם כָּל יְצִיר נִבְרָא / לְעֵת נַעֲשָׂה בְחֶפְצוֹ כָּל
אֲזַי מֶלֶךְ שְׁמוֹ נִקְרָא / וְאַחֲרֵי כִּכְלוֹת הַכֹּל, לְבַדּוֹ יִמְלֹךְ נוֹרָא /.[47] Again, every one of
the ten lines of the Ashkenazic-Italian version of *Adon Olam*, every one
of the fifteen lines of the Sephardic-Eidot Hamizraḥ version, every one
of the sixteen lines of the Yemenite version, is parallel to every other
one, because each has this eight-syllable pattern (˘ – – – ˘ – – –). In the
metrical cases I just cited, the parallel is purely rhythmic. But a parallel
might also result from rhyme, from the fact that lines end with a syllable that sounds more or less identical to the last syllable of another
nearby line. In rhymed poetry, certain lines send us back in particular
to some lines and less so to others. Thus in the character Faust's first
statement in Goethe's poem of that name ("Habe nun, ach! Philosophie, /
Juristerei und Medizin, / Und leider auch Theologie / Durchaus studiert,
mit heißem Bemühn. / Da steh ich nun, ich armer Tor! / Und bin so klug
als wie zuvor"), rhyme links theology more closely to philosophy than to
medicine or law; even more importantly, the rhyme of *Tor* ("fool") and
zuvor ("previously") links the line concerned with cleverness (*so klug als
wie zuvor*) to the one about foolishness.[48] There are other sorts of sound-
based or phonological parallelism besides meter and rhyme. One such
type results from the fact that each line is largely alliterative, even though
various lines' alliterations are based on a different letter (thus the opening
lines of *Beowulf*: "Hwæt. We Gardena in geardagum, / þeodcyninga, þrym
gefrunon, / hu ða æþelingas ellen fremedon. / Oft Scyld Scefing sceaþena
þreatum, / monegum mægþum, meodosetla ofteah, /...").[49] Parallels may
be rhythmic without being metrical: as long as the lines tend to be of more
or less similar length, they will share a cadence. Consequently, even free

---

46. In the system of medieval Hebrew meter, the *shewa* and all *ḥataf* vowels are considered short, as is the *shuruq* meaning "and" at the beginning of a word. All other
vowels are considered long. Note that any *shewa* that is grammatically *naḥ* can be read
as *naʿ* (and thus as a short vowel) if necessary for the meter. Similarly, any *shewa* or
ḥataf vowel can be considered a silent vowel (viz., a *shewa naḥ*, and thus as no vowel
at all) when necessary for the meter.
47. Following the norm for scanned medieval verse, the poetry requires us to treat
the *ḥataf-pataḥs* in נַעֲשָׂה and in וְאַחֲרֵי as a silent, as if each were a *shewa naḥ*. Also, the
shewa in כִּכְלוֹת and in יִמְלֹךְ is treated as a *shewa naʿ*.
48. Johann Wolfgang Goethe, Faust I, Verse 354.
49. To get a sense of the alliteration, one can go, of course, to YouTube: https://
www.youtube.com/watch?v=CH-_GwoO4xI, or https://www.youtube.com/watch
?v=ozorjJzrrvA.

verse that eschews both meter and rhyme will nevertheless consist of lines that resemble each other simply because the speaker pauses again and again after each line. The mere fact of pausing after relatively brief units of discourse itself creates a loose but noticeable—more specifically, audible—form of parallelism.[50] Parallelism comes in many forms and sounds, and of course in most cases, there are several types of parallelism that link line to line. Rhymed poetry is often metrical. (In fact *Adon Olam* also displays rhyme, as do the lines I quoted from *Faust* have meter.) Lexical parallels inevitably involve syntactic parallels at a surface level, while semantic parallels often involve syntactic parallels at a deep level.

If we accept Jakobson's definition of poetry, it follows that poetry is always cyclical: verse constantly goes back even as it moves forward, for every new line echoes a line that came before it, whether in its semantic content, its rhythm, or its phonology. Consequently, poetry lends itself especially well to suggesting linkages (of one idea and another, of one character and another, of moods, of events), because as one line echoes a previous one it also implies some connection between its content and that of the previous line, even if they display no explicit meaning-based parallelism.[51] For this reason, the literary critic Northrop Frye, in his essay "Rhetorical Criticism: Theory of Genres," identifies a basic contrast between prose and poetry. Frye identifies prose as "the rhythm of continuity" and observes that "the rhythm of prose is continuous, not recurrent, and the fact is symbolized by the purely mechanical breaking of prose lines on a printed page ..."[52] "Lyric," on the other hand, is "the rhythm of association": "The lyric is ... the genre which most clearly

---

50. It is here, I think, that the enormously helpful work of James Kugel (Yaakov Kaduri) and of F.W. Dobbs-Allsopp breaks down. Both of these scholars deny that parallelism is at the core of biblical poetry (see Kugel, *Idea*, 51, 56–57, and cf. 59–61; Kaduri, "Biblical Poetry," 289–91; Dobbs-Allsopp, *On Biblical Poetry*, 3, 56, 143, 271), arguing instead that the core of biblical verse is the simple act of saying something brief, pausing, and then continuing with another brief statement which may or may not echo the lexica or semantics of the previous utterance. But Kugel and Dobbs-Allsopp adopt far too narrow an understanding of parallelism. What Jakobson and scholars like Cooper, Geller, and Berlin show us is that the simple fact of uttering and then pausing, uttering and then pausing, again and again itself creates a type of audible parallelism.

51. Jason M.H. Gaines, *The Poetic Priestly Source* (Minneapolis: Fortress, 2015), 36, phrases this point well in his discussion of Jakobson's conception of poetry: "All poetry asks the reader to consider whether a second line relates to its preceding line, and to what degree."

52. Northrop Frye, *Anatomy of Criticism: Four Essays* (Princeton: Princeton University Press, 1971), 263.

shows the hypothetical core of literature, narrative, and meaning in their literal aspects as word-order and word-pattern."[53] Both these critics point to something essential about verse, which is its circular nature, its tendency (in relative contrast to prose) in every new line to progress but also to return. Even when poetry narrates—that is, when it relates what happened first, then second, then third[54] so that it moves its characters and its audience forward in time—it also moves back, and back again, and back again, as each line echoes an earlier one, thus associating what came before with what follows. Others have noted these core tendencies of prose and poetry as well. At around the same time that Jakobson presented his approach, the literary theorist Barbara Herrnstein Smith wrote,

> Repetition is the fundamental phenomenon of poetic form ... All the principles that have been or may be used to generate formal structure in poetry are describable in terms of the repetition of either a certain physical feature in language—as in rhyme and alliteration—or a relationship among such features—as in stress patterns and syllable counts. The fundamental unit of poetic form is the line ...[55]

The 19th-century poet Gerald Manley Hopkins already contended that parallelism is the constitutive quality of poetry, as Jakobson himself points out at the outset of one of his most famous articles on poetry:

> When approaching the linguistic problem of grammatical parallelism one is irresistibly impelled to quote again and again the pathbreaking study written exactly one hundred years ago by the juvenile Gerard Manley Hopkins: "The artificial part of poetry,

---

53. Frye, *Anatomy*, 271.

54. Here, it is useful to recall that in many languages a verb meaning "to count" is related to a verb meaning "to narrate," since narrating at its most basic involves enumerating events in order. This is true in Semitic languages (Hebrew: לִסְפּוֹר, לְסַפֵּר), in Indo-European languages (English: to count, to recount; German: zahlen, erzählen), and in Finno-Ugric (Hungarian: szamol, beszamol).

55. Barbara Herrnstein Smith, *Poetic Closure: A Study of How Poems End* (Chicago: University of Chicago Press, 1968), 38. Repetition, of course, encourages a poem's audience to note equivalence. Thus Jakobson made the same point when he wrote, "The poetic function [of language] projects the principle of equivalence from the axis of selection into the axis of combination. Equivalence is promoted to the constitutive device of the sequence" (Jakobson, "Linguistics and Poetics," 358). Similarly: "In poetry similarity is superimposed on contiguity and hence equivalence is promoted to the constitutive device of the sequence" (Jakobson, "Poetry of Grammar," 602).

perhaps we shall be right to say all artifice, reduces itself to the principle of parallelism. The structure of poetry is that of continuous parallelism, ranging from the technical so-called Parallelisms of Hebrew poetry and the antiphons of Church music to the intricacy of Greek or Italian or English verse."[56]

Another, more recent, source that underscores the circular nature of poetry is the film, *Paterson*, which is above all a film not only about a poet (and bus driver) but about poetry. You will notice that the opening event and closing event of the movie, separated by a week, are identical: like a poem, the film moves back even as it moves forward. Pay attention also to the constant presence of circles in the film: for example, in the painting, the clothing, and the cupcakes of the main character's companion. In the Cheerios the main character eats each morning—and don't miss the several close-ups of his watch, lingering long enough for us to notice the cyclical sweep of its seconds-hand. No less important: each day the main character drives a bus route, a large circle. (The Muse, disguised as a Japanese tourist, remarks to him, "A bus driver in Paterson? Ah. This very poetic.") While the film's connection to the New Jersey poet William Carlos Williams (whose very name exemplifies the cyclical aspect of poetry!) has been widely noted, I am not sure that anyone pointed out its thoroughly Jakobsonian conception of poetry, perhaps because, as the example of Hopkins makes clear, one does not need to read Jakobson or Herrnstein Smith or Frye to arrive at their conclusion; one only needs to read poetry.

At the risk of reducing varied and complex cross-cultural phenomena to broad generalizations, I think we can follow these theorists by noting that poetry tends to be cyclical and prose linear. We can see this especially clearly in the Bible when the same event is treated in prose and poetry. Consider the following examples. In Judges 4:19, a prose narrator describes the meeting between Yael and Sisera in sequence:

---

56. Jakobson, "Grammatical Parallelism," 399, quoting from Humphry House and Graham Storey, eds., *The Journals and Papers of Gerard Manley Hopkins* (London: Oxford University Press, 1959), 89.

וַיֹּאמֶר אֵלֶיהָ הַשְׁקִינִי־נָא מְעַט־מַיִם כִּי צָמֵאתִי וַתִּפְתַּח אֶת־נֹאוד הֶחָלָב וַתַּשְׁקֵהוּ וַתְּכַסֵּהוּ׃

He said to her, "Let me have some water, please, for I am thirsty."
Then she opened a container of milk and let him drink, and then
she covered him up.[57]

But the poet in Judges 5:25 describes the same event without regard
for sequence, moving ahead in time and then returning in a rhythmic back-and-forth:

מַיִם שָׁאַל / חָלָב נָתָנָה / בְּסֵפֶל אַדִּירִים / הִקְרִיבָה חֶמְאָה׃

Water, he asked; / milk, she gave; / in bowl fit for princes / she
brought forth cream.[58]

The structuring here is one of intensification (water, milk, cream), not
temporal sequence. The same contrast is evident as the prose narrator and then the poet describes Sisera's death in Judges 4:21 and 5:26–
27 respectively:

וַתִּקַּח יָעֵל אֵשֶׁת־חֶבֶר אֶת־יְתַד הָאֹהֶל וַתָּשֶׂם אֶת־הַמַּקֶּבֶת בְּיָדָהּ וַתָּבוֹא אֵלָיו בַּלָּאט
וַתִּתְקַע אֶת־הַיָּתֵד בְּרַקָּתוֹ וַתִּצְנַח בָּאָרֶץ וְהוּא־נִרְדָּם וַיָּעַף וַיָּמֹת׃

Then Yael, the wife of Ḥever, took a tent stake and placed a
hammer in her hand. Next, she came to him quietly and drove
the stake into his forehead, and he sank onto the ground. (He
had fallen asleep, exhausted.) Then he died.

יָדָהּ לַיָּתֵד תִּשְׁלַחְנָה / וִימִינָהּ לְהַלְמוּת עֲמֵלִים
וְהָלְמָה סִיסְרָא / מָחֲקָה רֹאשׁוֹ / וּמָחֲצָה וְחָלְפָה רַקָּתוֹ׃
בֵּין רַגְלֶיהָ כָּרַע / נָפַל שָׁכָב
בֵּין רַגְלֶיהָ כָּרַע / נָפַל בַּאֲשֶׁר כָּרַע / שָׁם נָפַל שָׁדוּד׃[59]

Her hand she sent forth to the stake,
    her right hand for the workmen's club.

---

57. The אות איח"ן דגוש ו+אות of the *waw*-consecutive introduces what happens next in a
sequence and thus can accurately or literally be rendered not simply as "and" but
more precisely as "then" or "next." I translate it that way in some cases both here
and below.
58. More literally, curds or butter—that is, some sort of creamy solid food derived
from milk.
59. My lineation departs from the Masoretic indications of syntax, which puts a more
major stop on נָפַל, which would suggest the lineation:

בֵּין רַגְלֶיהָ כָּרַע / נָפַל שָׁכָב / בֵּין רַגְלֶיהָ כָּרַע / נָפַל
בַּאֲשֶׁר כָּרַע / שָׁם נָפַל שָׁדוּד׃

And clubbed Sisera,
>   crushed his head,
>   and smashed and broke his temples open.
Between her legs he bowed,
>   went down, lay.
Between her legs he bowed,
>   he went down right where he bowed,
>   there he went down — assaulted, ruined, crushed.

The prose carefully limns a temporal sequence, carefully noting a parenthetical pluperfect by using disruptive word order (וְהוּא־נִרְדָּם) so that
what happens when is quite clear. The poetry, on the other hand, gives
multiple impressions of the same actions, repeating itself, providing a
new angle, hinting (in ways my translation tries to capture) at the physical humiliation of the warrior at the hands of a woman. To do all this,
the verse dispenses entirely with any concern for temporal sequence.[60]
This difference between prosaic and poetic descriptions of the death of
Sisera reflects two ways of understanding God's involvement in history.
As John Goldingay points out, the prose account of Deborah and Barak's
victory in Judges 4 "celebrates Yhwh's involvement in events but pictures
Yhwh working via human processes, while the poetic account [in Judges
5] speaks more figuratively about the stars fighting from heaven and a
torrent sweeping Sisera's forces away."[61] In both, God's presence in events
here on earth is hidden, in one case behind normal historical process, in
the other behind overwhelming natural phenomena.

   With these broader ruminations on poetry's tendency to cycle back
on itself and thus to link what comes earlier with what comes later, I
would like to turn to one more biblical poem, Psalm 114. While it is not a
narrative poem—in fact, the Bible lacks the narrative poetry so typical
of the ancient world—Psalm 114 does refer to narratives found elsewhere

---

60. The same may be said of poems like Exodus 15 and Psalm 78 as wholes: though
they refer to events, they are not really narratives because they do not recount events
in order, in a manner that establishes the events' chronological sequence. Instead,
moving back and forth in time as the poems progress, Exodus 15 and Psalm 78 use
parallels from one section of the poem to another in order to link disparate or even
blur separate events.

61. Goldingay, *Psalms 1–41*, 260. For analogous reflections on complementary ways of
perceiving God's activity in the world in Exodus 7–15 (in this case involving not only
prose and poetry but different Pentateuchal sources), see Mordechai Breuer, *Pirqei
Mo'adot*, [in Hebrew] 2 vols. (Jerusalem: Horeb, 1993), 1:193–265.

in the Bible. Consequently, it will be worthwhile to observe the way in which it associates the events it mentions with their temporal sequence. Let's take a look at this lyric poem.

מזמור קי״ד.

בֵּית יַעֲקֹב מֵעַם לֹעֵז:	1 בְּצֵאת יִשְׂרָאֵל מִמִּצְרָיִם
יִשְׂרָאֵל מַמְשְׁלוֹתָיו:	2 הָיְתָה יְהוּדָה לְקָדְשׁוֹ
הַיַּרְדֵּן יִסֹּב לְאָחוֹר:	3 הַיָּם רָאָה וַיָּנֹס
גְּבָעוֹת כִּבְנֵי־צֹאן:	4 הֶהָרִים רָקְדוּ כְאֵילִים
הַיַּרְדֵּן תִּסֹּב לְאָחוֹר:	5 מַה־לְּךָ הַיָּם כִּי תָנוּס
גְּבָעוֹת כִּבְנֵי־צֹאן:	6 הֶהָרִים תִּרְקְדוּ כְאֵילִים
מִלְּפְנֵי אֱלוֹהַ יַעֲקֹב:	7 מִלְּפְנֵי אָדוֹן חוּלִי אָרֶץ
חַלָּמִישׁ לְמַעְיְנוֹ־מָיִם:	8 הַהֹפְכִי הַצּוּר אֲגַם־מָיִם

PSALM 114

1   When Israel went forth from Egypt,
     the House of Jacob from people speaking a foreign tongue,

2   Judah became His holy property,
     Israel, what He ruled.

3   The sea saw and fled,
     the River Jordan turned itself around.

4   The mountains danced like rams,
     hills, like little sheep.

5   What's with you, Sea, that you're fleeing?
     Jordan, that you're turning around?

6   Mountains, that you're dancing like rams,
     hills, like little sheep?[62]

7   At the presence of the Lord, writhe, O earth!
     At the presence of Jacob's God!

8   Who turns the rock into a pool of water,
     flint, into a bubbling fountain.

---

62. On the rendering of בני צאן ("sheep" generally, or more specifically "lamb, young sheep," see Adele Berlin, "Rams and Lambs in Psalm 114:4 and 6: The Septuagint's Translation of X // בן Y Parallelisms," *Textus* 24 [2009]: 107–17, who defends the former.

This is a deceptively simple poem. With the exception of the rare word לֹעֵז,
its vocabulary is accessible; it displays crystal-clear lexical and syntactic
parallelism; and from its very first word (בצאת) it refers to one of the
Bible's most central and well-known events, the exodus (יציאת מצרים). On
closer examination, however, it poses several surprises, a few of which
I would like to examine here.

A key to understanding this poem is that it alludes not only to an event
known from the Pentateuch but to a particular text from the Pentateuch
as well. Given the fact that the poem begins by mentioning the exodus
explicitly and goes on to speak of the splitting of the Reed Sea, we might
expect that the source text to which it alludes will be Exodus 14 or 15.[63]
In fact, however, the main source of this allusive poem is another text
altogether. Let us recall the opening line of our poem again:

בְּצֵאת יִשְׂרָאֵל מִמִּצְרָיִם׃

When Israel went forth from Egypt ...

Now note Exod 19:1:

בַּחֹדֶשׁ הַשְּׁלִישִׁי לְצֵאת בְּנֵי־יִשְׂרָאֵל מֵאֶרֶץ מִצְרָיִם בַּיּוֹם הַזֶּה בָּאוּ מִדְבַּר סִינָי׃
In the third month after the **Israelites** had **gone forth from** the
land of **Egypt**, on that day, they arrived in the Sinai desert.

As the emphasis I gave these words indicates, the first line of Psalm 114
is borrowed from Exodus 19:1, which supplies each of the psalm's first
three words and their order. Of course the word-for-word nature of this
borrowing is more noticeable in the original Hebrew than in translation. Psalm 114's opening verset is a boiled-down version of Exodus 19's
first verse. The psalm's first line takes the prose of the Torah and translates it into the poetry of the psalm. This boiling-down or translation
reflects the fact that poetic language tends to be terse and charged with

---

63. The psalm is often viewed as basically a Passover psalm. See, e.g., Hans-Joachim
Kraus, *Psalms 60-150*, CC, trans. Hilton Oswald (Minneapolis: Fortress, 1993), 371-
73. See also Gunkel, *Psalmen*, 493: "Der Psalm behandelt das große, grundlegende
Ereignis der Religion und des Volkstums, die *Auszugsgeschichte*." Note, however,
that Gunkel significantly nuances his position, adding (p. 494) that the poet "hat ...
eine bei weitem wirksamere, lebendigere Vergegensärtigung des Geschehens and
die Stelle gesetzt." Rashi, commenting on b. *Ber.* 56a, explains that the Hallel prayer
consisting of Psalms 113-118 is known as the "Egyptian Hallel" (הללא מצראה or הלל
המצרי) because it is read on Passover. Of course these psalms are read on all the
pilgrimage festivals and several other occasions, but Psalm 114 seems to associate
them especially with Passover.

implicit meaning, where prose tends to be wordier and its meaning more unpacked. What I am calling the poet's act of translation in Psalm 114:1 takes the information from the prose that is Exodus 19:1 and reduces it to its absolute essential.

Now, the identification of the source text is surprising, since Exodus 19 narrates not the exodus from Egypt but the revelation at Sinai. Why would a text that seems to be about one event allude to a text that speaks of another?

Before we answer this question, let us look at a few more oddities in this poem. The first verset of the poem's second line, הָיְתָה יְהוּדָה לְקָדְשׁוֹ (which I have rendered, "Judah became His holy property"), seems straightforward. First-semester Hebrew students are likely to know all three vocabulary items. The more we think about them, however, the stranger they become. First of all, why is the verb הָיְתָה feminine, given that the subject, יְהוּדָה, is masculine? Second, what exactly does the noun mean here? Finally, the pronominal suffixes it contains (meaning "His") are unusual: normally, pronouns refer back to a previous noun. Here, while it is pretty clear who we are talking about (God), nevertheless the words אלהים or ה' or their equivalent are nowhere to be found earlier in the poem. The poem's third line (הַיָּם רָאָה וַיָּנֹס הַיַּרְדֵּן יִסֹּב לְאָחוֹר) — "The sea saw and fled") prompts a question as well. What did the sea see? What did the sea and the Jordan River witness that prompted such fear? The verb ראה lacks a direct object. In the compact language of poetry, this absence is hardly unusual, but we should note that, as often in poetry, the text is assuming something here, and demanding that we think about the assumption.

Let us address these questions in reverse order. What sight, above all, causes dismay and prompts flight in the Bible? Think of verses like Isaiah 6:1, in which Isaiah tells us he saw God directly. Isaiah goes on to tell us in 6:5 how he reacted to seeing God: with dismay and fear that he was about to die. Similarly, at Mount Sinai the Israelite nation were frightened when they saw God and moved away: וַיַּרְא הָעָם וַיָּנֻעוּ וַיַּעַמְדוּ מֵרָחֹק — "The people saw, and they trembled and stood far away" (Exod 20:18). This reaction is not exclusive to humans. Mount Sinai itself behaved just like the Israelites at that same event: Exodus 19:16 tells us that the Israelites quaked at Sinai, while 19:19 tells us that God's presence caused the mountain itself to quake (the same verb, וַיֶּחֱרַד, is used of both the people and the mountain.) Elsewhere in the Bible, even the sea responds to the sight of God in the same way; Psalm 77:17 reads:

רָאוּךָ מַּיִם אֱלֹהִים / רָאוּךָ מַּיִם יָחִילוּ / אַף יִרְגְּזוּ תְּהֹמוֹת:

The water saw you, God / The waters saw you and writhed / Yea,
the deep shuddered.

This last text is especially important, since its context resembles that
of the psalm we are discussing. Psalm 77:16 speaks of how God rescued
(גאל, a verb frequently used of the exodus) the בני יעקב (a term that recalls
בית יעקב in 114:1). Psalm 77 goes on to speak explicitly of the exodus event
led by Moses and Aaron (v. 21) in which the people took a path through
the sea (v. 20); it also speaks of earthquake (v. 19), which recalls the mountains skipping and dancing in Psalm 114:4.

So I think we can say with confidence that the missing accusative in
Psalm 114:3 is God: what the sea saw was a theophany. Once we realize
that, the fact that the psalm alludes to Exodus 19:1 becomes less odd; that
verse, after all, introduces the Bible's core narrative of theophany. The
connection between Psalm 114 and Exodus 19 solves other problems in
the psalm as well, because Exodus 19 contains additional vocabulary and
motifs that influenced the psalm. In Exodus 19:3, we read,

וּמֹשֶׁה עָלָה אֶל־הָאֱלֹהִים וַיִּקְרָא אֵלָיו ה'
מִן־הָהָר לֵאמֹר כֹּה תֹאמַר לְבֵית יַעֲקֹב וְתַגֵּיד לִבְנֵי יִשְׂרָאֵל:

Moses went up to God, and Yhwh called to him from the mountain, saying, "Speak thus to the **House of Jacob** / Tell this to the
children of Israel."

The words in bold reappear in Psalm 114:1b, which continues the allusion
the first half of the verse began. A few verses later, in Exodus 19:5-6,
we read:

וְעַתָּה אִם־שָׁמוֹעַ תִּשְׁמְעוּ בְּקֹלִי וּשְׁמַרְתֶּם אֶת־בְּרִיתִי וִהְיִיתֶם לִי
סְגֻלָּה מִכָּל־הָעַמִּים כִּי־לִי כָּל־הָאָרֶץ וְאַתֶּם תִּהְיוּ־לִי מַמְלֶכֶת כֹּהֲנִים וְגוֹי קָדוֹשׁ

So now, if you really obey me and keep my covenant, then
you will be My **personal treasure** from among all nations. Of
course, all the world is Mine, but you will become My **kingdom**
of priests, My **holy** people.

The idea that the Israelites are God's סגלה, His personal treasure or special possession,[64] and therefore his גוי קדוש, reappears in Psalm 114:2: היתה יהודה לקדשו—"Judah became God's קדש. The word קדש has various meanings, but especially in light of the allusion, it is clear that the relevant meaning here is the sense it has in many ritual texts: "property belonging specifically to God."[65] As Leviticus 22:2-3, 9-10 makes clear, consuming a קדש or harming it is a personal affront against God. As Meir Weiss astutely notes, recognizing the role of Exodus 19:1-6 as the source of the extended allusion in Psalm 114 solves the problem of the feminine verb in 114:2: the verb היתה is feminine because its subject is conceived of as the ממלכת ("kingdom," a feminine noun) of Exodus 19.6![66] As the poem boils down language to its essentials, the whole phrase ממלכת הכנים וגוי קדוש ("a kingdom of priests and holy nation") is reduced to יהודה ("Judah"), but even in that boiled-down format, the phrase retains the feminine singular form of its source. Similarly, the absence of explicit reference to God before the pronominal suffixes of verse 2 is no absence at all; the antecedent nouns do appear after all, abundantly, in our poem's source text.

The allusion to Exodus 19 emerges as more contextually sensible as we move further into Psalm 114, because the images in the poem's middle and last verses connect up with the events at Mount Sinai: the dancing hills and the trembling earth of verses 4, 6, and 7 recall the mountain's quaking described in Exodus 19:18.[67] Further, the reference to God turning rock

---

64. See Moshe Greenberg, *Studies in the Bible and Jewish Thought* (Philadelphia: Jewish Publication Society, 1995), 273-78, and cf. Moshe Held, "A Faithful Lover in an Old Babylonian Dialogue," *JCS* 15 (1961): 11-12.

65. This meaning is derived from ritual law but not limited to it. For a metaphorical use of this legal term in a poetic which, like Psalm 114, refers to the exodus, see Jeremiah 2:1-3.

66. Meir Weiss, *The Bible from Within: The Method of Total Interpretation*, Publications of the Perry Foundation for Biblical Research in the Hebrew University of Jerusalem (Jerusalem: Magnes, Hebrew University, 1984), 93-100; see also the commentary by Moshe Garsiel to Psalm 114 in Nahum Sarna, ed., *Olam Hatanakh: Tehillim* [in Hebrew] (Tel Aviv: Dodezon-Itti, 1995), 2:170-71.

67. Here I disagree with Weiss, *Bible*, 366-68, and Adele Berlin, "The Message of Psalm 114," in *Birkat Shalom: Essays in Honor of Shalom Paul*, eds. Chaim Cohen, Jeffrey Tigay, and Baruch Schwartz (Winona Lake: Eisenbrauns, 2008), 353, who argue that "if a theophany is implied, it is not the revelation at Sinai but the presence of God manifest in the exodus and its aftermath," as Berlin puts it. Indeed, Berlin even doubts that the poem deals with theophany at all, arguing that "only the context can determine whether or not a theophany is depicted." But the context is rich in markers pointing back to the story of the theophany at Sinai in Exodus 19. Those markers make clear,

into water in Psalm 114:8 takes us back to Exodus 17:6 and other passages describing Israel's journey through the wilderness, in which God brings forth water from a rock.

But the middle verses of the poem remain surprising. While verses 4 and 6–8, with their references to mountains dancing and rocks bringing forth water, match the source in Exodus well, verses 3 and 5 seem out of place. What caused the sea to flee, I noted above, was the theophany at Sinai. But the Reed Sea split three months before the theophany, as Exodus 19:1 carefully noted in wording that the allusion in Psalm 114 leaves out: "In the third month after the children of Israel left Egypt, they arrived at Sinai." The sea reacted in the first month to an event that did not occur until the third! The second half of the line in question is almost as strange, as it refers to an event that occurred forty years later: the splitting of the River Jordan at the end of the Israelites' journey through the wilderness. We are told in this psalm that nature reacted to the Sinai theophany three months early as well as forty years late—and also right on time. The mountains and hills were punctual; the waters were not.

But this is precisely what we should expect as the psalmist translates the prose of Exodus into poetry. To someone who objects that the poem gets the timing all wrong, the poet might impatiently respond: that is just the sort of insignificant, prosaic detail that poetry wants to move us away from. What matters to the poet are the deeper affiliations among events that undue attention to narrative sequence will obscure. The liberation from slavery and the giving of the law are not two events, separated in time; they are simply two facets of a single reality. So is the crossing of the Jordan River by the nation Israel into its own land, where it will live freely under that law. God who redeems, God who reveals, God who guides into the promised land—these are all one God. The redemption, the revelation, the guidance are, from the poet's point of view, a single occurrence. Only from a limited, prosaic point of view do these things seem separate.

This difference between the prose writer and the poet is exactly what literary critics like Jakobson and Frye would lead us to expect. The prose writer in Exodus instructs us about sequence and history. The poet in Psalm 114 encourages us to view things *sub specie aeternitatis*, from a perspective outside time. For the author of Exodus 19, what happened

---

albeit through the subtle art of allusion, that Psalm 114 is, from its very first words and repeatedly thereafter, reminding us of the theophany at Sinai.

when is of prime importance, and that author employs the instruments of Hebrew prose—the *waw*-consecutive, disruptive word order, longer sentences that have room for details that specify months and days—to lay out the events one after the other. The author of Psalm 114 exploits the main building block of poetry—parallelism—along with literary allusion to highlight correspondences of more profound significance that transcend connections of mere temporal sequence. The six versets of verses 1–3 move seamlessly back and forth in time among the moment of the exodus (alluded to in verse 1, and also in the reference to the splitting sea in verse 3a), the moment at Sinai (described in verse 2, with its allusion to Exodus 19:5–6; but also described in verse 1, almost all of whose vocabulary comes from the Sinai narrative Exodus 19:1 and 19:3), and as far forward as the nation's entry into the promised land (v. 3b). These six versets also hint at the moment of the world's creation, as the parallelism between the Reed Sea and the River Jordan in verses 3 and 5 implies. After all, the parallel of ים ("sea") and נהר (often translated "river," but also "ocean current" or "a river in the sea") is a standard motif of theomachy and creation language in biblical texts, which draw in turn on older Canaanite poetic conventions that frequently link these terms as lexical parallels in adjacent versets.[68]

In making these cross-temporal linkages, our poet is far from unique. Several biblical poems that describe the exodus or the crossing of the Reed Sea emphasize the ways in which that event echoed or recapitulated or continued God's primeval act of creation. Some also make clear that the exodus prepared for the erection of Yhwh's temple. The use of old Canaanite mythological motifs to link exodus and creation, along with reference to the erection of the temple, is famously evident in the Song of Moses in Exodus 15, as scholars including Moshe David Cassuto and Frank More Cross have demonstrated.[69] The linkage of creation and

---

68. The bibliography is of epic proportions. See especially John Day, *God's Conflict with the Dragon and the Sea: Echoes of a Canaanite Myth in the Old Testament*, UCOP (Cambridge: Cambridge University Press, 1985), as well as Frank Moore Cross, *Canaanite Myth and Hebrew Epic: Essays in the History of the Religion of Israel* (Cambridge: Harvard University Press, 1973), 112–44 (and, on the relationship between Baal and Yhwh more generally, 145–94). A helpful review of the main primary texts is provided by Samuel E. Loewenstamm, *The Evolution of the Exodus Tradition*, trans. Baruch Schwartz (Jerusalem: Magnes, 1992), 240–57.

69. See, e.g., Umberto (Moshe David) Cassuto, "The Israelite Epic," in *Biblical and Oriental Studies* (Jerusalem: Magnes, 1973), and the same author's treatment of Exodus 15 in Umberto (Moshe David) Cassuto, *A Commentary on the Book of Exodus*, trans. Israel

exodus along with reference to the temple on Mount Zion is also evident in Isaiah 59:9-11 and Psalms 74, 78, and 95.[70] The double-linkage of exodus to creation on the one hand and to the erection of the deity's palace on the other is no coincidence, since cosmology and temple-building were closely connected in ancient Near Eastern mythology.[71]

To be sure, we should not overstate the case. Prose writers can and do suggest typological linkages among events far removed in time, using repeated vocabulary items and motifs to establish important associations. In fact, the story of the crossing of the Jordan River in Joshua 4 does just that, making clear that the crossing of the Jordan re-enacts the crossing of the Reed Sea. It is also perfectly possible to narrate in verse, as *The Iliad*, *The Gilgamesh Epic*, and *Paradise Lost* all make clear, even if biblical narrators eschew this possibility. But the cyclical, associational nature of poetry as understood by Jakobson and of lyric as understood by Frye show that poetry is particularly apt at erasing the boundaries of time so that a poem's audience will quickly sense the ways in which seemingly distant events are in fact repeating manifestations of a deeper reality.

Let me go a step further in contrasting prosaic and poetic approaches to time and eternity. Two Jewish thinkers address a similar contrast. Neither was discussing Psalm 114 or questions of literary genre, but both were discussing what happened, or happens, at Mount Sinai. The Ḥasidic rebbe, Avraham Yehoshua Heschel, asserts in a discussion of Sinaitic revelation that the categories of past, present, and future are irrelevant from a divine point of view:

באדם שייך עבר ועתיד, אבל אצל הש"י אינו שייך זה,
ובכל יום ויום הוא נותן התורה לעמו ישראל

Past and future apply to humans but to God (praised be His name) this does not apply. Each and every day God gives the Torah to the people Israel.[72]

Abrahams (Jerusalem: Magnes, 1967); Cross, *Canaanite Myth*, 121-144 (and note Cross's discussion of Psalm 114, pp. 138-139).

70. See Berlin, "Message," 349-50, 356, 359.

71. On these linkages in biblical literature and their ancient Near Eastern background, see Moshe Weinfeld, "Sabbath, Temple Building, and the Enthronement of the Lord," [in Hebrew], *Beit Mikra* 69 (1977): 188-93, and Bernd Janowski, "Tempel und Schöpfung: Schöpfungstheologische Aspekte der priesterschriftlichen Heiligtumskonzeption," *Jahrbuch für Biblische Theologie* 5 (1990): 11-36.

72. Avraham Yehoshua Heschel, *Oheiv Yisroel*, [in Hebrew] (Zhitomir, 1864), 172, first printed in 1788.

The same point is expressed by another Jewish theologian who bore the same name:

> What God does, happens both in time and in eternity. Seen from our vantage point, it happened once; seen from His vantage point, it happens all the time. About the arrival of the people at Sinai we read ... "In the third month after the children of Israel were gone forth out of the land of Egypt, on this day they came into the wilderness of Sinai" (Exodus 19:1). Here was an expression that puzzled the ancient rabbis: on *this* day? It should have said, on *that* day. This can only mean that the day of giving the Torah can never become past; that day is this day, every day. The Torah, whenever we study it, must be to us "as if it were given us today."[73]

The poetic point of view, as described by בֶּן־יֵעֲקֹב or Jakobson, is precisely what the two Heschels describe as the divine point of view: one in which past, present, and future recede in the face of something beyond temporality.

We have seen that Psalm 114 argues that the events of the first and third months of the Israelite's first year in the wilderness, redemption and revelation, are a single occurrence. From a rabbinic point of view, we might paraphrase the thrust of Psalm 114 in phrasing that, while anachronistic, is in no way inappropriate, especially for a study with the title "Prosody and Preaching." In rabbinic terms, one might say that the message of our poem is that Passover and Shavuot are a single holiday, and if one observes the former but not the other (as most modern Jews do), one

---

73. It would be prosaic to note that these lines appear in a book published 168 years later than the lines quoted immediately beforehand, but that is what footnotes are for: Abraham Joshua Heschel, *God in Search of Man. A Philosophy of Judaism* (New York: Farrar Straus and Giroux, 1955), 215, quoting sources including Rashi to Exod 19:1 and *b. Ber.* 63b. Heschel makes explicit his dependence on the *Oheiv Yisrael*, written by his namesake and great-great-great-grandfather in *Heavenly Torah as Refracted Through the Generations*, edited and translated by Gordon Tucker (New York: Continuum, 2005), 672. On time, eternity, event, and process in the later Heschel's work, see further Shai Held, *Abraham Joshua Heschel: The Call of Transcendence* (Bloomington: Indiana University Press, 2013), 129-33. The opportunity to quote this last work shortly after n. 63, especially in a footnote prompted by the continuity of Heschel's younger and older, is what is known in late rabbinic Hebrew as a סְגוּלָה. So is the fact that my own son Avraham called me, while I was in the midst of writing this note, to tell me he was just accepted into the Talmud class taught by Gordon Tucker's son (and Shai Held's colleague), Ethan. Here we might quote Prov 10:11 four times over.

has observed no Jewish holiday at all.[74] Liberation from slavery without acceptance of the law would be no liberation; freedom without responsibility is freedom perverted. A poem that on the surface is about one event but whose allusions and parallelism prove it to be about another comes to present an argument: the crossing of the Reed Sea is not the culmination of the exodus but one part in the creation of a covenant between God and Israel.

COMPLAINT AND PRAISE IN LIGHT OF SEQUENCE AND CYCLE

Our discussion of the cyclical nature of lyric suggests we turn back to Psalm 27 to consider its sequence one more time. Can we rightly say that the poem moves definitively from faith to doubt (or from simple faith to mature faith) with the latter receiving the last word?[75] Poetry encourages us to go back even as we move forward, to re-read and reconsider; indeed, it is not too much of a stretch to say that poetry encourages us to repent. If this is so, then we need to be on guard against putting too much emphasis on the ordering of the stanzas in Psalm 27. Lyric, because of its parallelism, resists closure in a way that is not characteristic of prose. To be sure, as Barbara Herrnstein Smith notes in her classic treatment of poetic closure, "The manner in which a poem concludes becomes, in effect, the last and frequently the most significant thing it says."[76] But she goes on to note that "closural effects will be minimal when ... the last allusions are to beginnings or to unstable events, and when concluding assertions are qualified and tentative."[77] This sentence beautifully suits the last two lines of Psalm 27, with their incomplete sentence followed by a repeated call to the reader to wait expectantly. What the psalmist tells us—or himself?—to wait for, of course, is the confidence the very first line of the psalm proclaims. The poem's tentative ending alludes to its beginning, reminding us that just as faith can be at once threatened and enriched by doubt, doubt can lead to faith.[78] For everything there

---

74. Note that b. Pesaḥim 118a associates Psalm 114 for two reasons (vv. 1 and 3) with Passover but also (v. 4) with Shavuot.

75. I am indebted to Walter Moberly for encouraging me to think more carefully about this point.

76. Smith, Poetic, 196.

77. Smith, Poetic, 210.

78. Seen in this light, the cyclical structure of this psalm recalls Walter Brueggemann's thesis that the Psalter moves from the theme of obedience in Psalm 1, through the

is a season, and Psalm 27's is one that can turn us around, can turn God around, and can use a poem's last stanza to turn us back to its first.

7

"With Fists Flailing at the Gates of Heaven":[1] Wrestling with Psalm 88, A Psalm for Chronic Illness

Shai Held

Psalm 88 is undoubtedly one of the darkest of the psalms. One scholar labels it "the most desperate of all laments";[2] another writer asserts that it presents "a wintry landscape of unrelieved bleakness";[3] and a third insists that the text is "unrelieved by a single ray of comfort or hope."[4] Yet Psalm 88 is even bleaker and more desolate than most scholars seem to realize—or allow.[5]

In a recent essay David Howard, Jr. goes so far as to refer to Psalm 88 as "the mother of all laments"[6] and in terms of the bold and unapologetic voice it gives to human grief and suffering, it may well be. Yet (as Howard

---

1. I borrow this phrase from Kristin Swenson's interpretation of Psalm 88, in Kristen M. Swenson, *Living Through Pain: Psalms and the Search for Wholeness* (Waco: Baylor, 2005), 141.

2. David M. Howard Jr., "Psalm 88 and the Rhetoric of Lament," in *My Words Are Lovely: Studies in the Rhetoric of the Psalms*, eds. Robert L. Foster and David M. Howard Jr. (London: T&T Clark, 2008), 132-146, at p. 132.

3. Martin E. Marty, *A Cry of Absence: Reflections for the Winter of the Heart* (Grand Rapids: Eerdmans, 1997), 68.

4. Artur Weiser, *The Psalms: A Commentary* (London: SCM, 1962), 586.

5. For two notable exceptions see Carleen Mandolfo, "Psalm 88 and the Holocaust: Lament in Search of a Divine Response," *BibInt* 15 (2007): 151-70; and Beth Tanner, "Psalm 88," in *The Book of Psalms*, eds. Nancy deClaissé-Walford, Rolf A. Jacobson, and Beth Laneel Tanner (Grand Rapids: Eerdmans 2014), 668-73. I came across Tanner's commentary as I was completing my own study.

6. Howard, "Psalm 88 and the Rhetoric of Lament," 133.

himself acknowledges) Psalm 88 stands out as much (if not more) for how it differs from other psalms of lament as for how it typifies them. In order to get at the spirituality of the psalm, we need to take careful stock of these divergences from the standard form.

Recall Gunkel's enumeration of the common features of lament.[7] Among the most significant are an invocation; a complaint or character-ization of the psalmist's predicament; an appeal for help; appeals and curses against enemies (sometimes coupled with wishes for the faithful); motivations for divine intervention; expressions of trust; articulation of certainty of being heard; and a vow of future action. Now, a psalm need not contain all of these elements in order to be considered a lament, but it is nevertheless striking how many are missing from Psalm 88. The psalm begins with an invocation (v. 2) and continues with an appeal to be heard (v. 3).[8] Most of the rest of the psalm is the complaint, though one could argue that the rhetorical questions of verses 11–13 provide motivations for intervention. Psalm 88 contains no explicit appeal for help,[9] which Gunkel considered the most important element of the psalms of lament.[10] The psalm contains no expression of trust[11] and does not give voice to a certainty of being heard, nor does the psalmist take a vow to praise God when he is saved. Most crucially, the core arc of the lament, the movement from lament to praise, is entirely absent from the psalm. The psalm ends where it lives: in darkness.

---

7. The rest of this paragraph summarizes (and closely follows) Robert C. Culley, "Psalm 88 Among the Complaints," in *Ascribe to the Lord: Biblical and Other Studies in Memory of Peter C. Craigie*, eds. Lyle Eslinger and Glen Taylor (Sheffield: JSOT, 1988), 289–302, at pp. 292–93.

8. Yet as we'll see, one could suggest that the appeal to be heard in verse 3 is in fact a quotation of an earlier cry for help, mentioned in verse 2. It would thus not be a present-day appeal. So Erich Zenger, in Frank-Lothar Hossfeld and Erich Zenger, *Psalms 2: A Commentary on Psalms 51–100* (Minneapolis; Fortress, 2005), 394.

9. The distinction between appealing to be heard and appealing to be helped may (biblically speaking, at least) be artificial; I am honestly not sure. In any case, as we'll see, the psalm contains only one explicit petition and even this may in fact be a reference to a past petition rather than a present-day one.

10. Hermann Gunkel, *Einleitung in die Psalmen: Die Gattungen der religiösen Lyrik Israels* (Götttingen: Vandenhoeck & Ruprecht, 1985), 218.

11. Toni Craven asserts that "One of the remarkable things about a lament is that despite the fact that God is frequently held responsible for the distress, the psalmists usually express unqualified trust in God's good intention for them." The author of Psalm 88 evinces no such trust and the psalm thus represents a dramatic exception to the rule. Toni Craven, *The Book of Psalms* (Collegeville, MN: Liturgical Press, 1992), 27.

Consider, too, how much of what is conventionally said of psalms of lament does not apply to Psalm 88. Richard Clifford, for example, writes that laments could more aptly be referred to as petitions, "since [their] purpose is to persuade God to rescue the psalmist."[12] In psalm 88, however, petition is marginal, if it is present all.[13] If anything, the psalm is relentlessly focused on the ways that God has failed to respond to the psalmist's repeated petitions for deliverance. Clifford adds that "The lament offers oppressed and troubled individuals a means of unburdening themselves before God and receiving an assurance."[14] One who recites Psalm 88 may well unburden herself, yet she will find no assurance at all in the psalm. Clifford further avers that "The lament enables the worshiper to face threats bravely and learn to trust in God."[15] Yet, as we will see, it is far from clear that Psalm 88 evinces much by way of trust. On the contrary, the worshiper who engaged with this psalm may well hear only that the psalmist's trust in God has yielded nothing but vexation and frustration.

Emphasizing the importance of the *waw* adversative in psalms of lament, Claus Westermann notes that it serves to introduce a turning point where lamentation gives way to confession of trust or assurance of being heard. "The 'but,' " Westermann writes, "designates the transition from petition to praise."[16] Yet in Psalm 88 the *waw* does quite the opposite: it leads into one final outpouring of lament, this one "all the more insistent on YHWH's rejection of the psalmist in spite of his constant pleading"[17]: "But as for me, I cry out to you ... Why, O Lord, do you spurn me?" (vv. 14–15). Westermann maintains that "In the Psalms of the O.T. there is no, or almost no, such thing as 'mere' lament and petition. ... The cry to God is always underway from supplication to praise."[18] But as

---

12. Richard J. Clifford, *Psalms 1–72* (Nashville: Abingdon, 2002), 21.

13. It may be present in verse 3 and is arguably implicit in the rhetorical questions of verses 11–13.

14. Clifford, *Psalms 1–72*, 21. In this context note also Bernhatd Anderson's suggestion that "The laments are really expressions of praise, offered in a minor key in the confidence that YHWH is faithful and in anticipation of a new lease on life." Bernhard W. Anderson with Steven Bishop, *Out of the Depths: The Psalms Speak for us Today*, 3rd ed. (Louisville: Westminster John Knox, 2000), 60. Needless to say, Anderson's claim has no purchase whatsoever on Psalm 88 (which, to his credit, he recognizes).

15. Clifford, *Psalms 1–72*, 22.

16. Claus Westermann, *Praise and Lament in the Psalms* (Atlanta: John Knox, 1981), 72–73.

17. A. Chadwick Thornhill, "A Theology of Psalm 88," *EvQ* 87 (2015): 45–57, at p. 46.

18. Westermann, *Praise and Lament*, 75.

its subversive use of the *waw* adversative shows, Psalm 88 constitutes a dramatic (and deliberate!) exception to Westermann's rule.[19]

Psalm 88 thus essentially strips away the glimmers of hope we conventionally find in the psalms of lament. Just how deep is the rupture between the psalmist and God? An array of scholars finds in verse 2a's אֱלֹהֵי יְשׁוּעָתִי, "God of my salvation," a hint of hope and even praise. Thus Marvin Tate, for example, writes that "Praise seems far away from Psalm 88, but in reality it is not; it even glimmers in the opening affirmation: 'YHWH, the God of my salvation.' "[20] Others suggest emending the text so that it reads אלהי שועתי, "My God, I cried out."[21] The emendation helps establish parallelism in an otherwise difficult verse,[22] but to the best of my knowledge there are no manuscript variants to support it. Moreover, if one thinks that אלהי ישועתי introduces a glimmer of hope into a very dark psalm, emending the text eliminates that sole glimmer and "the only redeeming expectation present in the psalm is turned into yet another plea to God."[23]

I would suggest we consider a third alternative, namely that the psalmist does indeed refer to YHWH as "God of my salvation," but that he does so at least somewhat ironically.[24] After all, the God to whom he calls has been anything but a God of deliverance to him. If the notion

---

19. See, for example, Thornhill, "Theology of Psalm 88," 46–47. And see also John Goldingay, *Psalms, Volume 2: Psalms 42–89* (Grand Rapids: Baker Academic, 2007), 644.

20. Marvin Tate, "Psalm 88," *RevExp* 87 (1990): 91–95, at p. 91. See also Leonard Maré, "Facing the Deepest Darkness of Despair and Abandonment: Psalm 88 and the Life of Faith," *OTE* 27 (2014): 177–188, at p. 181.

21. In (admittedly weak) defense of the emendation, one should note that the phrase אלהי ישועתי appears nowhere else in the Hebrew Bible, though ישועה does appear with other names for God. See, e.g., "El" in Isa 12:2 and Ps 68:20; and "Tzur" in Deut 32:15 and Ps 89:27. See Pyles, "The Depths of Darkness," 16, n. 11.

22. Thus yielding something like: "Lord, my God, by day I call for help, by night I cry out in Your presence."

23. Thornhill, "Theology of Psalm 88," 51. Erich Zenger, among others, argues for maintaining the MT since "with its salvation perspective, [it] establishes the 'positive' contrast with the dominant negative statements, which is indispensable to the psalm." Hossfeld and Zenger, *Psalms 2*, 390.

24. As I completed work on this essay, I was delighted to discover that Beth Tanner's commentary had anticipated my own: "This is the first and last line of the psalm that is not one of anguish. Indeed, by the end of the psalm, this one line will scarcely be remembered for all the pain that pours out. In fact, by the end of the psalm, one may wonder if this epithet is an expression of great faith or great irony." Nancy deClaissé-Walford, Rolf A. Jacobson, and Beth Laneel Tanner, *The Book of Psalms* (Grand Rapids: Eerdmans 2014), 671.

that the psalmist is speaking ironically seems far-fetched, consider what follows: 1) the declaration in verse 4, שָׂבְעָה בְרָעוֹת נַפְשִׁי, "I am sated with misfortunes," is clearly ironic, since it is usually some form of goodness or blessing that "sates" the psalmist (see, e.g., Ps 63:6: "I am sated as with a rich feast"; and Ps 65:5: "May we be sated with the blessings of Your house").[25] To announce oneself sated with sorrows is obviously to speak in a highly ironic way. 2) the opening of verse 6, בַּמֵּתִים חָפְשִׁי, is extremely elusive. But some have suggested that the psalmist says this ironically, since he is "free" only "from everything that makes life meaningful and enjoyable; free to be as good as dead."[26] 3) The use of the word סָמְכָה in the accusation of verse 8, עָלַי סָמְכָה חֲמָתֶךָ, "Your fury lies heavy upon me," is jarring, since the root ס-מ-כ often calls to mind God's faithful and steadfast support. These three examples suggest that the psalmist is no stranger to irony,[27] and that he is unafraid to employ it in direct address of God. Whether God is really the God of "my salvation" is one of the questions that most agonizes him.

As these examples of irony indicate, the psalmist is unabashed in calling God to account. In a subtle way the psalmist says so explicitly. Reminding God that he has been praying constantly, incessantly,[28] the

---

25. For other negative uses of "sated," see Job 9:18 and 10:15; and Lam 3:15.

26. Davidson, *Vitality of Worship*, 290. This is cited virtually word for word, though without attribution, in Leonard Maré, "Facing the Deepest Darkness of Despair and Abandonment: Psalm 88 and the Life of Faith," *OTE* 27:1 (2014): 177–188, at p. 183. Somewhat more soberly, Tate writes that חָפְשִׁי in the psalm means "set free," that is, "relieved of the normal obligations of life, because family and community already judge the speaker to be dead and thus 'free' of the responsibilities of the living." Tate, "Psalm 88," 91. In the same vein, see also Anthony R. Pyles, "Drowning in the Depths of Darkness: A Consideration of Psalm 88 with a New Translation," *Canadian Theological Review* 1 (2012): 13–28, at p. 17. Also worth noting in this context is John Goldingay's astute comparison of "free" here to the expression "let go" used in business contexts to describe someone who wants to keep on working but is no longer wanted. Goldingay, *Psalms, Volume 2*, 649. Second Kgs 15:5, where בֵּית הַחָפְשִׁית is used to refer to a place where lepers are quarantined, is likely also relevant here. Noting that the term חָפְשִׁי "usually denotes a free slave" (see Exod 21:5), Willem VanGemeren characterizes it as a "paradoxical expression, as though death brings freedom." Willem A. VanGemeren, *Psalms*, Expositor's Bible Commentary 5 (Grand Rapids: Zondervan, 2008), 659.

27. The phrase הָיִיתִי כְּגֶבֶר אֵין-אֱיָל "I am a man without strength," can also be taken ironically. The term גֶּבֶר suggests strength and vigor; the psalmist is thus a man of strength and vigor devoid of ... strength and vigor. On this, see Goldingay, *Psalms, Volume 2*, 648.

28. Clinton McCann astutely observes that the psalmist's use of three different words for crying out (צעק, קרא, שוע) serves to indicate that he "has exhausted every approach

psalmist declares בַּבֹּקֶר תְּפִלָּתִי תְקַדְּמֶךָּ, which NJPS renders as "Each morn-ing, my prayer greets you" (v. 14). The Hebrew תְקַדְּמֶךָּ can indeed be taken neutrally, but it can also suggest hostility and confrontation,[29] as in Psalm 17:13: קוּמָה יְהוָה קַדְּמָה פָנָיו, "Rise up, O Lord, confront them!" I wonder whether that meaning is at least hinted at here as well: the psalmist has not uttered gentle hymns each day but has accosted God and pleaded his case with passion (and, perhaps, with no small degree of fury too). In a similar vein, Tate points out that the reference to morning contains a note of bitterness, since morning was considered the time to expect God's help, help that in the psalmist's case never did come.[30]

The strife between the psalmist and God is brought to the surface by another anomalous feature of the text. In psalms of lament we typi-cally expect to encounter three parties: the psalmist, the enemies who persecute him, and the God he prays will save him. But Psalm 88 lacks any mention at all of human enemies, and one wonders whether that is because God has been cast in the role of the enemy instead. After all, it is God who is declared responsible—again and again and again—for the psalmist's woes.[31]

Why is the breach between the psalmist and God so profound? Psalms of lament depend on a longstanding relationship with God; part of what animates them is the fact that the psalmists have a past with God to draw on. Although the psalmists find themselves mired in affliction, as a rule they are confident—and they know from experience—that the God to whom they appeal is faithful and steadfast. As the psalmist's situation was once, so it can be again.

With this in mind, I would argue that the key word of the psalm has been overlooked (or at least underappreciated) by most commentators. Towards the end of the psalm, we learn something crucial about the

---

to God"—to no avail. J. Clinton McCann, "Psalms," *NIB* 4 (Nashville: Abingdon, 1996), 1027.

29. For this possibility, see Marvin E. Tate, *Psalms 51–100*, WBC 20 (Dallas: Word Books, 1990), 398; and Beth Tanner, in deClaissé-Walford, et al., *The Book of Psalms*, 671.

30. Tate, *Psalms 50–100*, 403; see Ps 46:6; 90:14; 143:8; and Zeph 3:5.

31. For an interpretation along these lines, see, for example, Richard J. Clifford, *Psalms 73–150* (Nashville: Abingdon, 2003), 86. There appears to be some tension between the psalmist's charge that God has actively assaulted and abused him, on the one hand, and his notion that God has turned God's face away from him, on the other. In any case, the former image is dominant here. For another example of a lamenter who moves between accusing God of inexcusable passivity, on the one hand, and active cruelty, on the other, see Psalm 44 (compare vv. 11–15 with vv. 24–25).

psalmist's life, something that forces us to see his misery in a radically new light. The psalmist's present predicament is no anomaly for him; he is not wrestling with a new, unforeseen torment after a lifetime of wellbeing and contentment. On the contrary, he has been גֹוֵעַ מִנֹּעַר, "dying since youth," that is, he has been forced to endure lifelong, crushing chronic illness.[32] It is one thing to struggle with acute illness after a lifetime of health; it is quite another to grapple with a debilitating illness of longstanding. In theological terms, the psalmist's problem is not that God seems to have suddenly abandoned him after long years of protecting him but rather that God forsook him long and that his life has been defined by that forsakenness.

Imagine a strong, loving, durable marriage that suddenly encounters difficult times and then compare it to a lengthy marriage that has been fractured for decades. It is obviously far more difficult to find a basis for hope in the second scenario than in the first. The psalmist's relationship with God is more akin to an irreparably broken marriage than to a fundamentally solid one that has suddenly reached an impasse. It would be difficult to overstate the importance of this distinction. The psalmist in Psalm 88 has no personal past to which he can turn for hope and assurance. Even if we take his invocation of God as "the God of my salvation" at face value, the psalm unfolds in a way that mimics the way his life has unfolded: by the time we have encountered the endless litany of suffering and woe, the "God of my salvation" is little more than a distant and faded memory.[33] For all intents and purposes, the only God this psalmist knows is a God of inexplicable wrath and abandonment.

---

32. Although it seems extremely likely to me that Psalm 88 is about (chronic) illness, I do think it is possible to take the illness as metaphorical and to interpret the psalm as referring to some other form of (relentless, enduring) suffering. Note similarly Tate, who thinks the psalmist is ill but admits that "There appears to be no language in Psalm 88 which necessitates a direct reference to illness." Tate, *Psalms 51–100*, 400. Tate is correct, unless we take מַחֲלָה in verse 1 to be a reference to illness (which Tate does not). See also McCann, "Psalms," 1027, who notes that although the psalm seems at core to be about terminal illness. The language is metaphorical and stereotypical enough to express other life-threatening situations" as is evident from the fact that many traditional interpreters, both Jewish and Christian, understood the psalm to be giving voice to the suffering of an exiled people. See, for example, the commentaries of Rashi and Rabbi David Kimhi to the psalm.
33. For a similar reading, see Beth Tanner, "Psalm 88," in deClaissé-Walford, et al, *The Book of Psalms*, 671.

ing only near the conclusion of the psalm is jarring, even devastating. Perhaps we had held out hope for him—and by extension for ourselves; perhaps we were put off by the unrelenting nature of his complaint— surely life is not *all* bleakness and heartache; and then it hits us: life has been this way for as long as the psalmist can remember. His lament reflects the reality of his life: the misery and the suffering just go on and on. At the end of the tunnel there is ... only more darkness.

It is worth noting how at the opening of each of the three sections of the psalm (verses 2–10a, 10b–13, 14–19), the divine name moves backward one place in the sequence of words. Thus, verse 2 begins with יְהוָה אֱלֹהֵי יְשׁוּעָתִי (first place); verse 10b with קְרָאתִיךָ יְהוָה (second place); and verse 14 with וַאֲנִי אֵלֶיךָ יְהוָה שִׁוַּעְתִּי (third place). As Erich Zenger insightfully explains, "The invocation presented in all three sections with the Tetragrammaton underscores the intensifying drama. ... The hiding of God's face that is complained of in verse 15 is literally put into words."[34] The more the psalmist prays, the further away God seems to be. Subtly but palpably, God's abandonment of the psalmist is rendered concrete.

Strikingly, as the psalm progresses the psalmist effectively ceases to petition God. In what appears to be the psalm's one and only explicit petition, in verse 3 the psalmist implores God: תָּבוֹא לְפָנֶיךָ, תְּפִלָּתִי הַטֵּה אָזְנְךָ לְרִנָּתִי, which NJPS renders as "Let my prayer reach You, incline Your ear to my cry."[35] It's worth noting that verse 3 could be interpreted as a memory of past cries for help, mentioned in verse 2, rather than a present-day prayer, in which case the psalm would be completely devoid of petition.[36] But by the time we get to verse 10, קְרָאתִיךָ יְהוָה בְּכָל-יוֹם, "I call to You, O Lord, each day," more than petitioning, the psalmist is complaining about God's stubborn inaction in the face of his own constant outpouring. The same applies to verse 14, וַאֲנִי, אֵלֶיךָ יְהוָה שִׁוַּעְתִּי, "But as for me, I cry out to You, O Lord." The psalmist is praying but he is not really petitioning so much as remembering—and reminding God—just how fruitless his long history of petition has been.

When the psalmist unleashes a torrent of rhetorical questions—"Do You work wonders for the dead? Do the shades rise to praise you? ..."

---

34. Hossfeld and Zenger, *Psalms 2*, 393.
35. NIV and NRSV are similar. As Howard reminds us, הַטֵּה is the only imperative verb form in the entire psalm. Howard, "Psalm 88 and the Rhetoric of Lament," 42, n. 26.
36. See Erich Zenger in Hossfeld and Zenger, *Psalms 2*, 394.

(vv. 11–13)—there is an element of petition to his words.[37] The psalmist reminds God of the desperate urgency of his plight; if God wants his praise, God ought to understand that they are both running out of time. Yet to the extent that we interpret the psalmist's questions as petitions, we should note that they are only implicit, indirect ones. It's as if the psalmist has been so hurt and so disappointed that he can't quite bring himself to petition God directly. The psalmist still needs help, so he gestures at pleading for salvation; but he's also exhausted and crushed, so much the most he can do is remind God of petitions past and hurl questions at God that (arguably) intimate a present-day request. As Artur Weiser astutely observes, the psalmist "cannot even nerve himself to make any more direct requests for God's help."[38] As for Job, so for the psalmist speaking does not help, but silence does not seem like a live option either: "If I speak, my pain is not assuaged; and if I forbear, how much of it leaves me?" (Job 16:6).

In a number of psalms of lament, the pain of being distant from God comes coupled with the agony of social isolation. The author of Psalm 42–43, for example, complains of being far from God and God's temple but also misses the "festive throng" with whom he once walked in pilgrimage to Jerusalem (42:5); for him the sound of "joyous shouts of praise" has been replaced by the very different sound of "breakers and billows" sweeping over him (42:5, 8). For the psalmists, to be separated from God is to be separated also from God's people.

Psalm 88 picks up on this theme and forcefully amplifies it. Not only has God unleashed God's fury on the psalmist, but God has turned his friends—those who might have comforted him in his affliction—away from him, making him "repulsive" in their eyes (88:9). Those of us stricken with chronic illness know this frustration well: just when we need our friends most, they move on, forgetting the depth of our suffering, or perhaps, being frightened off by it (it does not seem much of a stretch to connect "repulsion" at illness with fear of it). More than that,

---

37. Pyles declares that "The questions ... are themselves a kind of plea" (Pyles, "Drowning in the Depths of Darkness" 19). Culley writes more colorfully that "Darkening the picture can be a form of persuasion." Culley, "Psalm 88 Among the Complaints," 291.

38. Weiser, *The Psalms*, 586.

the psalmist is shut in, feeling "imprisoned" by his body and abandoned by his companions. He is desolated by isolation.[39]

Where does the psalm leave us? The concluding verse remains something of a crux; it is difficult to know how to punctuate, let alone translate, it: הִרְחַקְתָּ מִמֶּנִּי אֹהֵב וָרֵעַ מְיֻדָּעַי מַחְשָׁךְ. The two final words might mean "my companions are in darkness" (NRSV) or "darkness is my closest friend" (NIV). Although I cannot make a compelling grammatical argument for it, I am drawn to the suggestion that we take the Hebrew to be interrupted after מְיֻדָּעַי, thus yielding: "You have caused lover and friend to shun me, my companions (you have caused to shun me)—darkness!"[40] However we render the final phrase, the key point is that "Like it or not, forsakenness has the last word in Psalm 88."[41]

What are we to make of this agonized prayer? Many writers insist that despite its grave doubt and burning anger, Psalm 88 is a document of great, even heroic faith. Kathleen Harmon, for example, writes that "While Psalm 88 may appear to indicate loss of faith ... it actually does quite the opposite. The very act of speaking to God when God does not respond is an expression of profound faith. The person who no longer believes would simply walk away."[42] This is true as far as it goes, but it raises a question rarely if ever asked by scholars: just what does the psalmist's "faith" consist of? Faith is, obviously, a word that means many things to many people, and I wonder how helpful it is to use it without really attempting to flesh out what we mean by it. To be more concrete: the psalmist may still have something we would call "faith" in God, but does he still trust in God? Does he see God as reliable and faithful?[43] Can there be genuine faith without trust? The answer may well be yes, but it

---

39. Perhaps worth mentioning in this context is Carole Fontaine's observation that "Those who suffer find their whole world bounded by experience of their pain. In a very real sense, every sufferer suffers alone and neither talk nor silence blurs that one reality." Carole R. Fontaine, "'Arrows of the Almighty' (Job 6:4): Perspectives on Pain," *AthR* 66 (1984): 243–48, at p. 244.

40. Tate, "Psalm 88," 93.

41. Mandolfo, "Psalm 88 and the Holocaust," 156.

42. Kathleen Harmon, "Growing in Our Understanding of the Psalms, Part 2: Persisting in Prayer when God is Silent," *Liturgical Ministry* 20 (2011): 52–54, at p. 53.

43. Commenting on this psalm, Zenger writes that "When and where God can no longer be praised, his divinity is in question." Zenger, in Hossfeld and Zenger, *Psalms* 2, 396. This seems overstated to me. God's *divinity* is not in question for the psalmist, but God's *goodness* most certainly is.

seems odd not even to consider the question. More fundamentally, at this late date does he still harbor hope that God will intervene to save him?[44]

Attempting to give some substance to the psalmist's faith, Leonard Maré writes that "He still speaks to God, he affirms his relationship (God of my salvation), he believes praise is the norm and wishes to return to it, he acknowledges YHWH's attributes (faithful love, faithfulness, righteousness, wonderful works)."[45] Yet Maré's suggestion requires significant nuancing. It is certainly true that the psalmist still addresses God and that he wishes that he could return to a life dedicated to praising God. But as we've seen, it is not clear that the psalmist unequivocally "affirms" his relationship with God (irony is in part an expression of equivocation); he may dream of being restored to a life of praise, but it seems unlikely that he trusts that this dream will be fulfilled; and he does mention God's attributes, but only as a distant memory, and in the context of anticipating soon being fully and finally cut off from them.[46] We will need to work harder to try and understand just what we mean when we speak of the psalmist's enduring "faith."[47]

Given the intensity and duration of the psalmist's suffering, given how many desperate prayers have gone unanswered; it is a wonder that he goes on praying at all.[48] Robert Culley wonders why the psalmist would "offer such a prayer if there is no hope for an answer or if there is no hope of persuading YHWH to rescue?"[49] Whether the psalmist is totally devoid

44. In the same vein Mandolfo writes: "There is no doubt that the supplicant in Psalm 88 contends and questions, but is there any evidence that she continues to trust or believe? And in what sense 'believe'? There is no indication that the supplicant trusts that God will rectify the situation, but she prays nevertheless." Mandolfo, "Psalm 88 and the Holocaust," 164–65.
45. Maré, "Facing the Deepest Darkness," 187.
46. More astutely, Zenger observes that the psalmist "evokes the image of the God who is proclaimed is Israel's great traditions—which God now makes simply absurd for the petitioner." Hossfeld and Zenger, Psalms 2, 395.
47. Additionally, we must resist the temptation to soften the edges of the psalmist's despair and thus to paper over the depth of his theological crisis. VanGemeren falls into this trap when he declares that "Though the psalm ends in a lament, faith triumphs, because in everything the psalmist has learned to look to the 'God who saves.'" Such an interpretation flattens the text and refuses to confront its irresolution. VanGemeren, "Psalms," 662.
48. See, e.g., A.A. Anderson, The Book of Psalms (London: Oliphants, 1972), 623; and Karl-Johan Illman, "Psalm 88—A Lamentation without Answer," SJOT 1 (1991): 112–20, at p. 120.
49. Culley, "Psalm 88 Among the Complaints," 291.

of hope or only mostly so I cannot answer,[50] but in any event I think the answer to Culley's question lies elsewhere. Despite his anger and disappointment, the psalmist refuses to sever his connection with God. Or perhaps, as he himself sees the situation, he refuses to allow God to sever God's connection to him. God may hide God's face, but the psalmist will go right on talking because otherwise he will be utterly alone. In a sense, the psalmist's ceaseless talking to God keeps God "present" even as the psalmist complains of God's absence.

There is, of course, a theological dimension of all this. Walter Brueggemann movingly maintains that the psalmist prays because praying to YHWH is simply what Israel does: "To be Israel is to address God, even in God's unresponsive absence."[51] Israel may feel abandoned, betrayed, abused but Israel will not be silence(d). As Brueggemann writes, "The faith of Israel is like that. The failure of God to respond ... leads to more intense address. This psalm, like the faith of Israel, is utterly contained in the notion that ... YHWH must be addressed, even if YHWH never answers."[52]

But there is also an existential dimension to all this that we must not overlook. The psalmist has endured unspeakable suffering. As if the sheer reality of enervating illness has not been enough, he has been forced to confront persistent feelings of abandonment—both the God to whom he turned for salvation and the friends to whom he looked for solace have effectively left him for dead. But he is not dead, and he needs to be heard. To give voice to his suffering—physical, emotional, and spiritual—is to reclaim his own dignity.

---

50. It is worth contrasting the words of Mandolfo—"The supplicant of Psalm 88 is making an appeal, but is not for the removal of suffering, so far as I can see ... she shows no sign of having any more hope of that happening[;] it is an appeal for explanation"—with those of Goldingay: "The one thing ['why?' questions] are not doing is asking for information, and if YHWH had an answer that could 'solve' the 'problem of suffering,' this would not mean that the suppliant could put away his or her pen and go home. The 'Why?' is more a challenge to action than in inquiry." See Mandolfo, "Psalm 88 and the Holocaust," 165; and Goldingay, Psalms, Vol. 2, 656. I'd be tempted to split the difference between these two approaches: the psalmist would obviously love for God to deliver him but by this point his hope has run thin (or perhaps run out), so barring salvation, he'd at least like an accounting of God's appalling behavior. Of course, he may well be convinced that no coherent or defensible accounting is possible and so his question is actually more an accusation than a query.
51. Walter Brueggemann, The Message of the Psalms: A Theological Commentary (Minneapolis: Augsburg, 1984), 81.
52. Brueggemann, The Message of the Psalms, 79.

AN (AMBIVALENT) THEOLOGICAL POSTSCRIPT

The author of Psalm 88 assumes that a very active providential hand is at work in his life; as Carleen Mandolfo puts it, "The supplicant of Psalm 88 never questions God's active omnipotence in the affairs of the world."[53] God (alone) is the source of his woe and God (alone) can be the source of his deliverance.

For many modern readers (and, frankly, for me too), all this no doubt raises an array of difficult questions: What kind of God do we need to believe in, and what notion, if any, of divine providence do we need to have, in order to utter these psalms with integrity? If we don't believe that God actively runs the world, or even if we don't believe that God runs the world in quite so micromanaging a way, can the psalms of lament still have a place in our religious lives?

The psalmists cry out to God because they believe that God can relieve their suffering; they don't just want to be heard, they want to be *answered*—and saved. The primary purpose of lament in biblical times was not catharsis but salvation. This leads some Bible scholars to assert that "Prayers of sorrow and complaint that expect no concrete answer have no point of contact with biblical lament."[54]

I am not so sure that they are right. In lament, regardless of response, "suffering is given the dignity of language."[55] Suffering can render us passive, voiceless, mute. As Rabbi Joseph Soloveitchik (1903-1993) teaches, there is something inherently redemptive about finding words for our pain. "A mute life is identical with bondage," he writes, "a speech-endowed life is a free life."[56] Even before they are saved by God—or even, for that matter, in situations when they are not saved at all—the psalmists accomplish something transformative simply by giving voice to their afflictions.

What I am describing here may in part be a psychological process, but it is primarily a relational one. It is not just that the psalmists speak; it is that they speak *to someone*—and not just to anyone, but to the One who

---

53. Mandolfo, "Psalm 88 and the Holocaust," 166.
54. Scott A. Ellington, *Risking Truth: Reshaping the World through Prayers of Lament* (Eugene: Pickwick, 2008), 29.
55. Claus Westermann, "The Role of the Lament in the Theology of the Old Testament," *Interpretation* 28 (1974): 20-38, at p. 31.
56. Joseph B. Soloveitchik, "Redemption, Prayer, Talmud Torah," *Tradition* 17 (1978): 55-72, at p. 56.

created them, loves them, affirms their dignity, and hears their cries.[57] In our own time many of us are more confident of God's solidarity than we are of God's salvation (though, looking around at the world each day, I cannot but have severe doubts about both). That may indeed represent a vast gap, or even a chasm, between us and our biblical forebears. Yet they have bequeathed us something precious and potentially transformational: the insistence that we need not lie about our suffering, the awareness that honesty is never a sacrilege, the courage to cry out, and the confidence that injustice is to be resisted rather than accepted.

Soloveitchik speaks of the redemptive power of *petition*—to give voice to our needs is to some degree to redeem ourselves. What I am suggesting, somewhat tentatively, is that a similar logic may apply to lament. In full-throatedly declaring that our suffering is too great to bear, and in unabashedly insisting that we do not deserve the anguish that we endure, we participate in our own redemption. Again, this has a psychological and existential dimension, but it has a powerful relational and theological dimension too. If suffering can make us feel passive and victimized, lament can restore our sense of dignity and agency. In mustering the audacity to speak to God in this way, the psalmist—and we who recite his words—declare, against all evidence to the contrary, that we matter, both to ourselves and to God.

It takes remarkable courage to remind God that when we die, we will no longer be able to sing God's praises (vv. 11-13). In these words we implicitly declare that we matter to God; that when we die, God will lose praise—but not just *any* praise, *our* praise. As Kristen Swenson writes, "Of all the other people in the world, or even simply within the psalmist's community, the psalmist assumes that God would lose out by allowing her, in all of her particularity, to die at this time."[58] If we die, we intimate, God will miss us.

Yet all of this notwithstanding, for many of us, to pray the laments is to make theological statements we do not mean. Responding to a recent query from me about what he makes of the psalms of lament, a prominent Christian theologian responded: "Lament gives us a true expression of the angst of the sufferer and a false view of God." But can one embrace liturgically what she rejects theologically? I am honestly not sure.

---

57. Coming at this from another angle, laments bind us to God even as we express disappointment with God; protesting God's absence paradoxically makes God present.
58. Swenson, *Living Through Pain*, 144.

8

Truth and Hidden Things: Reading Isaiah 45:9–25 as Scripture

Katie M. Heffelfinger

"The truth," quipped Oscar Wilde, "is rarely pure and never simple."[1] With characteristic irony, this simple statement appears to convey a certain amount of truth. However, there are voices who would call for religious faith to offer clear guidance to believers, and to proclaim the truth clearly and simply.[2] Words such as the NRSV's "I the LORD speak the truth, I declare what is right" (Isaiah 45:19) appear to lay claim to the nature of truth, and of divine speech. But this passage presents divine speech poetically, a form that conveys truth in a way that problematizes our affection for simplicity.[3] Biblical poetry invokes and glories in complexity. It renders truth rich and full by embracing the ambiguity inherent in human experience, by intensifying our encounter with the emotional element of our grasping truth, and by holding competing truths in juxtaposed and realistic tension. In short, biblical poetry offers to our contemporary faith

---

1. Oscar Wilde, *The Original Four-Act Version of the Importance of Being Earnest: A Trivial Comedy for Serious People* (London: Methuen, 1957), 9.
2. See Mark Oakley, *The Splash of Words: Believing in Poetry* (Norwich: Canterbury Press, 2016), xviii, for a description of such voices in the contemporary context.
3. For a description of current Western culture that resonates with this idea, see Iain McGilchrist, *The Master and His Emmisary: The Divided Brain and the Making of the Western World*, expanded ed. (London: Yale University Press, 2019), especially xxv.

contexts an urgently needed counterbalance to our tendency to valorize that which is simple, clear, direct, and paraphrasable by insisting that relationship with God invites us into a realm in which mystery, paradox, emotion, and imagination are profoundly relevant.[4]

What I am suggesting is that biblical Hebrew poetry can contribute significantly to faith communities in our current cultural context. I am not arguing that such encounters should be primarily explanatory or informational. Rather, engagement with biblical Hebrew poems should start from the attitudes and postures they invite through their own particular form. Individual poems will demand distinctive postures, but I would like to propose some attitudes that are both generally appropriate to biblical Hebrew poetry, and particularly appropriate to the text I intend to examine more closely. The cultivation of these postures, I suggest, are primary ways these texts exert influence on those who read them as Scripture.[5]

IMAGINATION VS. INSTRUCTION

First, we should approach poetry imaginatively. We arguably live in a culture that is experiencing the effects of imaginative impoverishment. This loss, already being heavily critiqued across a broad range of fields of study, has a negative impact on our capacities as readers of poetry, as ethical decision makers, and as people of faith.[6] In many ways, openness

---

4. I can only speak out of contexts that I know, and name my religious location as Protestant Christianity. It may well be the case that traditions not shaped by the same influences do not experience these impulses, or do not experience them to the same extent. However, it does seem to be the case, as pointed out by Malcom Guite, *Faith, Hope and Poetry: Theology and the Poetic Imagination* (London: Routledge, 2012), 2, that the post-Enlightenment context has some broader relevance to our attitudes to poetry in this regard. On post Renaissance Western culture and its relationship to these ideas, see further McGilchrist, *The Master and His Emissary*, 6.

5. See Oakley, *Splash of Words*, xv, on poetry generally: "ultimately poetry is not about factual information but human formation."

6. See Guite, *Faith, Hope and Poetry*, 1. On the role of imagination in human moral development see Martha C. Nussbaum, *Upheavals of Thought: The Intelligence of Emotions* (Cambridge: Cambridge University Press, 2001), especially 236–37. On "knowledge as formative process," see Arianna Borrelli and Alexandra Grieser, "Recent research of the aesthetics of knowledge in science and religion" in *Approaching Religion* 7 (2017): 8. On "attention" and "value," see McGilchrist, *The Master and His Emissary*, 28–29. On the negative impact of avoidance of imagination in theology, see O'Donoghue and Kelly in John O'Donoghue, Anne F. Kelly and Werner G. Jeanrond, "The Agenda for Theology in Ireland Today," *The Furrow* 42 (1991): 692–710.

to poetry's own way of being is one potential "redress" of this imbalance.[7] By conveying its meaning through images and by resisting didactic simplification, poetry enacts imaginative expansion.[8] Practicing a posture of imaginative openness invites biblical poetry to address us as Scripture.[9] In turn, biblical poetry forms us by enlarging our imaginative capacity across repeated encounters.[10] This attitude requires allowing ourselves to enter the "world" of the text.[11] It means listening with an openness to its images and metaphors as ways of making meaning. It means resisting the urge to translate our encounters with poetic texts into sources of didactic instruction.[12]

Embodiment and Emotional Encounter

Second, our approach to poetry should embrace a posture of patient expectancy. Much biblical poetry addresses the hearer directly, without the intervening frame of a narrative or discursive structure.[13] This feature produces immediacy and places the hearer into an encounter with the poetic speaker, which inevitably carries an emotional charge. Attentive openness to the poem's voice and its emotional world are crucial to interpreting and receiving the text on its own terms. Poetry demands attention to its own particular concrete expression.[14] Poems offer an encounter

---

7. The term "redress" is drawn from Seamus Heaney, *The Redress of Poetry* (London: Faber & Faber, 1995), esp. 4.

8. Jonathan Culler, *Theory of the Lyric* (London: Harvard University Press, 2015), 305, notes the capacity of lyric language for "enlarging imaginative resources."

9. See Ellen F. Davis, "Teaching the Bible Confessionally in the Church," in *The Art of Reading Scripture*, eds. Ellen F. Davis and Richard B. Hays (Grand Rapids: Eerdmans, 2003), 11, who articulates "The teacher's task" as involving the development of "imaginative skills for wondering fruitfully."

10. See e.g., Culler, *Theory*, 305, on the way lyric poetry works by embedding itself in memory.

11. See Paul Ricoeur, *The Rule of Metaphor: Multi-disciplinary Studies of the Creation of Meaning in Language* trans. Robert Czerny (London: University of Toronto Press, 1977), 220.

12. See, e.g., O'Donoghue, "The Agenda for Theology in Ireland Today I," 693, who describes the theology he diagnoses as suffering from "denial of imagination" as "wearingly didactic."

13. On the non-narrative and non-discursive tendencies of much biblical poetry, see F.W. Dobbs-Allsopp, *On Biblical Poetry* (Oxford: Oxford University Press, 2015), 185, concerning modes of address see ibid., 197, and on the relevance of this approach heuristically to much prophetic poetry, see ibid, 228.

14. For Christian readers of these texts, close attention to the speaking other of the text before us and embrace of that voice's complex concreteness aligns better

which cannot be abstracted into propositions without significant, if not overwhelming, loss.[15] Poetry's strangeness[16] works to draw us out of our human tendency toward self-orientation.[17] When we attempt to bend poetry to our expectation of what it should be, we resist its own concrete speaking and its ability to form us into slower, more attentive listeners, capacities which expand our openness to both the complex human other and to the real and living God.[18] Our posture toward biblical poetry, then, is one of surrender of our control over it, and of waiting. As Mary Kinzie remarks, "It may well put us closer to the truth of art to wait rather than interpret."[19] Again, the posture poetry demands has formational potential. Biblical poetry acts as Scripture, at least in part, by shaping habits of attentive openness to the otherness of God.

TENSION AND POETIC TRUTH

Third, poetry invokes a posture of vulnerable uncertainty. Poetry has the ability to chasten our over-familiarity and our desire for simple certainty.[20] Poetry exploits the tensions in language. As Jane Hirschfield

---

(however uncomfortably) than abstract generality with Christianity's insistence upon the concrete, embodied, particular expression of God in the Incarnation of Jesus Christ. See e.g., Guite, *Faith, Hope and Poetry*, 11; and Larry E. Axel, "Reshaping the Task of Theology," *American Journal of Theology & Philosophy* 8 (1987): 60.

15. On "event," see Jane Hirshfield, "Poetry and the Constellation of Surprise," in *Hiddenness, Uncertainty, Surprise: Three Generative Energies of Poetry* (Newcastle: Bloodaxe, 2008), 46; and Mark S. Burrows, "The Energy of Poetry in a Culture of Saturation," *ARTS* 24 (2013): 20. On the reductive nature of the move from concrete to abstract, see Axel, "Reshaping the Task of Theology," 59-60.

16. See Sarah Zhang, "How is a Love Poem (Song 4:1-7) Like the Beloved?" in *Biblical Poetry and the Art of Close Reading*, eds. J. Blake Couey and Elaine T. James (Cambridge: Cambridge University Press, 2018), 146.

17. On the importance of the "renunciation of infantile omnipotence" in human moral development, see Nussbaum, *Upheavals of Thought*, 218. On the historical role of "the arts and religion" in "counterbalanc[ing]" a "self-reflexive virtual world," see McGilchrist, *The Master and His Emissary*, 6.

18. On the necessity and ethical import of "sustained attention," see J. Blake Couey and Elaine T. James, "Introduction," in *Biblical Poetry and the Art of Close Reading*, eds. J. Blake Couey and Elaine T. James (Cambridge: Cambridge University Press, 2018), 11; on the need to "recover slowness," see Guite, *Faith, Hope and Poetry*, 26; and Davis, "Teaching the Bible Confessionally," 12.

19. Mary Kinzie, *The Cure of Poetry in an Age of Prose: Moral Essays on the Poet's Calling* (London: University of Chicago Press, 1993), x. See also McGilchrist, *Master and His Emissary*, 152-55, on "passivity" as opposed to "grasping" approaches to meaning.

20. On reading the Bible with an attitude that does not assume it already knows what the text means, see Davis, "Teaching the Bible Confessionally in the Church," 16.

comments, "good poetry helps us be more richly uncertain, in more profound ways."[21] Reading biblical poetry with openness to ambiguity means
resisting those aspects of our culture and our religious traditions which
exhibit what Malcom Guite names as "particular suspicion of the ambivalent or multivalent language of poetry."[22] This reading posture does not
look for complexity and ambiguity where they are not, but does celebrate
and embrace them where they occur.[23] It recognizes that in many and
important ways, the attempt to put human realities into words "inevitably [involves] paradox."[24] It assumes that the poem will make meaning
through tensive juxtapositions of words, through language that hides at
the same time as it reveals,[25] through images that play with the boundaries
between sound and sense, and between multiple layers of meaning.[26] It
resists harmonizing and flattening approaches to exegesis.[27] Embrace of
ambiguity has the capacity to form such virtues as humility, receptivity,
wisdom, and intellectual honesty in the face of that which transcends
our human modes of knowing.[28]

---

21. Jane Hirshfield, "Poetry and Uncertainty," in *Hiddenness, Uncertainty, Surprise:
Three Generative Energies of Poetry* (Newcastle: Bloodaxe, 2008), 43.
22. Guite, *Faith, Hope and Poetry*, 2.
23. See R.W.L. Moberly, "Faith and Perplexity," in *Old Testament Theology: Reading the
Hebrew Bible as Christian Scripture* (Grand Rapids: Baker, 2013), 240, on "premature" as
distinguished from "right use" of the ideas of "mystery"; and Guite, *Faith, Hope and
Poetry*, 29, on being "open to, and delighted with, ambiguity." See Christine Pilkington,
"The Hidden God in Isaiah 45:15 – A Reflection From Holocaust Theology," *SJT* 48 (1995):
287, on the danger of "ironing out inconsistencies."
24. McGilchrist, *Master and His Emissary*, 269.
25. Jane Hirshfield, "Poetry and Hiddenness: Thoreau's Hound," in *Hiddenness,
Uncertainty, Surprise: Three Generative Energies of Poetry* (Newcastle: Bloodaxe, 2008), 18.
26. See e.g., Culler, *Theory of the Lyric*, 304.
27. E.g., those Stephen A. Geller, "Were the Prophets Poets?" *Prooftexts* 3 (1983): 219,
considers problematic when he describes their treatment of "Ambiguities [as] ... only
problems to be eliminated, not opportunities for exegetical enrichment." Instead,
exegesis of poetic texts should aim for what William P. Brown, *A Handbook to Old
Testament Exegesis* (Louisville: Westminster John Knox, 2017), 66, calls "a deepening
of that sense of mystery—mystery deepened by understanding."
28. On "step[ping] back from hubris" and becoming "receptive, vulnerable and exposed," see Hirshfield, "Poetry and Uncertainty," 28; on wisdom, compare the reflections of Gerhard von Rad, *Wisdom in Israel*, trans. James D. Martin (London: SCM,
1972), 318; on intellectual honesty, consider the connection between the "concretely
real" and the ambiguous, as highlighted by Axel, "Reshaping the Task of Theology,"
60, and the related emphases of Guite, *Faith, Hope and Poetry*, 6, 11; and Hirshfield,
"Poetry and Uncertainty," 37.

READING ISAIAH 45:9–25[29]

With these postures in mind, we turn our attention toward the text.

In light of encounter, ambiguity, juxtaposition, and emotional tone, I argue that Isaiah 45:9–25 refuses to explain the LORD's ways. Instead, it produces a visionary world where resistance is utterly misguided and where gathering, bowing, and turning overwhelm "understanding." The "hidden" speaker exceeds "comprehension," speaking the standard by which all else that is spoken must be measured. The voice flaunts definition and revels in imagistic juxtaposition. In so doing, it has the capacity to undermine our compulsion to define, to designate, to clarify, and to delineate. The poem chastises the attempt to understand as pre-requisite for trust. Instead, it invites the embrace of a trust that is grounded in the majesty of one who is beyond the control of our knowledge.

The encounter this poem offers enacts a transformation of its hearer. It invites the audience into its imaginative world, to inhabit the space the poem's address creates. There the audience find their contentiousness rendered untenable, their self-aggrandizement misguided, and their grounds for faith reconfigured. They are invited not to comprehension, but to reverent wonder.

EMOTIONAL ENCOUNTER

A first avenue for consideration in this approach to the poem is an emotional clash which offers one of the poem's powerful modes of meaning-making. Opening indictment stands beside grand promise. The juxtaposition of these two tones dramatically re-positions the audience. While the impact of the opening indictment is profoundly humbling, the imagery also offers the audience a place of honor among people. Thus re-positioned the audience are shaped for re-apprehension of divine speech.

---

29. Unit delimitation in Second Isaiah is notoriously difficult; see e.g., the comments of Carroll Stuhlmueller, "Deutero-Isaiah: Major Transitions in the Prophet's Theology and in Contemporary Scholarship," *CBQ* 42 (1980): 1. The beginning of this poem is marked by a sharp paratactic shift in tone from an invitation to praise (v. 8), to indictment, and by change of addressee. John Goldingay and David Payne, *Isaiah 40–55*, ICC (London: T&T Clark, 2006), 2:31, also begin a unit here. Many scholars break the poetry into a new unit at verse 14, and there is a break at least at the level of a sub-unit there and at verse 18. The imagery is heavily linked throughout these lines, justifying treating them together, whether as closely joined, juxtaposed poems or as units within a larger poem.

The poem thrusts the audience into a direct encounter with a speaking voice, whose parallel deployments of *hôy* (45:9, 10) signal its harsh tone.[30] The parallelism's sound patterning draws attention to the comparison between the speaker and addressee. It is a comparison that emphasizes the sharp contrast between them.[31] The opening bicolon is ambiguous on several levels. It does not explicitly name those being indicted, characterizing them with descriptive participles. The one to whom *hôy* is announced is "one who contends with his fashioner."[32] Whoever the addressees are, they are invoked by a voice that characterizes them as disputing with the one who brought them into being. There are hints that Jacob/Israel is the addressee, particularly in the use of the verb "fashioner" (*yōṣĕrô*)[33] and in the use of offspring imagery (45:10 cf. 43:1), but the poetry avoids naming them as the addressee.[34] Instead, associations create an increasingly likely tie between the audience themselves and the indictee. By forcing the audience to come to this recognition themselves, the poetry increases the audience's emotional involvement. It implicates them in the act of assigning indictment to themselves through recognition.

---

30. The poem begins abruptly, moving without segue or introduction from the exhortation to praise with which it stands juxtaposed (45:8), to a stinging indictment. That is, it begins by employing a strong sense of poetic parataxis and an emotionally charged heightening of poetic presence through direct address. On the resonances of "*hoy*," see Goldingay and Payne, *Isaiah 40–55*, 2:31. Against e.g., Joseph Blenkinsopp, *Isaiah 40–55*, AB 19A (London: Doubleday, 2000), 251, and Bruce D. Naidoff, "The Two-fold Structure of Isaiah XLV 9–13," *VT* 31 (1981): 180, there is no need to re-divide the words. *Hoy* may be used with a "woe" meaning within Second Isaiah only here, but the word is clearly within the prophetic poet's vocabulary (Isa 55:1). Its resonances are perhaps strengthened by its rarity.
31. Two sets of sound-patterned groupings of three bicola draw attention to this juxtaposition in the auditory fabric of the poem, the first addressing the audience, the second declaring the speaker's presence. The opening sounds of these first three bicola of the poem begin in a pattern *hôy, hăyō'mar ḥōmer, hôy 'ōmēr*. This same pattern of three closely sound-linked bicolon openings expresses the self-presentation of the speaker: *'ānōkî, 'ănî, 'ānōkî* (45:12, 13). In contrast to the participle without any accompanying pronoun for the addressee, the divine speaker's first and third self-references employ both a first-person pronoun and a first-person finite verb, while the middle term of the construction modifies the pronoun "I" (*'ănî*) with the parenthetical "my hands."
32. All translations of the biblical text, unless otherwise noted, are my own.
33. This is one of Second Isaiah's favorite descriptors for the LORD and especially with respect to Jacob/Israel's formation (see, e.g., 43:1; 44:2, 24; 45:9, 11; 49:5). Blenkinsopp, *Isaiah 40–55*, 254, notes Isaiah 40–48's use of the term.
34. See e.g., Samuel E. Balentine, "Isaiah 45: God's 'I Am,' Israel's 'You Are,'" *HBT* 16 (1994): 106–107; and Goldingay and Payne, *Isaiah 40–55*, 2:34.

In heavily ironic rhetorical questions, the divine speaker develops a pair of resonances out of the opening image. Neither the unformed materials of the pot, nor the unborn child should be justified or able to correct the one who aids them into being.[35] These two imaginative out-workings of "fashioner" from the opening bicolon stand in an intensifying parallel relationship with each another. First, a pair of rhetorical questions asks the audience to consider the likelihood of earthenware objecting to the process of its own sculpting. The second pair of rhetorical questions shifts, intensifying the stinging tone. No longer hypothetical, no longer inanimate, and no longer speculative, the questions are placed on the indictee's lips and *hôy* is pronounced over the one who speaks them (45:10). Reiteration and reapplication disambiguate the "sons" and "my hands' work" with pronounced emotional impact as "the Holy One of Israel, and its fashioner" (45:11) is announced as the speaker.[36]

The divine voice employs creation motifs to paint its response onto a still broader canvas. It redeploys "making" (*taʿaśeh*) from the clay's query to claim the role of earth's maker (*ʿāśîtî*), applies the "hands" imagery to the creation of the heavens and picks up the language of "command" (*tĕṣawwunî*) to convey its own sovereignty (*ṣiwwêtî*, Isa 45:12) over the stars.[37] This is a profoundly humbling encounter which works emotionally at undermining resistance to divine activity.

In sharp and unexplained contrast to the chastising invective that begins the poem, the messenger formula announces a re-envisioning of the audience's relationship with other groups of people. They are offered a vision of themselves as those to whom powerful nations give honor

---

35. John D.W. Watts, *Isaiah 34–66*, WBC 25, rev. ed. (Grand Rapids: Zondervan, 2005), 153, rejects the association of the speaker with the one being conceived. While the "child" is not explicitly named here, the parallelism of the pot and the earlier reference to offspring support an implied reference to the child conceived.

36. Goldingay and Payne, *Isaiah 40–55*, 2:37, note the "confrontational edge." Both the handiwork and parental images are applied to refutation of the audience's "command" regarding "my hands' (*yaday*) work (*pōʿal*)." The pot querying the fashioner about his "work" (*pāʿālĕkā*) being without "hands" (*yādayim*) parallels this language while the reference to "sons" parallels the "father" and "woman" imagery. In his defense of the unity of verses 9–11, Naidoff, "The Two-fold Structure of Isaiah XLV 9–13," 183, points to a chiastic structure drawing on the fashioner and "work of hands" references.

37. The term for what is commanded here is "hosts" and the idea of commanding the hosts depends upon a militaristic metaphor for heavenly bodies cf. Goldingay and Payne, *Isaiah 40–55*, 2:39. I have translated "stars" here in light of the contextual reference to creation of the heavens and to capture some of the colon's alliteration.

and treasures (Isa 45:14).[38] Lavish glorification imagery collides with
the humbling trajectory already begun. Those honored among nations
(45:14), and those whose avoidance of shame and confounding stands at
variance with those around them (45:16), offer different images of the
audience.[39] The juxtaposition of humbling before God and exaltation
among humans invites the audience into a new imagistic and emotional
space. In this world it is possible to imagine themselves joining the community depicted in the bicolon "for to me every knee will bow and every
tongue will swear" (Isa 45:23).[40] These attitudes, and the juxtaposition
of emotional images that offer them, function to re-position the poem's
audience. Opening harsh and sarcastic invective undermines resistance
to the divine plan while contrasting promises of exaltation highlight the
audience's privileged position as beneficiaries of that plan. The poem's
imaginative world sets the audience into their "rightful place." It brings
them down from the self-exaltation that rejects the mysterious ways of
God, and simultaneously raises them up in contrast to those peoples who
do not know the Lord.

Meaningful Ambiguity

A second important approach to reading this poem poetically is an
embrace of its ambiguity. This is a difficult poem, which plays with its
words and is dotted with motifs of "hiddenness," "confusion" and "chaos."
It has a thick background which carries the attentive listener outside
the poem's boundaries to seek clarification in its resonances with other
poems.[41] As the poem forces its audience to grapple with its under-defined
and allusive claims, it reinforces the re-evaluation of their knowledge in
contrast to that of the speaking deity. In this way its mode of expression
embraces and conveys meaning.

---

38. On the addressee, see Goldingay and Payne, *Isaiah 40–55*, 2:43–44.

39. The imagery anticipates the poem's concluding bicolon which draws together
divine activity and glorification for the "seed of Israel" (45:25).

40. This response hinges on the poem's emphatic and repetitive stress on the singular
"righteousness" and only-ness of God, and presents such a response as an abashed
turning (45:22, 24).

41. Guite, *Faith, Hope and Poetry*, 27, points to the necessity of allowing intertextual
"interplay" in poetic interpretation. Within work on Isaianic poetry, the study of allusion has benefitted from the significant work of Patricia Tull Willey, *Remember the
Former Things: The Recollection of Previous Texts in Second Isaiah*, SBLDS 161 (Atlanta:
Scholars, 1997) and Benjamin D. Sommer, *A Prophet Reads Scripture: Allusion in Isaiah
40–66* (Stanford: Stanford University Press, 1998).

One of the poem's driving ambiguities is the absence of the impertinent potsherd's and its comparison partners' complaint. This elusiveness about the contention itself is part of the poem's imagistic work.[42] It hints that the audience's concerns might cluster around their inability to comprehend the deity's activities. Standing in unexplained parallel to the Creator's insistence upon having formed heaven and earth, humans and the heavenly host is the bicolon:

> I have roused him in righteousness,
> and all his ways I will straighten. (Isa 45:13)

The bicolon moves the frame of reference from cosmic creation to historical particularity, but without stating who "he" is. Divinely initiated re-creation becomes a motif of restoration from exile (Isa 45:13). A number of modern English translations supply Cyrus's name here,[43] signaling the problem that such ambiguity poses. While it is likely, though not certain, that the poem refers to Cyrus, it does so obliquely and this is part of the way in which the poem makes meaning.[44] The divine voice does not need to explain itself to the audience, as the poem's opening imagery illustrated. Instead, the bicolon focuses on the divine speaker's activity, rather than the identity of the one the LORD will raise up.

The ambiguity of this bicolon resists straightforward assimilation. Instead, it points outside of itself through allusive links with other lines and other Isaianic poems. The claim "all (kol) his ways (děrākāyw) I will straighten (ʾăyaššēr)" gestures toward Second Isaiah's opening poem, and the tie both to "way" and to levelling are significant.[45]

---

42. Multiple sources of allusion suggest themselves. Isa 40:27 cites Jacob's objections about hiddenness, while Isa 29:15-16, as pointed out by Goldingay and Payne, Isaiah 40-55, 2:37, employs hiddenness and pottery imagery. The complaint itself is not the problem, the relationship of complaint in which the creature queries the creator stands to the foreground.

43. See, for example, NIV, NRSV, NLT, and CEB which include the name Cyrus. Among those that do not are NET, NJB, and ASV.

44. There are significant elements of this poem's reference that hint at Cyrus, not least the use of the imagery of city rebuilding which appears in relationship to Cyrus where he is named in Isa 44:28. However, the language of "stirring up" which appears also in Isaiah 41 where the name of Cyrus does not appear, the commission to release exiles, and the description of being called "in righteousness" are related to the figure of the Servant in Isaiah 42. Goldingay and Payne, Isaiah 40-55, 2:40, note the parallel to Isaiah 41 and the absence of explicit reference to Cyrus here.

45. The injunction to prepare the "way (derek) of the LORD" (Isa 40:3) stands parallel to the imagery of "every" (kol) valley and mountain being transformed and the "rough

The pairing of "righteousness" (ṣedeq) and "straighten" (ʾăyaššēr) weaves this bicolon's ambiguity into the tapestry of interconnected meanings surrounding the divine voice's claims about itself as speaker.[46] A closely tied pairing appears in the parallelism:

> I am Yhwh, speaker of righteousness (ṣedeq)
> Spokesman of straightnesses[47] (Isa 45:19)

Both ṣedeq and mêšārîm are at play in the poem and gesture beyond simple associations, complicating and expanding the meaning of "truth" as a translation for ṣedeq here. The noun mêšārîm can carry a moral or ethical flavor, i.e., integrity,[48] but also has resonances with divine resolution of the audience's struggle. The echo here of the pairing of ʾăyaššēr with ṣedeq flavors this declaration with the imagery that announced the LORD's raising up one who would bring out the exiles and build the city (Isa 45:13). The creative, enacting divine word resonates with the declaration of deliverance. Carrying these associations, the freighted words convey both that the LORD's word is reliable, trustworthy, and true, and that

---

place" becoming a levelled one (lĕmîšôr). Sommer, *A Prophet Reads*, 159, describes a "split-up pattern" of allusion in which the prophet "separates a phrase from its source into two parts and inserts several words or even verses between them." Here, the dynamic seems to be a reversal of that movement, if Isaiah 40 is the source of the allusion and not the other way around. The poem draws together elements of parallel bicola combined into one colon composed entirely of the allusive elements. The "rough" there is heʿāqōb and sound play hints through this term at one of Second Isaiah's favorite terms for the audience yaʿăqōb. The sound play implies that the radical levelling, the straightening out, enacts a change that includes, if not primarily aims at, the audience. The poetry offers a visual image of cosmic re-landscaping through which to depict a radical re-alignment of the audience's realities. The "penalty" (40:1) is being reversed and deliverance announced, but alteration of the way also aims at Jacob's own "roughness," perhaps including Jacob's posture of complaint about that "way" being "hidden" (40:27).

46. Cf. Matthijs J. de Jong, "A note on the meaning of bᵉṣædæq in Isaiah 42,6 and 45,13," ZAW 123 (2011): 259-62, who emphasizes the "adverbial" (259) force and translates the word "legitimately" (261). While I would not rule out this meaning as an element of Second Isaiah's use of the term's resonances, the other occurrences of ṣedeq in the immediate context must also have an impact on its meaning here.

47. Goldingay and Payne, *Isaiah 40-55* 2:54, refer to mêšārîm as "a characteristic intensive or amplifying plural." Interestingly, the plural gets applied to ṣedeq in verse 24. See Goldingay and Payne, *Isaiah 40-55*, 2:60-61. I have kept this "amplifying plural" in translation to reflect the poetic intensity of the colon and to reinforce the alliteration.

48. See HALOT, 1:578. The noun employed here is based on the same root as the verb "straighten" in verse 13. BDB, 449, list both the noun employed here and the noun employed in Isaiah 40 within their larger entry on the root yāšar.

this word speaks deliverance into being. The creative, enacting word accomplishes what the LORD intends by it, and reference to "righteousness" which goes out from the divine mouth and will not return (45:23) resounds with the more expansive iteration of that motif in Isaiah 55.

That the divine word is creative and enacting, delivering as well as reliable is conveyed by the poetic juxtaposition in which it stands.[49] Isaiah 45:19 stands at an intersection between creation and salvation images. The self-declaration, "I am Yhwh" (v. 18), offered a resounding poetic conclusion to the description of the LORD as creator. The bicolon "I am Yhwh, speaker of ṣedeq, spokesman of straightnesses" stands parallel to it and offers itself as the climax of the series of bicola topicalizing divine speech.[50] Yet, it looks forward also. Ṣedeq, as Rendtorff has noted, seems heavily colored in Second Isaiah by its relationship to salvation terminology, and this occurrence is no exception.[51] "The nations' escapees" appear in the next verse and are placed in parallelistic juxtaposition with those "who pray to a god who does not save." Much more tellingly, the next declaration of divine uniqueness, self-predicates "a God of ṣeddîq and a savior (môšîaʿ)" (Isa 45:21).[52] Clearly ṣedeq belongs to the metaphorical domain of divine speech; the voice will go on to proclaim that it "went out from my mouth" (45:23). It characterizes the speech of a voice that commands worlds into being and pronounces deliverance. This is "truth" being spoken, but with expansive meaning and implications. It is a term with which the poem is playing, and one that resists precisely limited definition.

49. Goldingay and Payne, Isaiah 40-55, 2:55, note that these words are "set over against hiddenness, darkness, and emptiness."
50. This impression is strengthened by the following cola's shift to plural verb forms.
51. See Rolf Rendtorff, "Isaiah 56:1 as a Key to the Formation of the Book of Isaiah," in Canon and Theology: Overtures to an Old Testament Theology, trans. Margaret Kohl, OBT (Minneapolis: Fortress, 1993), 183. Salvation is certainly an aspect of the meaning that this poem develops around ṣedeq, though, as we have seen, it is not the only contextual impingement on the word's meaning.
52. Cf. Balentine, "Isaiah 45," 113, who reads this pairing as standing parallel to the hidden and savior pairing (45:15). He sees the divine voice's pairing as that to which the poem aims to elicit assent. Elsewhere in the poem ṣedeq appears alongside and paralleled to expressions of strength or might (Isa 45:24), which is not a difficult idea to relate to the concept of deliverance.

Mystery and Paradox

The voice who interjects "Surely you are a God who hides yourself" (Isa 45:15) highlights the experience of ambiguity this poem offers. Divine hiddenness in this poem directly intersects one of Second Isaiah's main tensions and illustrates the importance of its emotional, unsettling, and re-orienting work. The colon sits as a poetic interjection within its context and its ambiguity functions on several levels. Most obviously, it engages the mystery of divine hiddenness.[53] In addition, it is not altogether clear who is speaking these words within the poem's world, nor is it evident whether they are to be regarded as complaint, as a misunderstanding, or as a statement of truth.[54]

The immediately preceding cola place words on the lips of the nations (45:14). They take up Second Isaiah's motif of the LORD's uniqueness and tie that singularity to the audience's distinctive role. The immediate context, then, seems to express a recognition of reality from the perspective of the poem. If the nations' voice continues into the interjection "Surely you are a God who hides yourself," it expresses the mystery of divine hiddenness as fitting within the experience of the nations who recognize Israel's distinctive role and the LORD's unique sovereignty.[55]

But it is not altogether clear in the poem that the nations' voice speaks these words. In 45:14 the nations address a "you" but that "you" is apparently the poem's audience. The expression of divine hiddenness addresses the LORD as "you," enacting but not explaining its shift of addressee.[56] The poetic immediacy of this paratactic shift leaves significant ambiguity. The lines that follow do not directly take up the imagery of divine hiddenness. There confusion and confounding for the nations contrast with "unending salvation" for Israel (Isa 45:16–17). In its immediate poetic context "Surely you are a God who hides yourself" (Isa 45:15) stands under-determined. Its ambiguity leaves open the possibility that the nations continue speaking, or that another voice interjects. In either case, it is not clear whether this

---

53. Samuel E. Balentine, *The Hidden God: The Hiding of the Face of God in the Old Testament* (Oxford: Oxford University Press, 1983), 176, compellingly calls it "the absence of a present God."

54. Pilkington, "The Hidden God," 287–89, and Balentine, "Isaiah 45," 107–8, each describe the task of assigning a speaker here and illustrate alternative possibilities.

55. Goldingay and Payne, *Isaiah 40–55*, 2:42, read these words as spoken by "foreign peoples."

56. See Balentine, "Isaiah 45," 109, for illustration of the means by which the poetry emphasizes this shift.

assertion is to be taken as true, or as part of the "confusion" that differentiates Israel's experience from that of the idol worshipers (Isa 45:16–17).[57]

The ambiguity of this interjection is complicated by its tie to the motif of hiddenness in Second Isaiah. On the one hand, the parallelism immediately ascribing the title "savior" to this hidden God implies that the poem treats them as true, whoever it is that is speaking them. However, this truth is a complicated one as Balentine observes here, "hiding and saving, are joined in asserting a paradox of divine activity."[58] The word here, *mistattēr*, is a participial form of the word in Jacob/Israel's cited complaint in Isaiah 40:27, "Hidden (*nistĕrāh*) is my way from Yhwh."[59] In a climactic moment within the poetic movement of these chapters, the divine voice takes up language from both Zion's and Jacob/Israel's complaints declaring "for a short moment I forsook you, but with great compassion I will gather you; in a flood of fury I hid (*histartî*) my face for a moment from you, but with everlasting steadfastness, I will have compassion on you" (Isa 54:7–8). The language of the complaints moves tensely and paradoxically through the poems,[60] including this poem's earlier entanglement with the LORD's intention to level a way (Isa 45:13) and the resonance between this idea and the preparation of the LORD's way in Isaiah 40.[61] But the "hidden" imagery of Isaiah 45 relates not to Jacob's (or anyone else's) way, but to God and stands as an expression of apparent self-hiding. Here the divine voice does not immediately take up this language, complicating our sense of the relationship between the interjection, Jacob/Israel's complaint, and the divine voice's response.

Hiddenness appears again in verse 19 in noun form, where the divine voice relates it to its own speech. This bicolon carries its own ambiguity

---

57. Blenkinsopp, *Isaiah 40–55*, 258, indicates the possibility of both a "positive connotation" and "otherwise" for the claim that God hides himself.

58. Balentine, "Isaiah 45," 110.

59. I have chosen to translate the words in the order they appear, despite the normality of this word order in Hebrew, but not in English. By preserving this word order, it is possible to see the chiastic structure of the bicolon when the next colon inverts this word order.

60. The complaints of Jacob/Israel and Zion are each taken up in refutation (Isa 40:28–31; Isa 49:15–21). The paired terms of Zion's complaint are redeployed with the deity rejecting directly the claim of forgetfulness (Isa 49:15), issuing paradoxical commands about the audience's memory (Isa 43:18; 46:9), and proclaiming future forgetfulness for Zion (Isa 54:4), but embracing the language of "forsaking" while qualifying it with brevity (Isa 54:7).

61. Interestingly, Pilkington, "The Hidden God," 293, observes resonances with Isaiah 40 and 54 in her discussion of the "essential paradox [that] remains" in Isa 45:15.

offering what might be read less as a refutation of the interjection and
more as a complication of the picture of divine hiddenness.[62] Both this
bicolon and the next standing parallel to it begin with *lōʾ*, laying their
emphasis on what the deity claims not to have done. "In secret"[63] is itself
unclear. Does it indicate "where" such speaking did not take place, or
what the nature of that speaking was not, or is the imagery of the one
intended to convey the other? Gradually, these bicola's parallelism enacts
their intimation of disambiguation. "In secret" is accompanied by a parallel emphasizing place, the second bicolon adds an addressee, and both
"secret" and "darkness" are further amplified by the addition of *tōhû*.[64] The
image forming is that divine speech shares characteristics with divine
creation. The immediately preceding cola had, in a fashion typical of
Second Isaiah, underscored the LORD's uniqueness with reference to God's
role as "fashioner" of earth, creator and as one who created "not *tōhû*"
(Isa 45:18). Calling up resonances with both Genesis 1[65] and Isaiah 29,[66]
the poetry lays claim to divine speech as not "hidden," employing imagery that suggests divine speech creates and calls into being and sharply
contrasts with human speech and knowledge. Further complication and
expansion are added by language shared with Isaiah 45:3 where explicit
connection was made to Cyrus.[67]

---

62. Cf. Balentine, "Isaiah 45," 112, who treats the divine voice here as offering a "re-
interpretation of Israel's assertion." See Pilkington, "The Hidden God," 295–96, for a
helpful critique of Balentine's commitment to a Psalms/Prophets contrast in relation
to this theme and its application to this passage.

63. The NRSV also translates the phrase "in secret," which helpfully preserves the
potential ambiguity. Both "secrecy" and "hiding-place" are potential meanings for
this noun as indicated by *BDB*, 712. The initial context does not distinguish whether
the meaning should be one of mode or location, until the addition of *bimqôm* in the
parallel colon.

64. See David Toshio Tsumura, "*TŌHÛ* in Isaiah XLV 19," *VT* 38 (1988): 361, who highlights the variant translations offered for *tōhû* in this context illustrating both "loc-
ative" and "abstract" understandings.

65. Resonances include Genesis 1's accent on "darkness" in the primordial setting, its
recurrent reference to "seed," and its depiction of the elimination of *tōhû*, all accomplished through the divine word. Goldingay and Payne, *Isaiah 40–55*, 2:54, observe a
connection to Genesis 1.

66. Both "darkness" and "hide" are present in Isa 29:15, which Goldingay and Payne,
Isaiah 40–55, 2:36, linked to the earlier potter and clay imagery of this poem.

67. See Goldingay and Payne, *Isaiah 40–55*, 2:53.

Ambiguity here is not a problem to be solved or "interesting solely because it is a nuisance."[68] Ambiguity is a way in which the poem means. It invokes and creates the experience of divine hiddenness. The divine voice's ambiguity enacts and expands the human (and readerly) experience of divine mystery. In the world of the poem, the interjection "Surely you are a God who hides yourself" voices the reality of human limitation in knowing fully the mind and purposes of God.

DEMANDS THIS PASSAGE MAKES UPON
THE RECEPTIVE HEARER

The poem's ambiguity and its emotional encounter enact a humbling, an embrace of limitation, and a rightful re-orienting of attitudes and dispositions. The idea of divine mystery is, at least in part, embraced in Second Isaiah. The Lord is, for Israel, both revealed, in the divine, not secret, creative, redemptive, integrity-bearing word; and lofty, beyond containing, reducing, or controlling. Second Isaiah's climactic moment embraces the hidden "face" of God, qualifying it with brevity, placing it in the past (Isa 54:8), and pairing it with the rejection of the idea of "God-forsakenness." But the mysterious transcendence of the God whose word is effective, not hidden, comes through tensive, conflicted, ambiguous poetic speech.

"Surely you are a God who hides yourself" stands undesignated, and thus remains open to the audience, both the exilic historical audience, and the contemporary reader who reads this poem as Scripture. It offers an invitation to face the reader's own discomfort with divine hiddenness and to embrace the formative value of a poem that both contests self-exalting resistance to the deity and invites confidence in the utter "righteousness" of the Lord. As this voice seeks to affect a reorientation of emotions and attitude through engagement with its images, it plays with words and complicates their meanings through multiple, overlapping, and tensive redeployments. It conveys mystery. It offers abundance of meaning. It resists all forms of reduction. It invites its hearer, both ancient and

---

68. As Owen Barfield, *Poetic Diction: A Study in Meaning* (Middletown: Wesleyan University Press, 1973), 61, quipped about the attitude of those orientated toward "Logic" about the shifting of word meanings.

modern, to find themselves "read" by the voice which unmasks their pride and exposes the brokenness of their language.[69]

IMPLICATIONS FOR APPROACHING SCRIPTURE

In conclusion, biblical poetry offers an opportunity to reflect on what we mean when we speak about Scripture. Biblical poetry suggests that one way in which we might conceive of our relationship with Scripture is that of "formational encounter." Biblical poetry in general, and this poetic text in particular, offer formational encounters that shape readers in attentive openness, imaginative empathy, and humble embrace of complexity.

In the context of distraction, biblical poetry forms habits of attention, habits that may give rise to more healthily ethical encounters with others, habits that form the capacity for attention to God in prayer, for, as Weil observes, "prayer consists of attention."[70] While it may seem a truism that what we think about will shape who we are, there is interesting evidence that our brains are impacted by what we give attention to, and that this formation has a bearing on our future behaviors.[71] In this poem in particular, the emotionally intense encounter with the divine speaker forms attentiveness that maintains God's majesty and resists assimilation into our human designs and pre-conceptions.

When neglect of our imaginative capacity has the potential to undermine our ability to envision appropriately that which is outside of ourselves, biblical poetry confronts the prosaic world with worlds of its

---

69. Guite, *Faith, Hope and Poetry*, 30, offers the metaphor of a musical instrument for the readerly experience. As Davis, "Teaching the Bible," 15, comments, "Our language is broken by our denial of its uncertainty."

70. Simone Weil, "Reflections on the Right Use of School Studies with a View to the Love of God," in *Waiting for God*, trans. Emma Craufurd (New York: Perennial, 2001), 57, see also 64-65.

71. See McGilchrist, *Master and His Emissary*, 133, 167, 246-53. McGilchrist describes the importance of the mode and object of our attention in shaping our world and ourselves and as impacting our behavior (167). He points to the role of "mirror neurons" (250) in creating our empathetic engagement through imagination as well as to "cell memory" and the "way in which the structure of a neuronal connection in the brain changes with use, so as to promote preferential use of the same connection in future" (246). He cites both "primacy of affect" (184) and studies of imitation (245-256) and comments that "what we imagine is in a sense what we are and who we become" (250). On "mirror neurons" and imagination see also Mark Johnson, *The Meaning of the Body: Aesthetics of Human Understanding* (London: University of Chicago Press, 2007), 161-62.

own.[72] As Nussbaum has demonstrated, imagination plays an important role in the formation of ethical character particularly through the ability to "imagine another person's experience" and the imagination's role in enabling "differentiation of self from world."[73] This poem transforms an imagistic depiction of contentiousness, juxtaposing a lavish, glorious future. It moves the imagination from a setting of resistance to an invitation to worshipful wonder. It pulls its audience out of an attitude shaped primarily by their own perceptions, into one that views reality from the perspective of the other.

In a time of reductive simplification, biblical poetry insists that the central truths of humanity and the divine are complex.[74] The creation of abstract concepts and ideas out of precise particularities produces loss. This is true both of the encounter of poetry and of meaning as encountered through human interactions.[75] In this poem, ambiguity invites wrestling with divine speech itself, an encounter that has the capacity to shape us into more receptive, more engaged, more imaginative readers. It forces us to leave some questions open.[76] By engaging biblical Hebrew poetry in these ways, we practice the habits it forms in us, we engage in formational encounters, and we engage with it as Scripture.

---

72. Walter Brueggemann, *Finally Comes the Poet: Daring Speech for Proclamation* (Minneapolis: Fortress, 1989), 3, describes "*a prose world*" as one that "is organized into settled formulae" (emphasis original).

73. Nussbaum, *Upheavals of Thought*, 237. Nussbaum's reference points here are to the role of the "narrative structure" of human emotion, particularly in childhood development. However, the relevance of imagination to ethics arguably extends to the imaginative expansion enabled by poetry.

74. See McGilchrist, *The Master and His Emissary*, xxv, on reductionism.

75. Johnson, *Meaning of the Body*, 270.

76. This is an attitude that might well be associated with the virtues of wisdom. In the conclusion to his study of wisdom, von Rad, *Wisdom in Israel*, 318, comments that "it is the highest wisdom to abstain from the attempt to control wisdom in abstract terms, that it is much wiser to let things retain their constantly puzzling nature, and that means to allow them to become themselves active and, by what they have to say, to set man to rights."

9

The Dynamic Relationship between God and Man in the Book of Hosea: A Dynamic-Synchronic Reading

Yisca Zimran

Individual prophetic units in the Bible in general, and in the book of Hosea in particular, portray the prophet's concrete approach toward the events of his time. A reading of individual units might indicate the context of their authorship or redaction, the events that elicited the prophecy, and even specific reactions to these events, reflected in calamity, rebuke, and consolation. For example, Isaiah 7 is often perceived as a response to the Syro-Ephraimite War in 734 BC, and Jeremiah 39 is often attributed to the beginning of the siege in Jerusalem toward the end of 589 BC.

A reading of individual units requires a clear delineation of the unit's boundaries, based on acceptable and probable parameters. Additionally, an analysis is needed of the unit's arrangement, time of authorship, and stages of formation, especially when based on diachronic approaches. The purpose of an independent reading is to trace the unit's original intent, the social-historical background, and the cultural and ideological world it reflects. Through this method, the modern reader can be brought closer to the past.

However, this paper demonstrates a dynamic-synchronic reading in Hosea, which reveals ongoing links and processes *between* the units in the book: the paper is based on a synchronic approach to the canonical text of Hosea, and reads the text dynamically.[1] In other words, it focuses on the

---

1. For example: Brevard S. Childs, "The Canonical Shape of Prophetic Literature," *Interpretation* 32 (1978): 46–55.

relationship between the individual units and the manner in which the lexical recurrences challenge the original boundaries, and thus enables the creation of significant processes in the framework of the book's totality. The outcome of this reading might shed light on the prophetic work as a complete product, with dynamic internal significance which supersedes the original meaning of each individual unit. This type of reading involves the reader in the interpretive process, since it is the *reader* who creates new meaning in the text.[2] Therefore, this method enables modern readers to bring the text closer to their frame of reference.[3]

The book of Hosea is characterized by an inordinate volume of lexical recurrences and related wordplay. It is therefore an appropriate text for demonstrating the application of this reading method, which can theoretically be applied to any poetic biblical text due to the characteristic of poetry and the place of the addressee in this type of texts, as explained below.[4] The book's characteristics invite the reader to listen, interpret, and reformulate the content of the prophecies. Since the lexical recurrences create another layer of meaning in the unit, they should be perceived as an immanent part of the book's *content*—and part of the totality of components that support the meaning of the texts,[5] and not merely as a literary characteristic.[6]

THE SELECTED UNITS

As an example of the application of this reading method, I have selected a group of five units from the MT of the book, relating to five different themes. Each independent unit contains unique and closed content: 7:8–12 is a rebuke for creating an alliance with foreign nations. 9:1–6 relates to idolatry and is dedicated mostly to the description of future calamity in

---

2. Stulac uses the term "implied reader." For the characteristics and significance of the implied reader, see Daniel J. Stulac, *History and Hope: The Agrarian Wisdom of Isaiah 28–35* (University Park, PA: Eisenbrauns, 2018), 82–85.

3. See John Barton, *Reading the Old Testament: Method in Biblical Study* (London: Darton, Longman & Todd, 1996), 217–19.

4. See e.g., Martin J. Buss, *The Prophetic Word of Hosea* (Berlin: Töpelmann, 1969): 28–30.

5. As posited for example by Harold Fisch, *Poetry with a Purpose: Biblical Poetics and Interpretation* (Bloomington: Indiana University Press, 1988), 139; Paul Kruger, "The Divine Net in Hosea 7, 12," *ETL* 68 (1992), 132–36.

6. See e.g., Gerald P. Morris, *Prophecy, Poetry and Hosea* (Sheffield: Sheffield Academic, 1996), who believes that the book is only poetic, not rhetoric nor ideology.

light of the present situation. 11:1–7 returns to idolatry and emphasizes the contrast between this phenomenon and God's expectations of the relationship with the nation. 11:8–11 is a prophecy of consolation that describes returning the nation of Israel to its land due to the loving relationship between God and his people. 12:1–2 is a rebuke for creating political alliances while emphasizing their futility and presenting them as a contrast to the relationship with God. Why these five units?

The units I have selected are characterized by featuring the correlative pair "Assyria-Egypt," which should be defined as a motif.[7] In other words, this is a recurring idiomatic phrase which encompasses a broad abstract meaning that enriches the explicit text.[8] Each of the units presents the relationship with Assyria and Egypt as an alternative to the relationship with God. Therefore, the motif represents the distance from God. Despite the general prevalent mention of Egypt and Assyria in the Bible due to the centrality of the two kingdoms, their appearance as a correlative pair is unique to the book of Hosea, and particularly to the five units discussed in this paper.

The broad lexical links, demonstrated in the following table, strengthen the connection between the units and reinforces their suitability to demonstrate this reading method:

יונה	7:11; 11:11	הל"כ	7:11, 12; 9:6; 11:2, 10
לב	7:11; 11:8	לא יד"ע	7:9 [twice]; 11:3
יחד	11:7, 8	קר"א	7:11; 11:1, 2, 7
בית	9:4; 11:11; 12:1	אכ"ל	7:9; 9:3, 4; 11:6; [11:6 כלתה; 11:4 אוכיל]
עיר	11:6, 9	רו"מ	11:4, 7
שוד	9:6; 12:2	יר"ד	7:12; 12:1

---

7. For the definition of "correlative pair," see: Wilfred G.E. Watson, *Classical Hebrew Poetry: A Guide to its Techniques* (Sheffield: JSOT, 1984), 132. For defining them as a motif briefly, see James L. Mays, *Hosea: A Commentary*, OTL 13A (Philadelphia: SCM, 1969), 159.

8. For example, Shemaryahu Talmon, "The 'Desert Motif' in the Bible and in Qumran Literature," in *Biblical Motifs*, ed. Alexander Altmann (Cambridge: Harvard University Press, 1966), 39; Weston W. Fields, *Sodom and Gomorrah: History and Motif in Biblical Narrative* (Sheffield: Sheffield Academic Press, 1997), 19, emphasize that a motif may be based on a historical event, but contains the abstract principles which stem from this event and have implications on the other texts that integrate the motif. Cf. Robert Alter, *The Art of Biblical Poetry* (New York: Basic Books, 1985), 146, who defines a similar phenomenon as a "proverbial biblical image."

בֵּן	11:1, 10	רֵעַ״י	9:2; 12:2
קָדוֹשׁ	11:9; 12:1	הפ״כ	7:8; 11:8
עַמִּים	7:8; 9:1; 11:7	אה״ב	9:1; 11:1, 4
שׁוּ״ב	7:10; 9:3; 11:3 [twice], 7, 9	זב״ח	9:4; 11:2
יש״ב	9:3; 11:11	עש״י	9:5; 11:9
כח״שׁ	9:2; 12:1		

Limiting the dynamic-synchronic reading to a group of texts with similar characteristics defines the foundation for a joint reading of the texts and sets clear parameters for such a reading. By setting unequivocal parameters, we define a clear line that prevents an unlimited reading of texts based on the associations created in the reader's mind. However, limiting the scope to this group of texts does not negate the possibility of defining additional groups in the book and examining the meaning created by their dynamic-synchronic reading.

What, then, is the interpretive and ideological contribution of the links created between the five units?

DIALOGUE BETWEEN THE UNITS

Scholars who emphasize the unique literary qualities of Hosea relate them to the book's lexical recurrences in a variety of ways. For example, Buss utilized the recurrences to distinguish between original and later components in the prophecies.[9] Morris emphasizes not only the repetition, but also the distinctions in the use of each recurring phrase, while utilizing various meanings of idioms and roots. He views these as testimony to the prophet's poetic capabilities.[10] Uffenheimer demonstrates the difference between recurring phrases as an expression of the book's ideology.[11] He also illustrates how the prophet sometimes uses repetition to present a correspondence between units, which represents a dialogue between God and the nation. I would like to go one step further and demonstrate how the lexical recurrences are the foundation for a dialogue between the units, even when the units relate to entirely different matters. In this paper, the term "dialogue" describes the "revival" of

---

9. Buss, *Prophetic Word*, 29–33. For a critique of his work see: Morris, *Prophecy*, 68–69.
10. For example: Morris, *Prophecy*, 68–73, 110–31. Cf. Fisch, *Poetry*, 139–44.
11. Benjamin Uffenheimer, "Amos and Hosea–Two Directions in Israel's Prophecy," in *Zer Li'Gevurot*, ed. Ben-Zion Luria (Jerusalem: Kiryath Sepher, 1972): 294–98 [Heb.].

existing lexical similarities between the texts and instilling them with meaning that emerges from the relationship between the texts: interpretation, qualification, reinforcement, or judgment of the recurrences against one another. The dialogue need not correlate with the primary meaning of the units, and it is not explicitly present, but rather *founded* in the formulations and *developed* by the reader who notes the literary similarities between the units.[12]

My use of "dialogue" does not denote a unit that utilizes the content of an earlier unit to express judgment or ideological development. Dialogue as denoting a critique or successive use of previous units is founded in a determined chronological relationship between the units, and a historical study of the development of the book.[13] Moyise defines this as "dialogical intertextuality."[14] Additionally, despite the subjective element in the dialogue between the units, and the wide breadth offered to the modern reader, the term "dialogue" is not used here in the manner applied by Beal or van Wolde,[15] since the dialogues under discussion are not an application of the reader's independent associations with the totality of biblical texts.

In the next section I will demonstrate the significance of the "Assyria-Egypt" pair in the units and in the relationship between them. I will then track the roots שו«ב and הל«כ, which appear in four out of the five units. I will then demonstrate the relationship between phrases that appear in some, but not all of the units, by the verb root אכ«ל. Finally, I will address the "dialogue" between the pairs in two full units, 9:1-6 // 12:1-2

---

12. Similarly: Ronald E. Clements, "Patterns in the Prophetic Canon," in *Canon and Authority*, eds. George W. Cots and Burke O. Long (Philadelphia: Fortress, 1977), 42–55, here 46-48, who defines processes based on lexical and thematic similarities. However, Clements implements this method in the framework of different prophetic books in order to demonstrate the canonical reading of the text. As a result he observes in the texts a broad consideration of redemption, not only calamity.

13. Lena-Sofia Tiemeyer, "The Coming of the Lord-An Intertextual Reading of Isa 40:1-11; 52:7-10; 59:15b-20; 62:10-11 and 63:1-6," in *Let Us Go Up to Zion: Essays in Honour of H.G.M. Williamson on the Occasion of his sixty-fifth Birthday*, VTSup 153, eds. Iain W. Provan and Mark J. Boda (Leiden; Boston: Brill, 2012), 233–44.

14. Steve Moyise, "Intertextuality and the Biblical Studies: A Review," *Verbum et ecclesia* 23 (2002): 424–25.

15. Timothy K. Beal, "Ideology and Intertextuality: Surplus of Meaning and Controlling the Means of Production," in *Reading between texts: Intertextuality and the Hebrew Bible*, ed. Danna N. Fewell (Louisville: Westminster John Knox, 1992), 27–39; Ellen van Wolde, "Trendy Intertextuality," in *Intertextuality in Biblical Writings*, ed. Sipke Draisma (Kampen: Kok, 1989), 43–49.

[הפ«כ, יונה, לב, הל«כ, שו«ב], and 7:8–12 // 11:8–11 [רע«י, בית, שוד]. I will explain the meaning instilled in each phrase and root in the context of the specific verse, and the dialogue created through various occurrences.

The recurrences might catch the reader's eye and stimulate the dialogical process presented below, perhaps due to their uniqueness, such as the irregular recurrence of dove or šōd. In other instances, the recurrence of central and familiar phrases demands analysis to uncover meaning, as in the case of the root שו«ב.

RECURRING PHRASES

ASSYRIA AND EGYPT

In several occurrences of this motif, it serves as part of the description of sin. The motif symbolizes Israel's plea for help to Egypt and Assyria, or to foreign gods.[16] Such pleas symbolize attachment to Egypt and Assyria, which is perceived as ungratefulness and betrayal of God. In these cases, Israel contacts these nations willfully, and the motif indicates a distance between God and the nation following the latter's deeds. 9:3 utilizes the same motif to express the emotional distance created between God and the nation, and the punishment for their behavior: Ephraim shall return to Egypt and in Assyria they shall eat unclean food. In this occurrence, God responds to the nation's behavior, and it is God who initiates the nation's undesired contact with Assyria and Egypt as a punishment that indicates distance from God. The relationship with Assyria and Egypt that began as a derivative of the nation's will continues as a derivative of God's will. Finally, the same motif also expresses God's abstention from completely destroying the nation due to God's foundational love, which limits the scope and severity of the punishment: They will be roused like a bird from Egypt, like a dove from the land of Assyria (11:11). In this case, the motif's significance is in preventing its realization; God nullifies the relationship between Israel, Assyria, and Egypt as an outcome of his close personal relationship with the nation, and returns the nation to their land and to him. While the distance between God and the nation due to their relationship with Assyria and Egypt is the

---

16. Hos 7:11: they call upon Egypt and they go to Assyria; 11:5: he will not return to the land of Egypt, rather it is Assyria who is his king because they refused to repent; 12:2: they make a treaty with Assyria and oil is carried to Egypt.

result of the nation's willful action, God is the one to restore and renew the relationship.

שו«וב

In 7:10, the root שׁו"ב (qal perfect 3rd common plural) represents the persistence in Israel's betrayal of God, they do not שָׁבוּ (return) to the LORD their God, or seek him, for all this. 9:3 presents God's response to Israel's betrayal through a wordplay between the root שׁו"ב (qal perfect 3rd masculine singular) and the root יש"ב (qal imperfect 3rd masculine plural):[17] They לֹא יֵשְׁבוּ (shall not dwell) in the land of the LORD; but Ephraim שָׁב (shall return) to Egypt, and in Assyria they shall eat unclean food. God rejects and distances Israel, and the two roots are instilled with physical symbolism. The occurrence in 11:5 can be perceived as a response to the strong rejection expressed in 9:3: "He לֹא יָשׁוּב (will not return) to the land of Egypt; rather it is Assyria who is his king because they refused לָשׁוּב (to repent)."[18] While the words describe a distance between Israel and God, that stems from the fact that Israel did not return to God, this is not an absolute severance and essential nullification of the covenant. This type of distance might have been expressed in the verse if it had also mentioned a return to Egypt.[19] In this verse, the root שׁו"ב

---

17. The verb וְשָׁב might be derived from the root שׁו"ב ("return") or from the root יש"ב ("settle," "sit"), as expressed in the difference between MT and LXX (Francis I. Andersen and David N. Freedman, *Hosea*, AB 24 [New York: Doubleday, 1980], 525). However, see Hans W. Wolff, *Hosea*, trans. G. Stansell, Hermemeia (Philadelphia: Fortress, 1974), 150.

18. However, Mays (*Hosea*, 150) translates the verse: "He returns to the land of Egypt; Assyria—he is his king! Because they refuse to return (to me)." See similarly: Andersen and Freedman, *Hosea*, 583. Lena-Sofia Tiemeyer, *"When God Regrets"* (MA thesis, Hebrew University, 1998), 62, believes the verse should be read as a rhetorical question with a positive answer—"yes, they shall return to Egypt and Assyria." For possible corrections see, e.g., Gert Kwakkel, "Exile in Hosea 9:3-6: Where and for What Purpose?" in *Exile and Suffering*, eds. Bob Becking and Dirk J. Human (Leiden; Boston: Brill, 2009), 130-31; R. Scott Chalmers, *The Struggle of Yahweh and El for Hosea's Israel* (Sheffield: Sheffield Phoenix, 2008), 80.

19. The biblical perception asserting that taking a travelled path in the opposite direction signifies undoing the process represented by that path, would view the description of the new contrasting reality whereby the nation returns to Egypt (vv. 3, 6) as containing a deeper significance of terminating the bond between Israel and God as a result of their sin. Mays, *Hosea*, 126; Uriel Simon, *Reading Prophetic Narratives*, trans. L.J. Schramm (Bloomington: Indiana University Press, 1997), 140-41. See: Wolff, *Hosea*, 159: "Israel will be removed from Yahweh's land—thus experiencing final separation from Yahweh—to the unclean land of Assyria and

has a physical meaning of avoiding returning to Egypt (*qal* imperfect 3rd masculine singular), as well as a spiritual return, or more accurately avoiding return, to God's ways (infinitive).[20] The latter denotation of the root שו"ב might retrospectively affect the interpretation of the root in 9:3. Perhaps the idea that Ephraim שָׁב (shall return) to Egypt is not only a physical description, but also an expression of Israel's trust in and reliance on other nations. Thus, the physical dwelling in Egypt is instilled with symbolic significance of distance from God. Hosea 11:7 creates an opening for a renewal of the relationship between Israel and God: "My people are dependent on מְשׁוּבָתִי (my turning back)."[21] God recognizes the nation's dependence and emphasizes the possibility of a mutual return. Contrary to 7:10 and 11:5, which express the anticipation that the nation will return to God, this verse indicates the possibility that God will be the one to initiate the return, regardless of the nation's behavior. This return is given practical expression in 11:9, where an additional occurrence of the root expresses God's desire to sweeten the verdict, and decision to avoid punishing Israel: I will not execute my burning anger; לֹא אָשׁוּב (I will not again) destroy Ephraim (*qal* imperfect 1st common singular).[22] The practical return is presented in verse 11, through the

---

to the graves of Egypt, in which her entire history of salvation will also be buried," and ibid., 155.

20. In its original context 11:5 is understood by some as describing sin, e.g., Mays, *Hosea*, 155; Wolff, *Hosea*, 194, 200. Conversely, there are those who understand it as a description of punishment, e.g., Andersen and Freedman, *Hosea*, 583–84; Francis Landy, *Hosea*, Readings: a New Biblical Commentary (Sheffield: Sheffield Academic Press, 1995), 139; Hans M. Barstad, "Hosea and the Assyrians," in *"Thus Speaks Ishtar of Arbela": Prophecy in Israel, Assyria, and Egypt in the Neo-Assyrian Period*, eds. R.P. Gordon and Hans M. Barstad (Winona Lake: Eisenbrauns 2013), 99.

21. For מְשׁוּבָתִי denoting God's return to the nation, see for example H.G. May, "Fertility Cult in Hosea," *AJSL* 48 (1932): 83–84. Similarly, see: Andrew A. Macintosh, *Hosea*, ICC 13A.1 (Edinburgh: T&T Clark, 1997), 456. However, he assumes it is the nation who returns to God. וְאֶל עַל יִקְרָאֻהוּ יַחַד לֹא יְרוֹמֵם is a description of the nation's calling out to God. See Douglas K. Stuart, *Hosea-Jonah*, WBC 31 (Waco: Word, 1987), 180–81, who believes that the changes he applied to the verses instill an identical meaning to the one I explicated here. Cf. Gale A. Yee, *Composition and Tradition in the Book of Hosea* (Atlanta: Scholars Press, 1987), 223. See: Jan Joosten, "Targumic Aramaic a'wrm—'oppression' (Isa. XLVII 2, Hos. XI 7, Mic. VI 3)," *VT* 51 (2001): 552–55, who demonstrates the unique reading in Pseudo-Jonathan, which emphasizes the bondage embedded therein.

22. See: Reidar B. Bjornard, "Hosea 11:8–9: God's Word or Man's Insight?" *BR* 27 (1982): 18. Cf. Andersen and Freedman, *Hosea*, 590.

play with the root יש"ב (*hiphil* perfect 1st common singular): "I הוֹשַׁבְתִּים (will place them) in their houses."[23] Although the return anticipated of Israel in 7:10 was not realized, 11:11 describes a return to the primal state, which is the converse of the state described in the context of retribution in 9:3. If the exile from the land expressed distance from God, dwelling in the land expresses the renewed relationship between God and his people.

הל»כ

The root הל»כ in Hosea 7:11 expresses Israel's relationship with Assyria and Egypt (*qal* perfect 3rd common plural): they call upon Egypt but they הָלְכוּ (go) to Assyria.[24] "Going" in this verse expresses an act of trust. The recurrence of the root in verse 12 instills the relationship with these nations with a sense of betrayal of God, and indicates his complete control over his nation in every time and place: "As they יֵלֵכוּ (go), I will cast my net over them" (*qal* imperfect 3rd masculine plural).[25] In 9:6 the root expresses the transition from a destroyed land to exile; in other words, the punishment God will inflict on his nation and the geographical and emotional distance that will result (*qal* perfect 3rd common plural): "For behold, when they have הָלְכוּ (gone) from the devastated land (*šōd*)," Egypt shall gather them, Memphis shall bury them.[26] In this verse, "going" does not symbolize trust, but is rather portrayed as walking with a crouched posture which indicates the nation's

---

23. However, the Septuagint, the Peshitta, and others, translated from the root שו"ב: והשיבותים, which is more appropriate to the particle על (see e.g., William R. Harper, *Amos and Hosea*, ICC 13A.2 (Edinburgh: T&T Clark, 1994), 372; Macintosh, *Hosea*, 467; Wolff, *Hosea*, 193).

24. See Barstad's unique attitude toward Assyria and Egypt in this verse, based on his conceptual perception: Barstad, "Hosea," 96. However, cf. Stuart, *Hosea*, 121; Harper, *Amos and Hosea*, 304, who believe this to be a general objection to the relationship with other nations, not relating to a specific event.

25. Yee, *Composition*, 184, views the lexical repetition as evidence of a redactor's addition. On p. 185, Yee presents the verse as a punishment, but with the purpose of bringing the nation to repent. Cf. Harper, *Amos and Hosea*, 304; Kruger, "Divine Net," 135, who understand the verse as a description of punishment, based on the net imagery at its center.

26. Stuart, *Hosea*, 145, views the word תְּקַבְּצֵם as a reversal of the Exodus from Egypt—instead of gathering the nation to pull them out of Egypt—they are gathered in Egypt to be destroyed. The fact that Memphis was a burial city reinforces the content of the verse (Wolff, *Hosea*, 156; Macintosh, *Hosea*, 349).

severe state. The nature of הל«כ here instills a secondary meaning to previous uses of the root verb: while they are perceived by the nation as a wise step that will reinforce the nation's position, in retrospect this appears to be a turning point that worsens its situation in the future. Additionally, the root הל«כ has a negative connotation in 11:2, where Israel is portrayed as betraying God and placing its faith in others instead (*qal* perfect 3rd common plural): As I called them, they הָלְכוּ (went) from me. In this instance, the betrayal is expressed in idolatry. The final appearance of the root is surprising since it fails to mention the disconnect and distance between God and the nation, and instead emphasizes the connection between them, which is the derivative of a divine initiative (*qal* imperfect 3rd plural): They shall יֵלְכוּ (go) after the LORD, who roars like a lion (11:10).[27] The process that began with "going" that distanced the nation from God ends with a journey that expresses their renewed connection due to God's initiative. Here, the הל«כ reflects the appropriate trust in God, in contrast with all of the previous uses of the root. In this text the nation is no longer following other nations or foreign gods, or in a despondent posture expressing distance from God, but rather reflects the power of God's leadership.

PARTIAL REPETITIONS

אכ«ל

In Hosea 7:9 the root אכ«ל (*qal* perfect 3rd common plural) describes the control of other nations over Israel, and the loss of independent power as a result: "Foreigners אָכְלוּ (devour) his strength, but he does not know it." As a result of their actions, which differ from those described previously, and as a description of the resulting punishment, 9:3–4 utilize the root once more (*qal* imperfect 3 masculine plural; participle masculine plural construct): "Ephraim shall return to Egypt and in Assyria they יֹאכְלוּ (shall eat) unclean food. They shall not pour drink offerings of wine to the LORD, and their sacrifices shall not please him. Such sacrifices shall be like mourners' bread; all אֹכְלָיו (who eat of it) shall be defiled."

The fact that they do not bring their offerings to God's dwelling, eat in a foreign land, and are affected by their actions, attests to the physical

---

27. The recurrence of the root הל"כ in 11:2, 10, is perceived as a reversal by Andersen and Freedman, *Hosea*, 591; Marie T. Wacker, "Father-God, Mother-God, and Beyond: Exegetical Constructions and Deconstructions of Hosea 11," *Lectio difficilior* 2 (2012): 15.

and emotional dismissal of the nation.[28] The use of the root אכ«ל as an expression of distance between God and the nation, and the cultural and religious gap between Israel and the nations, retrospectively alters the meaning of the previous occurrence of the root. If אכ«ל in 7:9 was understood as denoting a political or military blow to Israel's strength, now an additional meaning is instilled, denoting damage to the nation's religious character. In 11:6 the root (*qal* perfect 3rd feminine singular) is an expression of the calamity that will befall the cities of Israel. This calamity is accompanied by the previously described exile, enhancing the punishment: The sword rages in their cities, it consumes their oracle-priests, and וְאָכְלָה (devours), all[[(?)]] because of their counsels.[29] However, another usage precedes this use of the root, which is reminiscent of the initial relationship between God and the nation: "With human cords I drew them, with bonds of love. I was to them like those who lift a baby to their cheeks. I bent down that I might אוֹכִיל (feed) him (4)."[30] This occurrence emphasizes the contrast between the identity of the provider and the quality of the food, compared to previous occurrences of the root. This contrast enhances the positive meaning of the verse. Mentioning the initial relationship in 11:4 demonstrates the distance between the initial and present relationships. On the other hand, it emphasizes the close relationship even in this difficult time, and creates hope that the relationship may be renewed in the future.

Whole Units

Three recurring phrases appear in units 9:1–6 and 12:1–2 of Hosea: רע«י, בית, שוד. In 9:1–6 the recurring phrases are included in the description of the punishment: threshing floor and wine vat לֹא יִרְעֵם (shall not give attention to them) (v. 2);[31] it shall not come to בֵּית (the house) of the LORD

---

28. For the symbolic meaning of eating unclean food and its effect on the nation's status, see: J. Andrew Dearman, *Hosea*, NICOT (Grand Rapids: Eerdmans, 2012), 238; Stuart, *Hosea*, 143; Andersen and Freedman, *Hosea*, 520.

29. The powerful impression of the destruction that will befall Israel is magnified with the sound play of the verbs וְחָלָה / וְכִלְתָה / וְאָכְלָה; see: Landy, *Hosea*, 140.

30. Mays, *Hosea*, 150; Wacker, "Father," 2–3, for example, translates as "feed"; and cf. Andersen and Freedman, *Hosea*, 582–83. Wacker, "Father," 4–5, emphasizes the ramifications of these readings on the mother's presence in the unit instead of the father. See also: Morris, *Prophecy*, 71, on Hosea's application of "a repetition of sound with variant spelling and meaning - in simple terms, wordplay."

31. Regarding the verb יִרְעֵם, derived from the root רע«י denoting "to tend to the needs of others," see e.g., Stuart, *Hosea*, 142; Dearman, *Hosea*, 237 n. 72; however, cf. Macintosh,

(v. 4); and "For behold, when they have gone from שֹׁד (the devastated land), Egypt shall gather them, Memphis shall bury them (v. 6)." These are, in fact, linked with the three stages of punishment: preventing agriculture in the land (רע«י), destroying the land (שוד), and exile (בית). In chapter 12 the very same phrases are used to describe the sin: "Ephraim has surrounded me with deceit, and בֵּית (the house) of Israel with treachery (v. 1), Ephraim רֹעֶה (concerns himself) with wind—he pursues an east wind everyday; he multiplies lies and שֹׁד (havoc) (v. 2)." The relationship between the units reinforces the relationship between sin and punishment, and the justification for punishment. For example, the lexical repetition creates the following connection: since Israel is characterized as engaging in lies and שֹׁד (havoc), they are likely to go from the devastated land, שֹׁד, to Egypt. Interestingly, as in other units, the sins differ in each of the texts, and a link is created between the political sin (v. 12) and the punishment for the sin of idolatry (v. 9). Therefore, the relationship between the units also links various sins which are perceived similarly as betrayal throughout Hosea.

7:8–12 // 11:8–11

The dialogue between recurring phrases in Hosea 7:8–12 and 11:8–11 correlates with the nature of the dialogues demonstrated above and advances the discussion toward the formulation of the overall conclusion regarding dialogues between the units: the unit in chapter 7 describes the relationship Israel forged with Assyria and Egypt. This relationship is criticized in the unit both for its inefficacy and for the fact that it negates a relationship with God and is perceived as betrayal. Ephraim is described as a cake not הֲפוּכָה (turned) (7:8), and criticized for the lack of ability to withstand the challenges ahead. The description "Like יוֹנָה (a dove) gullible and without לֵב (sense), they call upon Egypt, they הָלְכוּ (go) to Assyria" (7:11) is an expression of lack of judgment behind their political choices. Despite God's call to return, their choice is that they do not שָׁבוּ (return) to the LORD their God (7:10). Contrary to their use here, the recurring phrases in the unit in chapter 11 express the reversal in the relationship between God and his people. Moreover, the majority of roots describing the nation in the first unit are used to describe God in the second: the description לִבִּי (my heart) נֶהְפַּךְ (recoils) within me in verse 8 presents

---

Hosea, 340, who derives it instead from רע"י III denoting desire. Wolff, Hosea, 211, instills the occurrence in 12:2 with the meaning of רע"י II, "to associate with." For this debate see e.g., HALOT, 3:1262; DCH 7:520.

God's change of heart and his grief for the nation he had decided to pun-
ish.[32] In verse 9 the desire to avoid destroying the nation, despite their
sins, is expressed by the root שו«ב: "I will not execute my burning anger;
לֹא אָשׁוּב (I will not again) destroy Ephraim." Parallel to Israel pursuing
the nations (הל«כ), which expressed the disconnect between Israel and
God, verse 10 describes the nation's pursuit of God: "They יֵלְכוּ (shall go)
after the LORD, who roars like a lion." This pursuit is a derivative of God's
will to return the nation to the land, and to him: "They will be roused like
a bird from Egypt like יוֹנָה (a dove) from the land of Assyria (v. 11)." The
same "gullible dove" that represented Israel's lack of stability and betrayal
of God in the first unit, follows God back to the land as an expression of
the renewed relationship.[33]

POSSIBLE IMPLICATIONS OF THE
DIALOGUES BETWEEN TEXTS

THE RELATIONSHIP BETWEEN GOD AND THE NATION

All five units include lexical recurrences. However, instead of signifying
resemblance, the linguistic occurrences express a development in God's
relationship with Israel through various components such as sin, punishment, and redemption. In correlation, the repetitions include syntactic,

---

32. The root הפ"כ in the context of the verse is part of a representation of the tradition
of Sodom and Gomorrah (Tiemeyer, "When God Regrets," 63; Fields, Sodom, 161). The
root הפ"כ is utilized to express the will of God instead of the nation's punishment, as
part of the dual utilization of the motif in the unit; see Wolff, Hosea, 201; Jopie Siebert-
Hommes, "'With Bands of Love': Hosea 11 as 'Recapitulation' of the Basic Themes in the
Book of Hosea," in Unless Some One Guide Me, eds. J.W. Dyk et al. (Maastricht: Shaker,
2001), 171. The root הפ"כ here therefore denotes change, not an overthrow. Cf. Fisch,
Poetry, 142. See also: J. Gerald Janzen, "Metaphor and reality in Hosea 11," Semeia 24
(1982): 27–29. נְחוּמָי expresses God's compassion for his people; see Tiemeyer, "When
God Regrets," 65; ibid., "God's Hidden Compassion," TynBul 57 (2006): 198.
33. Göran Eidevall, "Lions and Birds as Literature: Some Notes on Isaiah 31 and Hosea
11," SJOT 7 (1993): 83; Grace I. Emmerson, Hosea: An Israelite Prophet in Judean Perspective
(Sheffield: JSOT, 1984), 42. Kruger, "Divine Net," 134, demonstrates the relationship between the two occurrences of the dove in the book (7:11, 9:11), as part of the illustration
of the relationship between imagery throughout the book. According to Kruger, one
occurrence of imagery prepares the ground for the appearance of another, in a variety
of ways. In fact, Kruger's approach toward imagery applies a synchronic approach to
the book, relating among other things to the relationship between and mutual effect
of recurring imagery. His approach is founded on the presumption that "images do
not exist in isolation, they are strung together to constitute a structured whole" (ibid.).

grammatical, and content variations. The various components are connected through the repetitions, which unravel the unit's boundaries, and prevents a view of the various stages as independent content.[34] Thus, the complete calamity described in 9:1-6, for example, is not just an independent principal, but also part of a process that ends with the return to God; going to Egypt (9:6 הָלְכוּ) ends when the nation follows God back to the land (11:10 יֵלְכוּ). Returning from exile in 11:8-11, for example, is not an independent message, but rather a derivative of sin and subsequent calamity, and the return to the relationship described at the start of the process; returning to dwell in their homes(11:11 הוֹשַׁבְתִּים) leans on the return to Egypt (9:3 שָׁב) and the refusal to "return" to God (7:10 וְלֹא שָׁבוּ). In correlation, a dialogical reading of the lexical recurrences prevents the view of one component as the be-all, end-all; the repetition prevents the possibility of viewing either the calamity or the redemption as representative of the entire relationship, and enforces a view of the totality of details as an expression of the relationship between God and his nation. Creating a context-based process between the units by using these recurrences therefore enables one to view the legal and emotional foundation of this process, as well as its potential. It enables a view of the shared foundation of various actions by God and the nation, and binds them into a relationship in which God and the nation are intertwined. This process also provides context for various points in the historical sequence, and imbeds them in the personal bonds of love that exist between God and his nation, thus instilling meaning in the individual components, and indicating the positive future relationship between God and the nation. The broader prism of the relationship created by this reading enables one to place the individual or national relationship with God in a broader context, which can be relatable in any era.

---

34. Barstad, "Hosea," 95, points to the fact that in the book of Hosea the calamity and redemption are intertwined (similarly: Andersen and Freedman, *Hosea*, 51-52). See the essential discussion regarding the possible existence of prophecies of calamity and redemption in one layer of authorship in: Hugh G.M. Williamson, "Isaiah: Prophet of Weal or Woe?" in *"Thus Speaks Ishtar of Arbela": Prophecy in Israel, Assyria, and Egypt in the Neo-Assyrian Period*, eds. R.P. Gordon and Hans M. Barstad (Winona Lake: Eisenbrauns, 2013), 283-84. Cf. Clements, "Patterns," 50-51, who emphasizes the possibility of viewing both layers in one book, particularly in the book of Hosea, but conversely also relates to the meaning of maintaining the two types of prophecies in different layers of the canonic text. Yee, *Composition*, 310-11, attributes the combination of verses and chapters that reflect the altered relationship between God and his nation and inspire hope to the presently-exiled nation to the second redactor.

As I mentioned earlier, in a dialogical reading, the units do not stand independently, or serve only the purpose for which they were authored, but also represent stages in the process of which they are a part. This relationship deepens the meaning of each of the units, and shifts its independent significance to part of a whole that creates new meaning. However, a dialogical reading does not uproot the original meaning of the unit, but rather adds an additional layer to the reading of a modern reader.

Ideological Insights

The abovementioned process, and its various components, define principles related to the relationship between God and the nation of Israel. For example, according to the dialogues, the nation is presented as sinning and not returning to God at any stage. God is portrayed as the one who punishes, with an emphasis on the fact that the punishment is just. However, God does not anticipate the nation's return, and instead initiates bringing about their return, based on the earlier relationship. The root שו«ב is a fine application of this principle: throughout the units, the root שו«ב specifically describes the nation who fails to return to God and instead betrays him (7:10; 11:5), and in correlation describes the justice of returning them to Egypt and/or Assyria (9:3, 11:5). Eventually the root even describes the nation's return to the land by the hands of God (11:11). While the root *could have been* used to describe the nation's return to God, this is avoided; nonetheless, the punishment is cut short, and the nation is returned to its land.[35]

These dialogues also demonstrate the essential relationship between God and the nation, a relationship that is in fact the reason for a renewal of the relationship despite the nation's stagnancy, and is a source of great disappointment from the sinning nation, with the definition of its sins as betrayal. A good example can be found in the recurring root אכ«ל, which is used to describe the sin (7:9), the punishment (9:3-4; 11:6), and the essential relationship between God and the nation (11:4).

As briefly mentioned in the analysis of the units, the lexical recurrences and the relationship between the units also create a connection between seemingly unrelated phenomena, such as idolatry, and turning to foreign nations for assistance—for which Assyria and Egypt are the clearest and most relevant examples from the prophet's era. Linking the phenomena creates a unified principle, namely, the betrayal of God,

---

35. Mays, *Hosea*, 159.

which is the root of all sin in Hosea, and it indicates the unique meaning instilled in the relationship between God and the nation in this book. For example, 7:11 utilizes the root הל«ל» as an expression of the reliance on foreign nations, and 11:2 utilizes the same root to describe the reliance on foreign gods. The relationship between the two also serves to emphasize the justice of the divine punishment, through the use of a single root to describe sin and punishment.

Interestingly, while a dynamic-synchronic reading yields an interpretation of phrases that differs from their original meaning, some of the ideological insights that emerge from a dynamic-synchronic reading of the units actually correlates with ideological insights that characterize the book of Hosea, both in the reading of independent units, and in the formulation of broad characteristic principles. The ideological correlation reinforces the modern interpretation of the text, even if such a correlation is not required.

The Modern Reader and the Prophetic Text

While the interpretive conclusions presented above relate only to the book of Hosea and the examples analyzed in this text, the reading method described in this paper contributes to the definition of an essential relationship between the reader and the text, particularly between the modern reader and the prophetic text. The complex relationship between God and the nation formulated above was not presented on the surface of the text, but is rather a derivative of the dialogue between the units. A person who reads the units in their entirety uncovers the links, places each phrase in its rightful place in the sequence of texts, and defines the ideological perceptions that emerge from the links between the units. These ideological insights are embedded in the units and in the links that bind them; however, the extraction of the meaning is only enabled by the reader's participation in the process.

The fact that this is a fixed text—since this paper discussed the canonical text of Hosea—emphasizes its characterization as a text that is embedded in its past. As I stated earlier, the independent reading of the units preserves this status. For this very reason, the way to revive the text and instill it with new meaning is to read the units side by side and examine their effect on one another. In other words, creating dynamic dialogues between the units and reading them in this light enables modern readers to become involved in the ancient text, and to some extent, turn them into part of the rewriting of the text without damaging the fabric of the original text. In fact, this paper demonstrates the dynamic movement of the units both in the horizontal axis within the book, and the vertical axis that develops in time: horizontally, this study demonstrated the relationship between the units and the manner in which a dialogue between them breaks the boundaries of the units and links them while defining a dynamic process. This horizontal dynamic also extracts the units from the historical context in which they were written. This extraction is performed by the modern reader, who is also connected to the texts through the process, instilling the units with new meaning. The five units discussed above are an example of the manner in which the reader might awaken the units and take them out of context, thus reviving them.

What justifies the modern dynamic reading of this fixed text? What is the foundation of the renewed reading of canonical texts, in a manner that does not correlate with the original meaning of the individual units? The dynamic reading and the renewed interpretation stem from the characteristic of biblical poetry, which invites the reader to become involved in the text and uncover layers of meaning. However, these take on unique meaning when applied in prophetic literature due to its specific characteristics and objectives. Firstly, the purpose of classic prophecy was to reflect reality from a moral perspective, and rouse the nation to another perspective on its reality. The prophet sought to involve the nation, and to open their hearts to his message. The multiple rhetorical means applied by the prophets attest to the purpose of prophetic activity, including the purpose of the poetic prophecies documented in prophetic works. However, this paper expands the basic principles of prophetic literature, and enables the reader not only to become involved in one limited prophetic unit, but rather to connect the units based on clear lexical criteria, in order to extract new meaning that deviates from the original intent of the units. This type of intervention by the reader characterizes the stage of written prophecy. In effect, the reader, who becomes involved in the units and creates new meaning, continues the prophet's work, which does not end with sounding the prophecies, but rather moves forward on another path from the moment they are written.

A discussion of the relationship between the units does not emerge only from the limitations of the modern reader, who approaches a fixed text in which the units can no longer be expanded, but also from the advantages of the modern reader's perspective. As David Carr has asserted, the reading of a biblical text as a whole was not possible for the ancient audience, and thus was irrelevant. It is specifically the modern reader, with his ability to view the text in its entirety, who can read, analyze, and apply these reading methods.[36] According to Clements, the canonical text has another effect on the type of modern reading suggested above: the very creation of a canon reflects the ability and the need to read the texts in their entirety (whether in one book, or multiple books) while maintaining an interpretive link between them that affects the interpretation of the texts through their unification.[37] While these interpretations do not reflect the original meaning of the units, they are legitimate once the units are assembled in the canonical text.

Secondly, the freedom that enables a renewed interpretation is not entirely novel; this phenomenon exists even in the prophetic works themselves, and is expressed in the redaction of the text, its canonization, and the additions embedded throughout the centuries. The same can be said of the relationship between the New and Old Testaments, as Wolff indicates in his discussion of the manner in which Hosea's messages in chapter 11 are broadly embedded in John (1 John 4:8, 16) or Paul (Rom 5:20).[38]

These phenomena reflect a prophetic principle according to which the prophet's words are perceived as a representation of God's words, but since they are directed at man, he can use them as he pleases. Approaching the prophetic text with interpretive freedom is a methodological reflection of its content and premise: the future transmitted in classic prophecies is not a description of future deterministic realities, and cannot be realized by God alone, according to his will. The prophecies are given to the people, and are susceptible to human intervention which affects the realization of their content. Just as the content of the prophecies is not fixed, so too their formulation and meaning. The interpretive freedom creates hope and persistent change, instead of portraying prophetic works as determining a clear future which is the application of a divine edict that simply restricts human freedom.[39]

---

36. David M. Carr, "Reading Isaiah from Beginning (Isaiah 1) to End (Isaiah 65–66): Multiple Modern Possibilities." in *New Visions of Isaiah*, eds. Roy F. Melugin and Marvin A. Sweeney (Sheffield: Sheffield Academic Press, 1996), 214–16. However, cf. Stulac, *History*, 85.

37. Clements, "Patterns," 48–49.

38. Wolff, *Hosea*, 204. See also: Clements, "Patterns," 43–45.

39. Ronald E. Clements, "Who Is Blind but My Servant?" (Isaiah 42:19): How Then Shall We Read Isaiah?" in *God in the Fray*, eds. Tod. Linafelt and Timothy K. Beal (Minneapolis: Fortress, 1998), 156.

Part Two

—

Contemporary Poetry in Dialogue

10

Poetry's Outstretched Hand

Richard G. Rohlfing Jr.

Both the reader and the interpreter of the Bible must alert their imagination when they read or study the biblical poetry. What has been written with imagination, must also be read with imagination, provided the individual has imagination and it is in working order.[1]

The following interlude of ten poems is presented as an invitation to the imagination. Biblical Hebrew poetry has, indeed, been written with imagination and it demands the depth of our own imaginative and existential engagement. Deep calls to deep, and we may suddenly find ourselves struggling to respond in a way commensurate to the depths of that call as it resounds within us. We may find our hearts soaring or grieving or completely bewildered. Our affective realm, so habitually marginalized or left latent, nevertheless stirs. To this end, perhaps there is a thing that only a poem or song can do.

The well-known injunction of *Mishnah Pesachim* 10.5, "to see oneself as one who personally went out from Egypt," is raised up as a guidepost before the first poem in this collection. In the spirit of this Mishnah, the majority of the poems selected for this volume are written in the first person: the participatory *me*; the *we* of liturgy. These little pronouns are gifts, so easily overlooked. They allow for adaptation, reuse, and personal performance. Murray Lichtenstein has described the effects of the Song of the Sea as it "move[s] the listener in and out of the event, surrealistically

---

1. Luis Alonso Schökel, *A Manual of Hebrew Poetics*. SubBi, 11 (Rome: Pontifical Biblical Institute, 1988), 104.

overriding the constraints of time and space."[2] We hope that you too will be moved. Edward Hirsch articulates the vocation of poetry as, "the outstretched hand of transfiguration."[3] Poetry invites us in, but it does not leave us as we are.

Our intent was to curate a collection of poems that was as much as possible organic to the originating context of the essays as it was a contemporary engagement with the poetry of the Hebrew Bible. For this reason, most of the poems selected for inclusion in this section were written by those in attendance at the New Song conference (Symmons-Roberts, Briggs, Rohlfing, Stein, Austin, Apichella).[4] The poetry of Edward Clarke and Jacqueline Osherow, however, was specifically sought out for inclusion since their work constitutes a vital contemporary conversation with Biblical Hebrew poetry.

Clarke refers to his *A Book of Psalms* as conversations with the Psalter, not so much translation as "transplantations." As such his work is an interesting conversation partner to the essay of June Dickie on Psalms "Translated" for life in the twenty-first century. His transplantation of Psalm 43 "Dear Inmost Soul" is a fruitful extension of Ellen Davis's reflections on and translation of Psalms 42–43. Osherow's "Darkness/Wings" is the fourth of her "Scattered Psalms" found in the collection, *Dead Men's Praise*. She leads us out into the untamed topography of the Bible's poetry where paradoxes shoot up like wildflowers and contrastive imagery, like some beautiful burr, snags upon our readerly imaginations. Her poetry is midrashic exegesis which, above all, encourages us to wonder. "Darkness/Wings" wrestles with a question which befits the volume, and often exercises parents trying to pass on the mysteries of the faith: "What do I tell / My daughter?" She does so with a haunting admixture of wit and pathos. At the level of content this poem pairs well with Katie Heffelfinger's essay "Truth and Hidden Things."

An attempt has been made to arrange the poems in relation to the general movement and themes of the essays. We begin with Richard S. Briggs riffing us through the biblical story in "The Song After the Night Before."

---

2. Murray Lichtenstein, "Biblical Poetry," in *Back to the Sources*, ed. Barry Holtz (2008), 113. Poetry collapses time, as Ben Sommer shows us, making the past somehow inhabitable.

3. Edward Hirsch, *How to Read a Poem: And Fall in Love with Poetry* (San Diego: Harvest Books/Harcourt, 2000), 60.

4. Micheal O'Siadhail, though not present at the conference, has offered up the perceptive response of a practicing poet to the *New Song* essays.

We are then gut-punched by Michael Symmons Roberts's poetic inhabiting of a well-known Genesis narrative with "Choreography." "Out of Our Depth" is my own personal answer in poem-form to *Mishnah Pesachim* 10.5. The poetry then moves into conversation with various psalms (Clarke and Stein), with longing, lament, bewilderment, and exile (Austin, Osherow, O'Siadhail), before turning finally to praise (Apichella). The whole section concludes with a transliteration and translation of the medieval Jewish hymn, *Adon Olam*. This is both a gesture toward the rich tradition of liturgical Jewish poetry, which stretches well beyond the biblical period, and also an opportunity, irrespective of Hebrew competency, for readers to sound out the sonorous Hebrew rhythm and rhyme.[5] Though we could suggest further points of connection between these poems and the volume's essays, such intertextual resonances seem better left to the reader's own reflections.

As stated in the introduction, the blending of poets in this section, the amateur alongside the accomplished, is purposeful. Unless otherwise noted, the poems in this section are original works received through the New Song conference. We hope this encourages you to respond with prayerful, perhaps even poetic, participation; responding to the depths of biblical Hebrew poetry with the depths of imaginative seriousness it calls for.[6]

---

5. Benjamin Sommer discusses the eight-syllable pattern of *Adon Olam* in chapter six of this volume, "Prosody and Preaching." The version I engage with is the Ashkenazi-Italian version. I would also like to register my thanks to Prof. Sommer for his thoughtful responses to my translation of *Adon Olam*. I gleaned much from his insights, encouragements, and constructive criticism. Of course, all shortcomings in translation remain my own.

6. "Full imaginative seriousness" is a phrase used by Walter Moberly to describe the need for interpretive diligence in order to imaginatively enter into the world of the text. Moberly gives an account of this concept in relation to second naiveté and the possibility of transformative encounter by means of immersion in the textual world in R.W.L. Moberly, *The God of the Old Testament*, (Grand Rapids: Baker Academic, 2020), 6–7. See also R.W.L. Moberly, *Old Testament Theology: Reading the Hebrew Bible as Christian Scripture* (Grand Rapids: Baker Academic, 2013), 285.

THE SONG AFTER THE NIGHT BEFORE

בְּכָל דּוֹר וָדוֹר חַיָּב אָדָם לִרְאוֹת אֶת עַצְמוֹ כְּאִלּוּ הוּא יָצָא מִמִּצְרַיִם

"In every generation one is obligated to see oneself
as one who personally went out from Egypt."

Mishnah Pesachim 10.5

(i) Genesis 3
One day out of Eden
All is not lost
We still have each other
Though Adam seems distracted
Asks who brought the fruit? And what are these skins for?
And is work, seriously, what it is going to be about?
He thinks *he* has problems, I say, *sotto voce*

(ii) Exodus 15
One day out of Egypt
All is not lost
No really – we have so much to be thankful for!
Sorry, I can't hear myself think
With the song of the sea
And the roaring of the sea
And the nothing ever going to be the same again

(iii) Exodus 33
One day after the golden calf
All is not lost ... I think
There was a lot of talking at the front of the camp
Moses was angry. God was angry. It is hard to tell the difference
Confident men say we learn from our mistakes
And will never do that again.
The wise are saying nothing.

(iv) 1 Samuel 21
One day out in the wilderness with David
All is not lost
We fly by night
We take food where we find it
Though whether showbread is fair game causes some dispute
And we circle endlessly around Saul, the Lord's anointed
Wondering where the anointing will land

(v) 1 Kings 12
     One day after the split
     All is not lost
     Though these new border checkpoints
     Were a thing that should not have been in Israel
     Or Judah, or whatever we are going to call it now
     And there are a lot of broken hearts on the ground
     Not that you would know that from the politicians

(vi) 2 Kings 25
     One day out of Jerusalem
     –Ach–
     All is lost

(vii) Ezra-Nehemiah
     We read the law
     We build the walls
     Life goes on
     Never the same again, again?

                                        Richard S. Briggs

CHOREOGRAPHY

His fist smashes my face.
That's no wrestler's move;
so it's bare knuckles now. Okay.

There's blood in my eye,
the lid swells to a hood.
I use my head and butt him.

His lips bloom like a rose,
but he's still ticking, clicking
his tongue on the roof of his mouth.

Gamesmanship: the harder
I hit, the louder he clicks.
We raise the stakes:

he jabs me on the nose
to get my hands up,
then with otherworldly speed

he lands a right hand in my guts.
Agony: I'm folded,
dumbstruck, gasping like a fish.

He backs off a moment,
then he knees me in the jaw.
My teeth split the tip of my tongue.

I'm spitting now, incensed.
I grab two fistfuls of his shirt,
swing my foot behind his legs.

Shove. He staggers, falls
with me on top of him.
We've landed in the Jabbok creek.
I dunk his face to cool him off,
to make him choke and talk.
He comes up clicking still;

I slap him. He stares at me.
Are angels speechless? This one's
wingless, solid without weight.

Perhaps he's trying to talk?
It could be 't' or 'c': some stammering
Gabriel with a message?

I relax my grip to listen,
he sees his chance and turns us,
rolls me in the stream,

taps the hollow of my thigh,
and something gives. He helps
me up. He's damaged me.

Somehow he's slid my hip
out of its bone-cup, left me
clipped and limping.

When I stand, his clicking stops.
It dawns on me; that was no stutter,
but a beat. The dance is over.

'You had me there', he says
'I had to do your leg to settle things.'
He brushes off his shirt,

I hobble to the water's edge to wash.
I shout to him 'What was your name?'
I don't know if he hears me.

                              Michael Symmons Roberts

OUT OF OUR DEPTH

What will wipe from us
    the Nile's blood?
Clear from our nostrils
    the stench of creation
    undone?

Silence the violent voices vaunting,
    This deliverance
    is nothing
    ...a snake in hand,
    ...a teeming of randy quails
    out on the horizon, bah!
    ...the blast
    of a ram's horn
    high on a mountain

Perhaps in this bane
    one becomes a son?

He
    brews the sea
    differently
Whipping up
    a wild East wind

We
    bruise our heels
    suddenly
We
    reeds still shuddering

We
    no trite tune for
    a timbrel
    singing,
        He shakes the *whole earth*
        like a drum!

We, a mere vapor
We, stars crossing
We, the dregs,
    spewed from Ba'al Tsephon
We, a dry seed
    fell from Haran
We but look on,
    trembling at the work
    of our ancestors' god,
    wandering, wondering,
      what have you become?
We, like those who dream,
    as a word *de profundis*
    stammers out
    over *S'fat Ha Yam*
    mi kamoka ba'ēlim Adonay?
as if from lips just circumcised
    as if,
    our eternal reprise

                                Richard G. Rohlfing Jr.

43 - DEAR INMOST SOUL

The Sons of Korah II

I'm at the end of a question asked
Right at the heart of your deep heart.
   'Why art
   Thou cast
Down, O my soul?' I ask, that I
Might climb, with someone else's harp,
The shaft of truths that lie
In light that's at the mouth of my heart.
How crouched you are to make your murmur,
   Dear inmost soul of mine:
Extend your hands a little further,
You might just touch a face divine.

Edward Clarke

PSALM 132

"Obedience has a history"
Eugene Peterson

A bit of history always helps
that half time pep talk, when you've missed
a chance, a goal, and now the wind
is in your face, the going hard.

Obedience has a long track record
in the storied lives of women,
men like David who knew hardship,
failed and found God's faithfulness.

For everyone a resting point,
a halfway house, a half time break
– including God, who rests in Zion,
leaving us to find that place.

A lamp, a long obedience,
a story making light and sense
of suffering in the present tense.

Jock Stein

LAST WILL AND TESTAMENT

Arrange for me a final tenancy
where I may dwell unmoved within the ground
until the year of Jubilee comes round
and every slave to death at last goes free.
Contract me to a small security,
a safe deposit in a six foot mound
by solemn covenant with Hades bound,
until the last return of Jubilee.

Give me a dark and quiet place to stay,
nor grudge me that I wander here no more
looking for temporary room and board
as long as evening is the end of day.
O let me rest a while from life's rigour
till God alone is landlord of the world!

                                        Kilby Austin

DARKNESS / WINGS

He mounted a cherub and flew, He swooped on the wings of the
wind. He made darkness His concealment, round Him
His shelter–the darkness of water, the clouds of heaven.
Psalm 18:11–12

You will light my lamp, God, my God, illuminate my darkness.
Psalms 18:29

I'll tell my daughter
Don't be afraid
It's only God
Hiding Himself
No need to worry yourself
About the dark
Imagine He's a rider
In a deep black cloth
What would lurk
In such a path?

And if she asks why God
Needs a hiding place?
Whom He's hiding from?
Who would know His face?
Do I tell the truth
Or keep it simple?
I could quote the psalm
For example
Fiery wrath
Wings outspread

But why the wings?
Why the cherub?
Why does God
Need a ride?
And what's it like
Mounting a cherub?

Does he buck
And flail his wings
Or nod
And glide?

And where
Will he alight?
Does he go far?
Maybe at the center
Of a dark ex-star
Whose energy
Gravity?
Is so compact
It's far too strict
To let out light

A lamp unto my feet
Concealed in darkness
A light
To illuminate
The dark
A whirl of black
Its mass
So dense
That it was once
Pure light

Maybe each black hole
Is God concealed?
What do I tell
My daughter?
If the light's let out
What exactly is revealed?
Darkness of water
Darkness of cloud
Don't be afraid
It's only God

Jacqueline Osherow

STRETCHING

So is all history one secret narrative of power
Broken in the brick and rubble of Babel's tower?

Hard-bitten Atlas, our hands thrown in the air
Are we too disillusioned now to bother to care?

Our stories become labyrinths of irony that turn
On irony. Fiddlers fiddling while a world may burn.

He breaks me down on every side and I am gone
O you who stalked the barren road to Babylon

Or walked the desert as second Jerusalem fell
And Titus of Vesuvius shattered Herod's temple

Show us again some end to shape our storyline.
A feast of rich food and well-aged wine ...

Isaiah's imagination stretches somehow to cope;
In Jeremiah's darkest scroll a jazz of hope

That stirs even in the deepest cries of silence:
Then shall the young women rejoice in the dance.

Micheal O'Siadhail

93

Before I die I want to roar
a song that judders
my neighbor's walls,
shakes you, my big-
eared God and stirs
David from his sleep.

I can't play the sax
I can't bang a drum
I can't work the flute
I can't pick the harp
but I can respond.

Maria Apichella

ADON OLAM

Adon 'olam, 'asher malakh	Lord of spacetime, who did reign
b'terem kol yetzir niv'ra	before into being all creation came
L'et na'sa v'ḥeftso kol,	When all was made in his good pleasure
Azai melekh sh'mo nikra	Then *King* his name was proclaimed
V'aḥ'rey kikh'lot hakol	And after the end of all we know
L'vado y'imlokh nora	Almighty, awesome, will he yet rule
V'hu hayah v'hu hoveh	He was, and he is
V'hu yih'yeh b'tif'arah	And he will be, arrayed in holy majesty
V'hu 'eḥad v'eyn sheyni	And he is One, there is no 'Two'
L'ham'shil lo l'haḥbirah	To compare him with, his ally be
B'li reyshiyt b'li taḥliyt	Without beginning, without end
V'lo ha'oz v'hamis'rah	His the power and the sovereignty
V'hu 'Eli v'ḥay go'ali	He is my God, my redeemer lives
v'tsur ḥevli b'eit tsarah	Rock against sorrow in time of distress
V'hu nisi 'umanos li	He my banner, a refuge to me
m'nat kosi b'yom 'ekra	Portion of my cup, in the day I call
B'yado af'kid ruḥi	Into his hand I entrust my all
b'et 'ishan v'a'ira	When I sleep, when I awake
v'im ruḥi g'viyati	And with my spirit, in my dying hour
Adonay li v'lo 'ira	The Lord is mine, I shall not fear

A Medieval Jewish Liturgical hymn, or *piyut*
Authorship unknown[7]

Integral to worship services in Jewish communities around the world for centuries, this hymn has also been associated with prayers around the deathbed.

---

7. Though *Adon Olam* has been attributed to Solomon ibn Gabirol, there does not seem to be concrete evidence for the attribution. Public domain.

Part Three

—

Responses

11

Response 1:
A Song "Forever New" in the Psalms

Susan Gillingham

What did the psalmists mean when they referred to a "new song?" The term is used in six psalms. I ask this question because it has not been asked explicitly in any of the other papers, although the evidence for a new song has been taken for granted. Indeed, this is not only part of the title of this publication but also the heading over Michael Symmons Roberts's initial poem, which speaks of a "new song" as a raw compulsion, singing "what you never could say," in good times and bad.

Most contributors have emphasized our need to bring "something new" out of ancient and often mysterious biblical poems. John Goldingay does this with Genesis 49, seeing the text as a collective replay of remembered tribal traditions for a later age. Robert Hayward, in examining the early Jewish and Christian liturgical use of Exodus 15, argues that its central role in worship is evidence of it being "forever new." David Firth reads Hannah's prayer 1 Samuel 2 in a similar way: its "Magnificat-like" emphasis on exalting the lowly is a theme found not only in the rest of 1–2 Samuel, but lives on in later Jewish and Christian texts. Other authors find the "newness" in the contemporary performance of selected psalms (for example Ellen Davis, especially using Psalms 38 and 42–3; Benjamin Sommer, focusing on Psalms 27 and 114; and Shah Held, on Psalm 88). Others see this is in the continuing relevance, through the ambiguity of the poetry, of texts such as Isaiah 45 (Katie Heffelfinger) and Hosea 7–12 (Yisca Zimran). June Dickie notes that "newness" is always a challenge in translation, as seen for example when translating Psalms 133 and 134 into Zulu. A wide spectrum is covered here: but no author has given an account of that actual phrase, "new song," a term used almost exclusively in the Psalter.[1]

The fact that the phrase occurs primarily in psalmody suggests that this is a liturgical formula. If so, it was adapted in many different ways. It is found in two psalms near the end of Book One, two psalms in the middle of Book Four, and two psalms near the end of Book Five.[2] The six examples are as follows:[3]

> Sing to him a **new song** (שִׁיר חָדָשׁ);
>> play skillfully on the strings, with loud shouts.
>
> Psalm 33:3

> He put a **new song** in my mouth,
>> a song of praise to our God.
> Many will see and fear,
>> and put their trust in the LORD.
>
> Psalm 40:3

> O sing to the LORD a **new song**;
>> sing to the LORD, all the earth.
>
> Psalm 96:1

> O sing to the LORD a **new song**,
>> for he has done marvelous things.
> His right hand and his holy arm have gotten him victory.
>
> Psalm 98:1

> I will sing a **new song** to you, O God;
>> upon a ten-stringed harp I will play to you.
>
> Psalm 144:9

---

1. The exhortation to sing a "new song" occurs also in Isa 42:10; Judg 16:1; and Rev 5:9 and 14:3.

2. Interestingly it does not occur in Book Two, with its more nostalgic tone of longing for Jerusalem and vindication from suffering, nor in Book Three, with its harsher judgmental tone in remembering the destruction of both the northern and southern kingdoms.

3. The translation and versification used here is from the NRSV.

Praise the LORD!
Sing to the LORD a **new song**,
>   his praise in the assembly of the faithful.

Psalm 149:1

Four of these references are exhortations to the congregation to sing the song with the psalmist (Psalms 33, 96, 98 and 149). Two psalms (33 and 144) also refer to the new song being accompanied by stringed instruments. So other than Psalm 40 (whose peculiar character we shall consider later), the new song clearly appears within a liturgical context.[4]

Is there any common theme that might point to the content of this new song? Four psalms praise God's sovereignty over the cosmos (Psalms 33, 96, 98, 149), but praise of God as Creator is also found in other "creation hymns" such as Psalms 8, 19, 29, and 104, and in other kingship hymns such as Psalms 95, 97, and 99. Another shared theme might be the belief that God is about to bring in a "new thing" (עֹשֶׂה חֲדָשָׁה) in history.[5] Each psalm, however, expresses this differently. In Psalm 33, this comes through the created order; in Psalm 40, it is in the life of the individual; in Psalms 96 and 98, it is on account of God's universal rule as King; in Psalm 144, it includes the restitution of the poor; and in Psalm 149, it involves a military initiative against other nations. This is probably why the compilers never brought these psalms together into a separate category, such as is the case with the Songs of Ascent (Psalms 120-134).

So is their newness about their being composed for a new tune, or a new accompaniment to an old tune?[6] Psalms 33, 98, 144, and 149 all have references to musical accompaniment and Psalm 40 has as its heading "to the chief musician." Only Psalm 96 makes no specific reference to accompanying music. Other psalms, however, refer to the harp (כִּנּוֹר) as in 43:4; 49:4; 57:8; 71:22; 81:2; 92:3; 108:2; 137:2; and 150:3; others refer to the trumpet (שׁוֹפָר) as in 47:5; 81:3; and 150:4; and a lyre (נֵבֶל) as in 57:8;

---

4. There are many other references in the Psalter to singing "a song." Examples include 26:7; 28:7; 42:8; 68:4; 69:30; 81:2; 83:1; 137:4; and 147:1. It is however the "*new* song" that is our concern here.
5. The fact the phrase "new thing" (Isa 43:19) or חדשׁות, "new things" (Isa 42:9; 48:6) is found in only in Isaiah suggests that the phrase "new song" is attributable to this prophet.
6. See R. Tomes, "Sing to the Lord a New Song," in *Psalms and Prayers: Papers Read at the Joint Meeting of the Society for Old Testament Study and the Oudtestamentisch Werkgezelschap in Nederland en België, Apeldoorn August 2006* (Oudtestamentische Studiën / OTS 55; Leiden: Brill, 2007), 239.

81:3; 92:3; 108:2; 147:7; and 150:3; a tambourine (תֹּף) as in 81:2; 149:3 and 150:4, and finally, strings (מִנִּים) as in 150:4. Seven psalms (Psalms 4, 6, 54, 55, 61, 67, and 76) have the rubric "with stringed instruments" (בִּנְגִינֹות) but none of these are in our selection. So although musical accompaniment is taken for granted in singing a "new song," this does not mark off our six psalms as being essentially different.

Furthermore, all six psalms use formulaic language found in other psalms, particularly those on each side of them.[7] For example, Psalm 33, one of only two psalms in Book One without a superscription, and probably a late psalm, has a close linguistic relationship with Psalm 32. The אַשְׁרֵי makarismos in verse 12 is also found in 32:1-2 (and 34:8); the concern with right "counsel" (Hebrew עֵצָה) in verse 11 is also found in 32:8, whilst the "eye of the Lord" in verse 18 is in 32:8; and like 32:10-11, verse 21 ends with an appeal to the people to "be glad" and "trust" in God.

Similarly Psalm 40, which has such an odd internal order, with its prayer for help following the thanksgiving, has clear links with Psalm 39. Its preoccupation with death in verses 2 and 14 echo 39:4-6, 11 and 13; the vow of silence in 39:1-2, 9 contrasts with 40:9, where the healed psalmist cannot "restrain his lips." Both psalms are strikingly physical: Psalm 39 speaks mainly of the mouth and tongue (vv. 1, 3, 9), whilst Psalm 40 is aware not only of the mouth (v. 3) and the lips (v. 9) but also of feet (v. 2), ears (v. 6), heart (vv. 10, 12), and life itself (v. 14).

Psalm 96, probably an exilic psalm, also has particular links with the psalm before it. Psalm 95:1-7 is about singing to God, and 96:1-6 develops this further. The God of "salvation" in 96:2 is also found in 95:1; and the celebration of the kingship of God in 96:4 and 10 echoes 95:3, where God is a "great king" (מֶלֶךְ גָּדֹול). His superiority over all other gods (עַל־כָּל־אֱלֹהִים) is found in both 96:4 and in 95:3. The hishtaphel form of the verb חוה (to bow down) in 96:9, albeit a common expression, is also found in 95:6. The theme of rejoicing in 96:12 is also found at in 95:1 (both using the verb רנן).

Psalm 98, perhaps another exilic psalm, has correspondences with both 96 and 97. As well as the identical call to "sing a new song" (96:1 and 98:1), we find the same jussive appeals to praise in 98:7-9 ("Let the sea

---

7. Much of what follows has been influenced by my reception history commentary on these psalms. See Susan Gillingham, *Psalms Through the Centuries: A Reception History Commentary on Psalms 1-72. Volume Two*, Blackwell Bible Commentaries (Oxford: Wiley-Blackwell 2018), and *Psalms Through the Centuries: A Reception History Commentary on Psalms 73-150. Volume Three*, Blackwell Bible Commentaries (Oxford: Wiley-Blackwell forthcoming 2021).

roar, and all that fills it; the world and those who live in it ...") and 96:11–13
("Let the heavens be glad, and let the earth rejoice; let the sea roar, and all
that fills it ..."). Psalm 98 also has associations with 97. Both are concerned
with "righteousness and judgement'"(97:2; 98:9). The personification
of the "earth" (אֶרֶץ) in verses 3 and 4, which "rejoices" and "sees" God's
salvation, is also found in 97:1 and 4. The mountains are also personified
in each psalm: in verse 7 they "shout for joy," whilst in 97:5 they "melt" at
God's presence. In verse 6 we read הַמֶּלֶךְ יְהוָה ("The LORD is king") whilst
in 97:1 the phrase is יְהוָה מָלָךְ ("The LORD reigns").

Psalm 144 is distinctive in that it is actually little more than an anthology of other psalms. It is likely to be a late psalm, making particular use of
Psalm 18 (which itself is linked to the almost identical 2 Samuel 22) and of
Psalm 8 (with its own distinctive links with Genesis 1). For example, the
blessing formula בָּרוּךְ in verse 1 is the same as 18:46, both in the context of
God as "rock." Other combined images of protection (fortress, stronghold,
deliverer, shield, refuge) clearly link verses 1–2 with 18:1–3. The theophany
account in verses 5–8 again indicates some borrowing from 18:7–19. Verse
10 reminds us of 18:50 concerning King David's archetypal dependency
on God for protection. The use of Psalm 8:4 in 144:3–4 ("what are human
beings that you regard them? ...") serves to democratize these royal promises. Hence the links with the preceding psalm are more general: Psalm
143 is also anthological in its use of other psalms (25, 69, 77, 86, 119), and,
like 144, it also uses Psalm 18.

Psalm 149, probably another late psalm, also takes up themes from
other psalms. In this second to last psalm in the MT Psalter its military
language about God's judgement on the nations (vv. 7–9) reminds us of
Psalm 2, also concerned with the kingship of God and Mount Zion. Psalm
149:8 speaks of God binding his enemies with chains of iron (בְּכַבְלֵי בַרְזֶל),
whilst Psalm 2:9 speaks of God breaking the nations with a rod of iron
(בְּשֵׁבֶט בַּרְזֶל). Perhaps in this case the "new song" is not only 149, but 150,
which can be seen as the "new song" for the entire Psalter. Both psalms
start with "Praise the LORD" (הַלְלוּ יָהּ) which takes place in the "assembly
of the faithful" in 149:1 and the "sanctuary" in 150:1.

It is interesting to observe that the concern in our two psalms in Book
One is with the God who has acted *in the past*, both in the cosmos (33) and
in the life of the individual (40), whilst the concern of Psalms 96 and 98
in Book Four is with the God who reigns as King *in the present*, and the
concerns of Psalms 144 and 149 in Book Five is with that God will do *in*

the future. In some ways this fits with the characteristic tone in each of these three books.[8]

A further observation is that although each psalm appears to be a self-contained unit, its proximity to its neighbors gives a second level of meaning to the "new song." Psalm 33 could be read as the new song following the confession and answered prayer for healing in 32; the first part of Psalm 40 could be read as the answer to the prayer in 39; Psalm 96 could be the song which is promised in Psalm 95:1–7; Psalm 98 becomes the song about God's reign anticipated in Psalm 97; Psalm 144 is the new song which, in terms of its reference to the king, fulfils the aspirations of Psalm 143. Perhaps most significantly of all, on this understanding, Psalm 149, which relates to the psalms before it, anticipates the greatest song of all, Psalm 150.

Thus far we have established that each psalmist adapted the formula "new song" to suit the form and contents of their own thanksgiving or hymn, and that the compilers may well have placed these psalms in an appropriate literary context where the song now takes on a newer orientation in relation to other psalms near it. *"Forever new"* is the watchword here. The song is "new" to each of the psalmists in question; but it also becomes "new" again as later compilers placed each "new song" in relation to a previous prayer or call to praise. But then each song continues to be "forever new" as it is used by Jews and Christians in different circumstances over the centuries. This affirms what has been said by other contributors regarding the performative nature of Hebrew poetry in general and psalmody in particular: each "new song" has a variety of afterlives within later communities of faith.

In what follows, I intend to explore briefly just how this "forever newness" works out with each of the six psalms in question.[9]

BOOK ONE: PSALMS 33 AND 40

In Psalm 33:3 the new song accompanies the "word of the Lord" which brings out the heavens, the waters of the deep and the inhabitants of the

---

8. More could be said about this. See for example S.E. Gillingham, "Psalms of David, Psalms of Christ," in *Rooted and Grounded: Faith Formation and the Christian Tradition,* ed. by Steven Croft (Norwich: Canterbury Press, 2019), 69–85, and the bibliography there.

9. Here I adapt again my work in *Psalms Through the Centuries.* See n. 7 above.

world (vv. 6–8). It is as if creation itself accompanies the song of the faithful, rather like the heavens telling the glory of God in Psalm 19:1–4, or the "voice of the LORD" in the storm in Psalm 29. It is somewhat disappointing, therefore, to find that early Christian writers diminish the creation-orientated aspects of the new song by applying it to the church rather than to the cosmos. Basil the Great, for example, reads the "new song" as about *us* as psalteries and *our bodies* as the instruments of praise.[10] The literal meaning of the "harp of ten strings" (33:2), the musical accompaniment for this song of creation, is even allegorized on account of the pagan associations of music. Augustine, for example, sees the ten strings are the ten commandments, and we "pluck the Psaltery" by *fulfilling* the Law: "Let nobody's thoughts revert to the musical instruments of the theatre."[11]

This bias is fortunately not evident in Renaissance art, when we see the "new song" as a hymn celebrated in music. One example is Raphael's painting of St. Cecilia with the Apostles Paul, John, Augustine, and Mary Magdalene: the choir of angels in the cloud above the scene are singing verses from 33:1–3.[12]

In another more recent image, dating from the 1930s, the cathartic power of this new song is also linked to the restorative power of music. Arthur Wragg's black and white cartoon is accompanied by a caption below which reads: *"Praise the Lord with the lyre ... Sing to him a new song (Ps 33:2–3)."*[13] Only the face of the man at the keyboard is seen above the lid of the piano, but it is clear that he is in some sort of theatre from the black and white images of faces caught in the shadows behind him. The man has an intent expression. The bitter world of the Great Depression is at present forgotten. It is impossible to know whether Wragg also had in mind verse 19 ("... to deliver their soul from death, and to keep them

---

10. *Homilies on the Psalms* 15.2 (Ps 33), in FC 46:229–30, cited in *Psalms 1–50*, ACCS 7, eds. by Craige A. Blaising and Carmen S. Hardin (Downers Grove, IL: InterVarsity Press, 2008), 247.

11. *Expositions of the Psalms* 33.6, in *The Works of Saint Augustine, A Translation for the 21st Century*, ed. by John E. Rotelle, trans. by Maria Boulding (Hyde Park, NY: New City, 2000), 3:398–99, cited in ibid., 247. We may also note that the reference to the "ten-stringed harp" in Psalm 144 is interpreted in the same way.

12. See https://www.pinacotecabologna.beniculturali.it/en/content_page/item/2811-st-cecilia-with-saints-paul-john-the-evangelist-augustine-and-mary-magdalen-ecstasy-of-st-cecilia.

13. Arthur Wragg, *The Psalms for Modern Life* (New York: Claude Kendall, 1934).

alive in famine") but what is clear is that here and now the music in this new song is transformative.

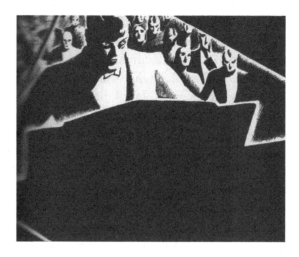

"Praise the Lord with the lyre ... Sing to him a new song" (Ps 33:2-3)

What of the afterlives of Psalm 40:3? Originally this seems to be a song of deliverance from near-death experience (vv. 2 and 14), and this is what is continued in Jewish tradition, where it is argued that David composed this new song after the illness in Psalm 39 had left him.[14] We noted earlier the linkage between Psalm 40 and Psalm 39, and this is also taken up in Igor Stravinsky's first two movements of his *Symphony of Psalms,* using Psalms 39:12-13 and 40:1-4.[15] Much of the second movement, from Psalm 40, is a four-voice double fugue. The "new song" is announced by a trombone, which re-uses some of the initial fugue (suggesting that this is not an entirely new song). The movement ends with a piccolo trumpet again recalling the initial fugue—as if the memory of waiting for God to act is being considered all over again.[16]

---

14. See Avrohom Chaim Feuer, *Tehillim: A New Translation with a Commentary Anthologized from Talmudic, Midrashic and Rabbinic Sources* (New York: Mesorah Publications, 2004), 497–98.
15. See https://www.youtube.com/watch?v=h3Swan5TF_8.
16. See Joel M. LeMon, "Symphonizing the Psalms: Igor Stravinsky's Musical Exegesis," *Interpretation* 71 (2017): 25–49. Psalm 150 is the third psalm analyzed here.

This new song in Psalm 40:3 has another well-known contemporary application since it became a watchword of the Irish rock band U2.[17] The song is called "40" by Bono, and was originally part of their 1983 album, *War*. This verse has been performed over four hundred times since then. At the end of every performance the band finishes with "40" and then leaves the stage—the singers first, then guitarists, and finally the drummer. The audience sings "How long to sing this song?," continuing as the lights go up and they turn to the exits. The repeated chorus goes:

> I will sing, sing a new song.
> I will sing, sing a new song
> How long to sing this song?
> How long to sing this song?
> How long, how long, how long
> How long to sing this song?

So thousands of U2 fans, with little knowledge of the Bible, let alone the psalms, are given the last word on Psalm 40. The full content of the "new song" might not be understood, but this does not prevent it having closure.[18]

We have noted how the new song in Psalm 40 is different from the other five in being a personal testimony of faith. Not surprisingly it has been re-used in this way. Two examples must suffice. One is Charles Wesley, having returned from his missionary work in Georgia, already ordained and still supporting the "Holy Club" in Oxford. Wesley, in hindsight, did not consider he had been converted until he read (on May 21, 1738) Psalm 40:3: "He put a new song in my mouth, a song of praise to our God." By the next day he had apparently composed "And can it be, that I should gain an interest in my Saviour's blood?"[19]

A second example is Gerard Manley Hopkins's version, composed in 1864, which combines Psalm 40:3 with imagery from Psalm 65:10–13:

> He hath abolished the old drouth
> And rivers run where all was dry.
> The field is sopp'd with merciful dew.

---

17. See www.u2.com/music/lyrics/2.
18. Cited in Bill Goodmann, "Assured Lament: U2 Sing the Psalms," 15–16, in https://relegere.org/relegere/article/view/483.
19. Susan Gillingham, *The Psalms Through the Centuries: Volume One*, Blackwell Bible Commentaries (Chichester: Blackwell, 2008), 207.

He hath put a new song in my mouth,
The words are old, the purport new ... .[20]

BOOK FOUR: PSALMS 96 AND 98

Psalm 96 addresses other nations, with their deities "dethroned," and calls the people to praise the true LORD (vv. 7–10). The twin themes of the new song and the nothingness of other gods are also used in Isaiah 42:10–12 and 43:16–21, which suggests that the exile in Babylon was the context for this psalm. It was known by the time of the Chronicler, who cites it in 1 Chronicles 16:23–33, after citing Psalm 105:1–15, in the context of the restored temple, and the new song in Psalm 96 is now read as a prophecy, that God will come to his people and judge the earth (v. 13).

God's kingdom is always entering history, and Christians have re-read Psalm 96 in the light of another prophecy, now fulfilled: the "new song" is now the song of the kingdom of God inaugurated through Jesus Christ. Jerome observes in his *Homilies on the Psalms*: "Sing to the LORD a new song; Who is to sing? Sing to the LORD, all the earth. If this is to refer to the Temple in Jerusalem, O Jew, why is *all the earth* called to praise?"[21] This ethos is implicit in several musical arrangements of the psalms, as various as Handel's Chandos Anthem no. 4, "O Sing unto the Lord a New Song" from 1718;[22] and the more contemporary version by Joseph Gelineau, "O Sing a New Song to the Lord," which also implies a Christian reading.[23]

Rashi, writing nearly seven centuries after Jerome, but aware of this reading, responds: "This Psalm refers to the distant future and its end proves this, saying: 'that he comes to judge the earth.' Everywhere a 'new song' refers to the future to come."[24] In Jewish interpretation this "new song' can only really be sung at the final act of restoration, when the Messiah comes, and, as in verses 7–10, all nations will acknowledge the God of the Jews.[25]

---

20. Cited in Paul S. Fiddes, "G.M. Hopkins," in *The Blackwell Companion to the Bible in English Literature*, eds. Lemon, R. et al. (Chichester: Wiley-Blackwell, 2009), 563.
21. Marie Liguori Ewald, trans., *Jerome: Homilies Volume I (1–59 on the Psalms)*, FC 48; (Washington, DC: Catholic University of America Press 1963), 109–18.
22. See https://www.youtube.com/watch?v=N42nSAaeb9M. Handel's Chandos Anthems were based on Psalms 93, 95, 96, 97, 99 and 103.
23. See https://hymnary.org/hymn/HS1991/706b.
24. Esra Sherevsky, "Rashi and Christian Interpretations," *JQR* 61 (1971):76–86.
25. Feuer, *Tehillim*, 1186 and 1190, citing Kimḥi; also A.Cohen, *The Psalms*, Soncino Books of the Bible, 2nd ed. (London: Soncino, 1992), 315.

Psalm 98:1 has also been read very differently by Jews and Christians. *Midrash Tanchuma*, with its teaching on the Torah, speaks of the "new song" in Psalm 98 as the last of the Ten Songs of Faith—the one to be sung at the end of time.[26] The date of the coming of the Messiah is known only to God (v. 2) but the tradition of the dedication of this psalm by Moses to the tribe of Naphtali, who were content in God's blessing (Deut 32:34), offers a model of patient faith and hope. This explains its use at *Kabbalat Shabbat*. The thirteenth-century *Parma Psalter* has been influenced by these earlier Jewish liturgical traditions. Its image is set within the first Hebrew word of the psalm: a figure, with his right arm raised, points with his left to a musical stave with five lines and ten square notes. Three hybrids, one to the left, one above and one below, each with open beaks, represent the choir which the figure leads.[27]

As with Psalm 96, Christians have read the "new song" and the victory of God in verse 1 to be about the reign of Christ. The reference in Psalm 98:3, to all the ends of the earth seeing the salvation of God, allows for the justification of the gentiles' inclusion within the Christian community. According to the church fathers, the "new song" is "the church's song to Jesus Christ—a song for Gentiles as well as Jews.[28] Cassiodorus reads the psalm as celebrating both the first and second coming of Christ.[29] This explains its use in Christmas liturgy, alongside the Gospel reading from John 1:1-14.[30] "Puer nobis natus est," a Gregorian Chant for Christmas Day, is based on the first verse of this psalm (and Isa 9:6).[31] James MacMillan's "A New Song" assumes a more general Christian theme; it was featured in the BBC Proms in July 2000.[32]

---

26. See Feuer, *Tehillim*, 1202.

27. *The Parma Psalter* fol. 139v; see M. Beit-Arie, E. Silver, and T. Metzger, eds., *The Parma Psalter: A Thirteenth-Century Illuminated Hebrew Book of Psalms with a Commentary by Abraham Ibn Ezra* (London: Facsimile Editions Limited, 1996), 88.

28. Eusebius, *Proof of the Gospel* 6.6 in *Proof of the Gospel* (trans. W.J. Ferrar, 1920; repr. Baker, 1981), 2:6-7, cited in *Psalms 51-150*, ACCS 8, ed. by Quentin F. Wesselschmidt (Downers Grove, IL: InterVarsity Press, 2007), 200. See also Élisabeth de Solms, *Bible Chrétienne V. Commentaires: Les Psaumes* (Quebec: Anne Signier, 2001), 473 (on Athanasius and Augustine).

29. See P.G. Walsh, trans., *Cassiodorus, Volume One: Explanation of the Psalms 1-50*, ACW 51 (Mahwah, NJ: Paulist, 1990), 430-31.

30. See Jason Mason Neale and Richard Frederick Littledale, eds., *A Commentary on the Psalms from Primitive and Medieval Writers*, 2nd ed (London: Masters, 1874-1879), 3:251, which lists a number of other Christian festivals which used this psalm.

31. See https://www.youtube.com/watch?v=8pZR9cK13so.

32. See https://www.youtube.com/watch?v=gwWM8Zth4ns.

BOOK FIVE: PSALMS 144 AND 149

The "new song" which is promised in verse 9 of Psalm 144 has the most interesting reception of all these six psalms, in the way that ancient legends and myths have been used to re-emphasize its newness. This reception plays upon two key themes: a political theme, stressing the opposition to imperial powers (vv. 1-2 and 10-11), and a theological theme, emphasizing the renewal of creation and the restoration of family and community life (vv. 12-14). These two themes are reinforced by two tropes: Goliath and the unicorn.

The LXX adds the superscription "against Goliath" and so gives this a particular Davidic emphasis. The connection might be due to the imagery of the hands and fingers used for warfare in verse 1 (1 Sam 17:49), the "sword" in verse 11 (1 Sam 17:45, 51), and the imagery of deliverance in 144:6-7. Just as King David took on the Philistine "giants" threatening the people, so now the people will be given the strength to take on imperial "giants" of their own day.

Early rabbinic tradition makes much of the Goliath motif, setting the psalm either after David's defeat of Goliath, as in *Midrash Shocher Tov*, or after his victory over his enemies (Abraham ibn Ezra and Radak).[33] The attitude to warfare is to imitate "servant David": "In this psalm David expresses the authentic Jewish attitude towards war and warriors ... Glory and fame are not for David, because it is God who grants salvation to kings (v. 10). ... The sword is needed to combat hostile powers, yet it should be deplored. Thus, David desires to compose a new kind of song to God (v. 9), not only about muscle and might ..."[34] On this account the psalm is often cited in the evening service as an introduction to *Motza'ei Shabbat*, being the first prayer of a new week, teaching that all our efforts at overcoming the "enemy" are not about us but about God.

Predictably, in Christian reception the warfare is not so much physical as spiritual.[35] Hence Cassiodorus argues that the reference to Goliath in the Greek and Latin headings is a prophecy of Christ's struggle with evil and his victory over death: "Just as David laid low Goliath by using a rock as the weapon of war, so the power of the devil was overcome by

---

33. Feuer, *Tehillim*, 1677, citing *Midrash Shocher Tov*.
34. Ibid., 1677.
35. de Solms, *Bible Chrétienne V. Commentaires*, 665-66.

the Rock which is the Lord Jesus Christ."[36] This re-reading of the "Goliath" trope is found in several illustrated Psalters, both in the west and the east. The Carolingian *Stuttgart Psalter* (folio 158v) depicts warriors with swords and shields and David with stones and sling. The heading reads "Goliath attacking David and David beheading the dead Goliath."[37] The Byzantine *Hamilton Psalter* (folio. 237v) shows David slinging at Goliath, who is holding his sword and shield and surrounded by an army of Philistines (*Hamilton Psalter*, folio. 237v). The *Bristol Psalter* (folio. 231v) adds two inscriptions: David is the "Personification of Might" and Goliath is the "Personification of Pride."[38] The same image and inscription are found, more faintly, in the *Theodore Psalter* (folio. 182r).[39]

The unicorn trope is partly inspired by verses 3–4, which use Psalms 8:4 and 90:5–6 to express themes of human fragility and divine permanence. As the giant Goliath featured many times in Byzantine Psalters as a symbol of the might of imperial power, so the mythical unicorn symbolized the power of inner temptation. The Byzantine *Kiev Psalter* actually contains "The Fable of the Unicorn" (from Archdeacon Spiridon's account) in its margin above Psalm 144, written in a tiny vermilion script, with an image of a unicorn below it.[40] Both the account of the fable and the image are also seen, again faintly, on the damaged manuscript of the *Theodore Psalter* (folio.182v). Here the unicorn is inscribed; under the man are the words "Personification of Luxury" whilst the tree has the inscription

---

36. P.G. Walsh, *Cassiodorus, Volume Three: Explanation of the Psalms 101–150*, ACW 53 (Mahwah, NJ: Paulist, 1991), 413. This is also found in Ambrose *Exp. Ps.* 118.11: see Walsh ibid., 519.

37. http://digital.wlb-stuttgart.de/sammlungen/sammlungsliste/werksansicht /?no_cache=1&tx_dlf%5Bid%5D=1343&tx_dlf%5Bpage%5D=324.

38. http://www.bl.uk/manuscripts/Viewer.aspx?ref=add_ms_40731_f231v.

39. http://www.bl.uk/manuscripts/Viewer.aspx?ref=add_ms_19352_f182r.

40. See Nadezhda Toranova and Erin-Lee McGuire, *The Kiev Psalter of 1397: An Analysis*, published online 2003 at https://www.medievalists.net/2009/06/the-kiev-psalter-of-1397-an-analysis/. The Greek version of this fable has been attributed to John of Damascus (675–749) and concerns one of the parables told by St. Barlaam to Ioasaph, a newly converted son of a pagan king. A man tries to escape a unicorn, represented here as a symbol of death, and attempts to climb a tree, an apparent symbol of life, whose branches are laden with honey; betrayed by the seduction of sweetness the man little knows that at the base of the tree, by day and night, a black mouse and white mouse are gnawing at its roots. Soon the tree and the man will fall into the pit as a gaping hole opens up beneath them. The story has links with Genesis 3 and the seduction of the fruit of the tree (in this case, of knowledge, although the tree of life is also present); here the unicorn's role is like that of the serpent's temptation of Adam and Eve.

"Personification of Deceit."[41] The day mouse and night mouse gnawing under its roots can also be seen, as also the dragon in the pit, inscribed "Personification of Hell." The *Barberini Psalter* (folio. 237v) is almost identical in this respect.[42]

Several other psalms have references to giants and unicorns in the Greek or the Latin translations. Psalm 144, however, is the only place where the two are brought together. It is a fine example of the ways in which the ambiguities in the poetry lend themselves to more mythical as well as metaphorical allusions, thus broadening again the meaning of this "new song."

Psalm 149, in Jewish tradition, again interprets the "new song" as the song of the Messianic age. Yet for Christian commentators such as Augustine, God's praise is no longer found in the synagogues of the Jews (any more than it is in the madness of pagans, or in the errors of heretics or in the applause of theatres); the new song, God's praise, is found *in the church of his saints:*[43] "The Old Testament is an old song, the New Testament a new song. In the Old Testament are temporal and earthly promises. Whoso loveth earthly things singeth an old song: let him desire to sing a new song, love the things of eternity ..." [44] Jerome concurs: the new song is for "a new people that sings a new song."[45] This is the sung to be sung to the Lord Jesus Christ for his having built a universal Jerusalem for all peoples (vv. 1–2).[46]

What of the "new song" today? We have seen its various outworkings in the early psalmists and noted its broader afterlife in the work of the compilers, and seen the very different readings of it, in commentaries, music and art, throughout the centuries. What of today? At the time of writing (in late 2020) religious communities are still working out a *new* understanding of singing in worship as they look to a post lockdown context in the midst of a somewhat fragile "new normal." Psalm 137:4 ("How could we sing the LORD's song in a foreign land?") has a poignant relevance, for Covid-19 has forced us to silence our songs, for fear of passing on the virus to others. Covid, like those Babylonian captors, taunts

---

41. See http://www.bl.uk/manuscripts/Viewer.aspx?ref=add_ms_19352_f182v

42. J.C. Anderson, P. Canart and C. Walter, The Barberini Psalter: Codex Vaticanus Barberinianus Graecus 372 (Zürich: Belser, 1989).

43. Sermon 34.6 WSA 3 2: cited in Wesselschmidt, *Psalms 51–150*, 168.

44. Anthony Uyl, ed., *Exposition on the Book of Psalms* (Woodstock: Devoted, 2017), 693.

45. Ewald, *Jerome: Homilies Volume I (1–59 on the Psalms)*, 424 (Homily 59).

46. Walsh, *Cassiodorus, Volume Three*, 457.

us to sing the songs we long to sing but can no longer do. To date, our instruments are just beginning to be used again as an accompaniment to a song sung by a choir. Yet that new song—whether about the order and beauty in creation, or about individual healing, or about recognizing God's universal sovereignty, or about justice for the poor, or about praise simply for its own sake, as in Psalms 149 and 150—is "forever new." It will return. When it does, and when we remove our face masks and sing as never before, we shall appreciate its newness all the more.

12

Response 2:
A Response to *New Song*

Micheal O'Siadhail

INTRODUCTION

I was delighted to be asked to respond to this fine book. Unlike my fellow responder Jason Byassee, I was not at the conference that gave rise to this excellent collection of deeply thoughtful and scholarly papers, and I did not experience the excitement and fellowship that he so joyously describes. This means that I approach this as a reader without being able to recall the personality of the presenters of these papers, and without the benefit of hearing their more informal remarks as they answered questions from their audience. I did however search the authors on the internet in order to understand a little of their background and field of interest, and, not least, to gaze for a moment or two at a photograph, which allowed me to imagine their presence.

As I read through the book I was over and over again astonished and almost overwhelmed by how the papers combine a fine combing of the poetry's detail and often hidden intricacies with such a profound and moving reverence for the work. I am neither a biblical scholar nor a theologian. I come to the discussion of this poetry with the fascination of a practicing poet who loves the psalms. As I will outline later, I have written contemporary responses to the psalms, and they are indeed the inspiration for work in hand.

But how should I best shape a response to these rich and challenging explications of the psalms both as meticulous and multi-layered literary works and as a continuing inspiration for contemporary liturgy? It seemed to me pointless simply to attempt a brief summary of each chapter as this has been so well done in the carefully crafted introduction by Stephen D. Campbell and Richard G. Rohlfing Jr. Instead, it occurred to me as I read the book that there were certain dominant themes, and that maybe I could make observations focused on a few such themes before describing my previous engagement with Psalms and suggesting how insights gained from the book inform my current work.

The themes I want to highlight, are:

1. The intricate form and structure of Biblical Hebrew poetry;

2. The question of the translation of this poetry;

3. The discussion of what is poetry;

4. The value of close reading of the poetry.

STRUCTURE AND FORM

Many are aware that a good deal of the Hebrew Bible is written in poetic form: Psalms, Lamentations, much of the wisdom literature, and some of the later prophets. But, as we learn in this book, it is also in interspersed texts such as Jacob's Testament (Genesis 49) and The Song of the Sea (Exodus 15). We will look more generally at what constitutes poetry below. For those of us who do not read Hebrew and come from traditions where we think of poetic form in terms of meter or rhyme or corresponding vowel patterns, or various combinations of all of these, both John Goldingay's and Benjamin D. Sommer's outline of how biblical Hebrew poetry works is fascinating.

This poetry apparently adheres broadly to the practices of ancient Middle Eastern poetry. Writing about Jacob's Testament, John Goldingay assumes that it is rhythmic poetry mostly "comprising of series of short self-contained sentences that divide into two parts with two or three or four stresses in each part" (page 13). Goldingay refers to the parts of the line as cola. We are also told, as one senses even in translation, "the second colon commonly restates the first or complements it or explains a question raised by it."

Goldingay also assumes that written texts and oral communication complement each other, and that the poetry was chanted. I find it

intriguing how he likens the prophet Amos to contemporary rap artists
who can vary the number of words in a line so long as they keep the
rhythm going.

Undoubtedly the formal feature that even those of us who read the
psalms in translation instinctively recognize is parallelism. Parallelism
is found in other literatures. It is, for instance, an outstanding feature of
the Finnish national epic, the Kalevala.

As we will discuss below and as Benjamin D. Sommer emphasizes,
there are many kinds of parallelism. He refers to the parallelisms we
perhaps notice most in translations of the psalms as lexical parallelism
and semantic parallelism. He gives a very clear example of lexical parallelism in the opening of Psalm 145: "I extol You my God and king, / I bless
Your name forever and ever."

It is interesting that Sommer notes, "because Biblical poetry is essentially a form of free verse, there is no scansion to determine where lines
begin and end. ... Usually the decision how to lineate is uncontroversial
but sometimes it is open to debate." Such decisions can have consequences
for the meaning. Here the uninitiated are in the hands of the translator.

I must say that, though I am not qualified to access any variant readings, I have found the discussions of form and structure in the book have
enriched my appreciation of the traditions of biblical Hebrew poetry. I
can imagine its complexities even as I read in translation, and it reaffirms
my belief that we humans have always been intrigued by the interplay of
sound and meaning. As such it heartens me in my own strivings to catch
in words the intensity of our precious lives.

TRANSLATION OF BIBLICAL POETRY

The translation of poetry of any kind has always been controversial.
Robert Frost maintained that the essence of poetry is what is lost in translation; others believe that the essence is what remains.

June F. Dickie gives us what she calls an abbreviated history of
approaches to Bible translation, followed by the changing definition of
what the concept translation means, and a discussion of reception theory.

Fundamentally, she is tracing the move from "the form of message"
to "the response of the receptor." The older focus was the enjoyment of
reproducing as many of the stylistic features of the original; but then
the goal became the achievement of "the functional equivalence" in the
"receptor language." The emphasis is on how the translation strikes the

person who receives the translation. This is in turn pushed further, so that the message need not be conveyed in language, but rather might include performance which can be in song, rap, spoken poetry, drama, dance, mosaic, drawing, or painting. Indeed, in a kind of translation experiment she involves four different groups in the translation of psalms into Zulu with engrossing results. The term translation gives way to the idea of localization.

It seems that there is a spectrum that stretches from literal translation to what almost seems a riffing process on the original, substituting what is a more meaningful version for the local community. For instance, where Psalm 93 (vv. 3–4) refers to "floods," "many waters," and "waves of the sea," these get replaced by other natural images "wind," "fire," "mountain," or "lion," all of which were locally threatening phenomena. This reminds me of a similar development that folklorists are aware of: when a particular type of folk telling spreads, the imagery is adapted and made more relevant for a different environment. It may be that this a feature of orality.

Interestingly, C. T. R. Hayward, in an examination of *Shirat Ha-Yam* ("The Song of the Sea"), compares in absorbing detail the original Hebrew with the version in the Septuagint. This has hints of an early case of "localization." I quote him: "it would be hazardous to draw any conclusions from this evidence, although it is reasonable to point out that the Greek translation at least 'opens doors' to thoughts about how this song might be appropriated by future generations."

While I believe that, depending on the circumstances, the full spectrum of translation possibilities should be available, in my experience of literary translation, I would tend to agree with June F. Dickie's quotation from Ernst R. Wendland: "The compositional procedure must be loosened up in order to allow gifted translators the freedom to more fully access and creatively utilize the stylistic and expressive resources of the receptor language." When translating, I think I choose the middle of the spectrum. I would start with a fairly literal rendition and move a little away from it, finding more natural idioms. Ironically, in moving away a little I have always found that I move nearer the spirit of a poem. As an artist friend of mine always said, "Start tight, finish loose." As one brief example of what I mean, below is the translation to German, Norwegian, and Japanese of the sextet of a sonnet of mine called *Transit*,[1] which describes an airport scene:

---

1. Micheal O'Siadhail, *Collected Poems* (Tarset: Bloodaxe, 2013), 267.

I watch a parting couple in their embrace and freeing
The woman turns, a Veronica with her handkerchief
Absorbing *into herself a last stain of a countenance.*
*She **dissolves** in crowds. An **aura** of her leaving glance*
Travels through the yearning air. Tell me we live
*For those faces **wiped** into the folds of our being.*

Dort ein Paar beim Abschied—Umarmung, Loslassung.
Sie dreht sich um, Veronika mit Taschentuch,
***nimmt in sich auf** die letzten Spuren eines Angesichts,*
***verschmilzt** mit der Menge. Die **Aura** ihres Abschiedsblicks*
schwebt durch die sehnsuchtsvolle Luft. Sag, daß wir leben
*für diese Gesichter, den Falten unseres Wesens **eingedrückt**.*

Eg ser eit par som omfamnar kvarandre og gjer seg fri.
Kvinna snur, ei Veronika meg lommeplagg
*Som **tek opp i seg** ein siste flekk av det opne andletet.*
*Ho **vert borte** i folkemasse, Ein **glans** av hennar siste blikk*
Dreg gjennom den lengtande lufta og seier me at me lever
*For dei andleta som er **tørka** inn i foldane av vårt sinn.*

親密な二人が抱擁をし割れてる行くのを僕は見見る、
彼女は振り返り、キリストヴェロニカのようにハンカチで
その顔にの残った最後の表情自分の中に取りこんだいく。
そして彼女は群集の中に消えていく。割れの時の彼女の一瞥の雰囲
　　気が
思慕の思持をあたりに流していく。存在の壁の中に
塗りこめた、そのいう顔を見るために僕たちは生きているのだ。

While none of them have attempted to reproduce rhyme, all three are beautifully achieved and work within their own world. I will point to just a few examples of how the German translators (Audrey and Walter Pfeil), the Norwegian translator (Helge Torvund), and the Japanese translator (Shigeo Shimasu) all can move slightly away from the original.

All three change the Latinate verb "absorb," choosing instead the more general equivalent of "to take up" or "take in." Similarly they avoid the Latinate "dissolves" choosing instead in the case of German "versmilzt" (merges), the Norwegian "vert bort" ("was off"), the Japanese has the verb 消える ("disappear," "vanish," or "go out of sight").

The German retains the word "aura," while the Norwegian has "ein glans" (a radiance), and the Japanese 雰囲気 ("mood," "atmosphere," or "ambience"). On the other hand, the Norwegian retains the word for wipe, "tørka." where German has "eingedrükt" (imprinted). Japanese differs here in having 塗りこめた... 存在の壁の中に ("I could paint ... into the fold of being").

Where the original has "travels through," the German has "schwebt durch" ("floats through"), the Norwegian has "dreg gjennom" ("goes," "leaves," or "sets out through"), and the Japanese has あたりに流していく ("is flowing around in").

Finally the Japanese offers an interesting cultural aid in referring to Veronica's handkerchief as キリストヴェロニカのようにハンカチ("Christ's Veronica's handkerchief").

It seems to me that these changes, along with several more, ultimately bring the translation nearer the spirit of the original than a more literal translation.

WHAT IS POETRY?

Here we are dealing essentially with two aspects of this question. In the first place, if, as in the case of Hannah's Prayer (1 Sam 2:1–10), poetry is embedded in a prose narrative, how do we know what is poetry, or how it works as opposed to prose? Then, secondly, there is the question, what is poetry in general and how should we describe it?

It appears that an inset poem, such as Hannah's Prayer, is identified by its heightened language and its complex poetic structure. Even more so, it is labelled in the surrounding text as a prayer that might or might not be also a song. Yet most importantly, as David G. Firth points out in his enlightening chapter, it interrupts the narrative and does nothing at all to advance it. Furthermore, he shows how this didactic praise poem adumbrates the reversal of fortunes motif in the prose narrative, and the words used in the prayer when prefiguring the kernel message are echoed in the narrative. In this way he points to how the poem offers a hermeneutical key by which we are to read Samuel from a theocentric perspective and provides a mechanism for commenting on almost all aspects of the larger story.

It occurs to me that an embedded poem such as Hannah's prayer works to create a platform for commentary in a similar way to how the chorus in Greek theater does, or Shakespeare's clown. I have personally always been fascinated by the possibilities a second level of this kind enables. In a form I have used and refer to by the portmanteau noun "saiku" (sonnet and haiku), I place between sonnets a haiku that allows a comment on the content of the sonnets.

The more general question is how to describe what biblical poetry is from the point of view of content and form. I have for many years known and admired Ellen Davis's work. In her appreciation of biblical poetry and its contemporary value, she shares George Steiner's dictum in *Real Presence* that "The best reading of art is art."[2] She characterizes biblical poetry as "a sustained capacity for eliciting a response, for generating the involvement of those who repeat or pray them, and thus potentially changing the conversation from the abstract and technocratic to something that is profoundly humane." In short, as she says, they are good lyric poetry.

In her interpretation of Psalm 38 through poetry and dance she remarks that "the 'I' of the lament psalms is not an insistent, self-absorbed ego but rather a true self, born of a crisis of the spirit—the generative condition for all personal lyrics, as the contemporary American poet Gregory Orr observes." Given the compelling description of how Gregory Orr first turned to poetry, I understand. I am also conscious of the words of Shai Held in his extremely moving chapter where he wrestles with that bleakest of psalms, Psalm 88. Interpreting this psalm as an expression of chronic illness, he writes that "there is something inherently redemptive about finding words for our pain." For my part, I still like to think that lyric poetry can also spring from a sense of the abundance of life, a delight in simply being. Indeed, in treating Psalm 42–43, Ellen Davis notes how in this lament "the progression between the two parts of the psalm shows depression gradually yielding to the remembrance and anticipation of joy."

She also speaks of poetry as giving comfort, and once again quotes from Gregory Orr's *Poetry as Survival* where he identifies the "survival function." Personal lyrics "help us express and regulate our emotional lives, which are confusing and sometimes opaque to us." Here I absolutely concur.

I survived the final illness and death of my first wife by chronicling this heartbreaking experience in a series of poems, wshthich I was to later publish as *One Crimson Thread*.[3] Like Ellen Davis, I can quote Psalm 63:8: "though the clouds of these arrows may hide all suns of worldly comforts from thee, yet thou art still under the shadow of his wings."

---

2. George Steiner, *Real Presences* (Chicago: University of Chicago Press, 1989), 17.
3. Micheal O'Siadhail, *One Crimson Thread* (Hexham: Bloodaxe, 2015).

Benjamin D. Sommer, on the other hand, addresses the question of what poetry is in terms of form. I have already mentioned the characteristic lexical parallelism of biblical Hebrew poetry. Sommer emphases the fact that there are many other kinds of parallel beside the familiar ones with lexical or semantic equivalents. These can include phonological echoes, syntactic structures or simply rhythm—or simultaneous combinations of these. Indeed, widening the concept of parallelism, he sees rhyme, meter, alliteration, and so forth as basically forms of parallelism. In a discussion of sequence and cycle in poetry he draws on Roman Jacobson who "clarified that all poetry is based on the principle of parallelism"—a conclusion that Gerard Manley Hopkins had also come to in his time. If this is so, he maintains, then poetry by definition is always cyclical.

A further interesting angle is his taking up of Northrup Frye's identification of prose as "a rhythm of continuity" whereas poetry is "a rhythm of association." So, from a formal point of view, poetry is ultimately distinguished from prose by being cyclical while prose in contrast tends to be linear.

While both the idea of defining poetry as either always a form of parallelism or as cyclical as opposed to linear prose is appealing, it is an oversimplification. Surely in both cases we are dealing here again with a spectrum that shades over from the highly formal with much parallelism and cyclical organization to where even the repeated use of the definite article might be deemed to constitute parallelism or circularity. For my part, I choose the point on that continuum that seems to me to be appropriate. For instance, in *The Gossamer Wall: Poems in Witness to the Holocaust,* the form is in certain narrative sections confined to what I have called "zigzag rhyme," that is one word anywhere in a line rhyming with the previous line and another rhyming with a word anywhere in the following line.[4] This was to achieve a low emotional charge and let the unspeakable narrative tell itself. Similarly, in *The Five Quintets,* in certain parts of both *Dealing* (about economics), and *Steering* (about politics), while there is a rhyme scheme, the rhyming words are far apart so as to

---

4. O'Siadhail, *Collected Poems,* 393–472.

increase the sense of linear narrative.[5] As against that, for example, both *Love Life* and *One Crimson Thread*, with lyrical themes, are highly formal.[6]

THE VALUE OF CLOSE READING

Literary criticism has abounded with various theories and "isms," providing a lens through which literature is read. I am sure that each of them has some valuable insights to offer, but one of the most impressive features of this book is the meticulous close reading of the poems. Like Jason Byassee, I find it hard to imagine the hard hours of study and the depth of talent that lies behind each of these chapters. There are so many examples of the benefits of close reading. I want just to mention two.

Firstly, how Shai Held interprets Psalm 88 requires a very sensitive close reading. This, as he shows, is a very unusual lament psalm. It has no trust in God, no promise of praise for God; so there is no shift from lament to praise. Instead, there is a list of times God has failed the psalmist. While some have sought to find glimmers of hope in the psalmist's unburdening, he suggests there are touches of irony. He reads, for instance, "God of my salvation" or the use of "sated" in "I am sated with misfortunes" as the ironic comment of one whom God has ignored.

Secondly, I see what Yisca Zimran in her informative chapter calls a "dynamic-synchronic" reading as a specific kind of close reading. The canonical text of Hosea has many words and wordplays that recur in different units and a close reading challenges the boundaries of units. The reader partaking in the interpretive process gains a new perspective on the book as whole. It is suggested that this type of reading can be applied to other books.

I have always been a close reader of work I admired, and the attention and care lavished on biblical poetry in this volume confirms my belief in such reading. When working for over ten years on *The Five Quintets*, I found that I did a great deal of close reading both of prose and poetry. In order to attempt to understand the makers and shakers of history, it is often the inconspicuous biographical detail that is the key. In the first

---

5. Micheal O'Siadhail, *The Five Quintets* (Norwich: Canterbury Press), 2019. The quintets are entitled "Making," "Dealing," "Steering," "Finding," and "Meaning."
6. O'Siadhail, *Collected Poems*, 473–552; *One Crimson Thread*.

quintet *Making*, extensive close reading of the works of the featured literary figures meant that I could attempt to see the world through their eyes
and indeed incorporate their words into the sonnets written in their voice.

WORKING WITH THE PSALMS

As an earnest of my personal involvement with biblical poetry, I mentioned above that I had engaged with the psalms. The American composer
and arranger, Rob Mathes and I were commissioned to come up with a
work based on the psalms and responses to them. It became *At Night a
Song is with Me*, a cycle of songs and psalms for singers, rhythm section,
and orchestra which was performed twice in Christ Church in Greenwich,
Connecticut in spring and autumn 2010.

With my closest friend, the theologian David Ford, I poured over favorite psalms and decided to suggest Psalms 16, 25, 42, 90, 121, 137, 71, 139, 16,
and 148 (in the order they were performed). I sent them to Rob Mathes
who set these psalms, or excepts from them, to music. I then wrote songs,
which broadly outline life's phases where I either echoed or prefigured
words from the previous or following psalm depending on how Rob organized it. For example: lines from Psalm 42:

> *As a deer longs for flowing streams,*
> *So my soul longs for you;*
> *Oh my soul it waits*
> *For the living God, the living God.*
>
> *By day the Lord commands*
> *His steadfast love*
> *And at night his song is with me.*
> *At night a song is with me.*

are echoed in:

> *Why is the song over too soon,*
> *Over before lovers are done?*
> *Cry for the sun, weep for the moon.*
>
> *Yearning you left childhood's cocoon,*
> *Craving the air, daring to leap –*
> *Cry for the sun, weep for the moon.*

Spring winds have blown, petals are strewn,
Mourn for a youth no one can keep–
Cry for the sun, weep for the moon.

April for May, May then for June,
Aching so long, longing so deep–
Cry for the sun, weep for the moon.

Endless desire winding its tune–
Surely my song has only begun?
Cry for the sun, weep for the moon.

This interaction led just a decade later to my current work on a psalter of personal psalms. Responding to this book has been a timely meditation on the nature of biblical poetry. I found Katie M. Heffelfinger's chapter on Isaiah 45:9–25 a wonderful encouragement to dare a direct, honest, and even complex conversation with God. She speaks of "render[ing] truth rich and full by embracing the ambiguity inherent in human experience, by intensifying our encounter with the emotional element of our grasping truth."

I also find very inspiring her recommendation that in reading biblical poetry instead of explanation we should adopt appropriate postures. She proposes imagination rather than instruction, a posture of patient expectancy and vulnerable uncertainty. I think such postures might apply equally well to the ambitious task of creating a personal psalter.

This book also contains a number of fine poems by Michael Symmons Roberts. Rather than offering any explanatory comments, in the spirit of Katie M. Heffelfinger, I recommend that they be read with due respect for the mystery and paradox that is poetry.

ENVOI

When some eighteen years ago I was writing *The Gossamer Wall: Poems in Witness to the Holocaust* I found the final section the hardest to write. How should I dare to conclude a book like this except to cry "never again," and pray that such broken trust might heal? After much thought I entitled the section *Prisoners of Hope*.[7] Benjamin D. Sommer has an epigraph by Michael Symmons Roberts: "the scandal of it/ the refusal to deliver a

---

7. O'Siadhail, *Collected Poems*, 457–70.

denouement," and he himself comments that "it is fateful for the Jewish religion that the Torah ends on a note of hope rather than fulfillment." Perhaps all of us who ponder deeply biblical poetry are indeed prisoners of hope.

13

Response 3:
A Response to the
New Song Conference

Jason Byassee

A church magazine I used to work for had a strict policy against covering
academic conferences. We academic types think we have done something newsworthy if we have had a *really* good conference. The magazine
knew better. "Scholars gather and read papers to one another" was no
attention-grabbing headline, even before the internet. As a staffer with
too many academics for friends, I appreciated that this gave me an out
whenever a scholar asked me to report on some confab: "sorry, we don't
do conferences."

One of the strange fruits of the deadly worldwide coronavirus pan-
demic of 2020 may be to show us what a gift it is to gather in person.
"How good and pleasant it is when brethren dwell together in unity," the
psalmist exults (Ps 133:1). Something about six feet of personal distance
challenges that goodness. The instantaneousness of Zoom is a marvel,
but the inability to touch and eat and drink with one another leaves it
a disappointment. We are embodied animals. God delights to make us
in God's own image in our bodies, and then, Christians believe that God
himself is a body (not just was—is).[1] The inability to be together in person
for months shows us anew the goodness of bodily gathering, even in

---

1. We are not alone. Benjamin Sommer, a presenter at the conference and in the
present volume, "wrote the book" (as they say) on this topic in ancient Judaism: see
The Bodies of God and the World of Ancient Israel (Cambridge: Cambridge University
Press, 2009).

conferences. It may not make a headline, but it makes our lives worth living to get together and do something as mundane as deliver papers, drink coffee, make small-talk, gossip, buy books, and worry about making our flight home. Lord hasten the day.

We had one such conference in the summer of 2019, long before any of us knew such gatherings would soon become impossible. The setting at Ushaw College at Durham University was remarkable. I had been in the UK for six months on a grant to study the church in the north of England.[2] I am the sort of nerd who noses around campuses, explores architecture, wanders into chapels, and I still had not seen Ushaw with my own eyes. This is no accident. Catholics built it not long after Catholicism was begrudgingly allowed back into England, by folks accustomed to hiding from the law for their faith. So Ushaw is massive, imposing even on the inside, but it hides from all but those who mean to find it. It rambles on forever, but you cannot even see it from the road of its mailing address. Once you are inside, it contains multitudes.[3] Chapel after chapel after chapel, one opening up to another. A sanctuary the size of some Church of England cathedrals. A refectory to seat hundreds. A medieval-style monastic close that kept me perpetually lost. Yet what a grand edifice in which to be lost! And a model of Durham Cathedral made out of toothpicks or matchsticks or something similarly small (and combustible). A reminder that Catholics are not quite ready to let go of the burial shrine of Sts. Cuthbert, Bede, and Oswald, et. al. The Church of England may prize Durham Cathedral as one of its crown jewels, but Catholics look at it not just with outsider's envy, but with a dispossessed insider's possessiveness: this used to be *ours*. The chapel (yet another) in which we met for the conference had angels carved into the rafters. The space could not be more Catholic. Sure, now it houses a college of Durham University focused on Catholic education, but this was a building with the history of the church in the north of England etched into its fabric. A history of loss for Roman Catholics, to be sure. But our story shows what God can do with lost things. As Chesterton said, our God knows the way out of the grave.

---

2. See now Jason Byassee, *Northern Lights. Resurrecting Church in the North of England* (Eugene, OR: Cascade, 2020).

3. Walt Whitman's famous response to being found in contradiction with himself is also the title for conference participant Katie Heffelfinger's book on Isaiah: *I Am Large, I Contain Multitudes: Lyric Cohesion and Conflict in Second Isaiah*, BIS 105 (Leiden: Brill, 2011).

I listened to the poems and papers collected in this volume with awe. Just imagine the decades of learning required to produce erudition like this, the oceans of talent and hard work and courage. Their work made me want to preach. They sparked a fire in the bones, that cannot but flash out (Jer 20:9).

Perhaps it was the focus on poetry. Poetry demands personal involvement. You cannot read it right without being changed. Beauty demands community. I was in Vancouver recently cycling along when I noticed the cherry trees had only recently exploded into their annual pink grandeur. I stopped the first stranger I could find: look at that will you?! She agreed, magnificent. There is something about awe that simply must be shared, it cannot be kept to oneself or it rots, like manna kept overnight on a day other than the Sabbath. The focus of this conference on biblical poetry meant that it could not *not* preach. We were all involved. The beauty created and cultivated is intended by God to be shared. This was not because of any common worship, of course. We were Jews and Christians and others gathered not for prayer but for study. Yet worship kept creeping in: scraps of liturgy, lines of exultation, bits of invocation. The line between worship and not got blurry indeed. We were sharing beauty. How could it not?

I regret to inform you that not all that beauty could be stuffed into this volume. It kept overspilling, squirming out of the organizers' hands, overrunning the boundaries. Such is the nature of conferences. Scholars make offhand comments, leave off their carefully cultivated manuscripts, reveal more in asides or in Q&A than they are normally willing to commit to in print. The great Michael Symmons Roberts confessed that "I lost my atheism in my 20s," and has been trying ever since to find the right balance between faith and doubt. He noted that his home, Manchester UK, managed to be the birthplace of capitalism, and also of communism. It is the cradle of British suffrage and of radical politics in the UK. It might be thought of in Britain as a gritty backwater of a city, but it is actually the birthplace of revolutions. Not a bad spot for a poet on the prowl. He defended his craft, uh, craftily: poems will not surprise anyone else if they do not surprise their author. If you spy an idea for a poem, kill it. Folks tend not to read novels at funerals. Referencing Seamus Heaney, there is something about poetry that has kept it from becoming entirely secularized, unlike much of our culture. Poems are living things, slippery and unreliable: they defy meaning as well as create it. The Brits are particularly prone to fail at praise. After *Seinfeld* the entire consumerist west seems only ever to praise with a heavy dollop of irony. But the psalms offer "unalloyed praise." Not a bad practice to take up.

There was June Dickie, Bible translator in southern Africa, illustrating the way poetry listeners in KwaZulu-Natal will snap along with the poet's recitation. If they stop snapping, she stops reciting. Her own snap and video footage of the practice made the point unmistakable: poetry is a communal exercise. This is not the scholar at her carrell, it is the wordsmith on the street. Dickie went on to conclude—with courage in a room full of scholars—that adaptability to the present listeners may be more important than fidelity to the past: "because we trust the Holy Spirit." So the psalmist's deadly waves and breakers become, in KZN, the repeated attack of a lion. Translation is not just plodding over a dictionary for historical fastidiousness. It is also the making of a new art, as bold as the original.

Here is Ben Sommer saying he would name the Psalms "the book of faith and doubt." It was an aside, not in his paper, perhaps so close to him he hardly bothers to put it in writing, but it rings true. His fellow American Jews tend to celebrate Passover with eagerness but to neglect Shavuot. This is a mistake, he argues—to revel in freedom but not in the law—a typically American mistake. There is no freedom without common obligation. Perhaps the coronavirus is re-teaching that to all of us.

There is another panelist quoting Iris Murdoch: "if you pay attention to art, you will also pay attention to people." Here is another citing Patrick Miller: "the psalms lack specificity on purpose." That allows all kinds of readers to enter into scripture with their own circumstances. There is yet another presenter citing Murray Lichtenstein: "poetry in the psalms makes 'personal involvement' inevitable. We cannot not read the I as, well, I. Also as the "we" of the praying community, for this book is only ever delivered to us in community, extended in space and time. Here is another presenter, my teacher Ellen Davis, promising that "anything worth doing is worth doing badly." Sure, we were all taught to mistrust poetry. It resists truth, it wiggles out of our grasp, it refuses to be stapled down and autopsied for fixed, dead data. We abused poetry when we joylessly memorized and recited it. Read it anyway. Badly at first. Even more badly subsequently. It is worth doing because it delights in words, and will help you and your community to love God and neighbor anew. Eventually.

Not that there are not plenty of glorious moments in these essays themselves. C.T.R. Hayward pointing out that the Greek word *doxa* first appears in the Septuagint in the Song of the Sea. "Gloriously he has been glorified," *doxa* is used twice as soon as it appears once, doubling up on glory, not shrinking from superlative. David Firth on the didactic nature of poetry: the books of Samuel deploy poetry to show that those who exalt themselves wind up humbled, and vice-versa. Shai Held showing that Psalm 88 is even bleaker than you thought: it mentions no enemies because *God* is the psalmist's enemy (but hey, at least it implicitly reinforces divine omnipotence!). Katie Heffelfinger showing that good poetry chastens our over-familiarity with Scripture and undoes simple certainty. Yisca Zimran arguing that ancient poetry seeks to reflect reality in *moral* perspective—and marveling that God gives prophecy over to such fickle recipients as us human beings, to put to new use (a frightening responsibility that!). These scholars do not leave the cookies on the high shelf. Scripture's poetic treasures are here made available to all of God's people.

Maybe my old employer is right and conferences are not newsworthy. But it felt to me like something happened that week at Ushaw College. The world shifted just a bit. I learned anew that scripture is made for our delight. I left wanting to share that with the first stranger I saw, and then again with God's gathered assembly on the next Lord's day.

MANUMISSION

Not a slow dissolution of salt into water,
a folding down of dead leaves into earth,
a curl and ink-out smoke of letters in a fire,
a rise and gone of breath in open air,

but an awakening in skin so real it hurts,
a stretch and flex and flinch under a sun that burns,
a rain that makes us blink and spit,
in clothes like none we knew but all a perfect

fit and our city rebuilt brick by brick so
hard it casts the old place as a ghost, so we
tread the streets to trace the ones we love
and find them all, remade but recognizable,

take them in our arms, kiss them, hold them
fast as if we fear to lose them all again
but never will, which is the scandal of it,
the refusal to deliver a denouement.

Michael Symmons Roberts

Bibliography

11th century, Psalter with 14 odes and the apocryphal Psalm 151, MS 40731, Monastic Psalters, British Library, London. http://www.bl.uk/manuscripts/Viewer .aspx?ref=add_ms_40731_f231v.

Abusch, Tzvi. "The Form and Meaning of a Babylonian Prayer to Marduk." *JAOS* 103 (1983): 3–15.

Aejmelaeus, Anneli. "Hannah's Psalm in 4QSama." Pages 21–37 in *Archaeology of the Books of Samuel: The Entangling of Textual and Literary History*. Edited by Philippe Hugo and Adrian Schenker. Leiden: Brill, 2010.

Alexander, Philip S., trans. *The Targum of Canticles with a Critical Introduction, Apparatus, and Notes*. Volume 17A of the *Aramaic Bible*. Collegeville: The Liturgical Press, 2003.

Alter, Robert B. *The Art of Biblical Poetry*. New York: Basic Books, 1985.

———. *Book of Psalms*. New York: W.W. Norton, 2007.

Anderson, A.A. *The Book of Psalms*. London: Oliphants, 1972.

Anderson, Bernhard W. with Steven Bishop. *Out of the Depths: The Psalms Speak for us Today*. 3rd ed. Louisville: Westminster John Knox, 2000.

Andersen, Francis I. and David N. Freedman. *Hosea*. AB 24. New York: Doubleday, 1980.

ApRoberts, Ruth. "The Multiplication of Similitudes." Pages 65–71 in *Approaches to Teaching the Hebrew Bible as Literature in Translation*. Edited by Barry N. Olshen and Yael S. Feldman. New York: Modern Language Association of America, 1989.

Axel, Larry E. "Reshaping the Task of Theology." *American Journal of Theology & Philosophy* 8 (1987): 59–62.

Ave Christus Rex. "Gregorian Chant - Puer Natus Est (Latin & English)." Video. YouTube, February 10, 2019. https://www.youtube.com/ watch?v=8pZR9cK13so.

Bailey, Randall C. "The Redemption of Yahweh: A Literary Critical Function of the Songs of Hannah and David." *BibInt* 3 (1995): 213–31.

Balentine, Samuel E. *The Hidden God: The Hiding of the Face of God in the Old Testament.* Oxford: Oxford University Press, 1983.

———. "Isaiah 45: God's 'I Am,' Israel's 'You Are.'" *HBT* 16 (1994): 103-20.

Barfield, Owen. *Poetic Diction: A Study in Meaning.* Middletown: Wesleyan University Press, 1973.

Barton, John. *Reading the Old Testament: Method in Biblical Study.* London: Darton, Longman & Todd, 1996.

Bassnett, Susan. *Translation.* London: Routledge, 2014.

Barstad, Hans M. "Hosea and the Assyrians." Pages 91-110 in *"Thus Speaks Ishtar of Arbela:" Prophecy in Israel, Assyria, and Egypt in the Neo-Assyrian Period.* Edited by R.P. Gordon and Hans M. Barstad. Winona Lake: Eisenbrauns, 2013.

Batiffol, Pierre. *History of the Roman Breviary.* Translated by Atwell M.Y. Baylay. London: Longmans, Green, 1912.

Bäumer, Dom Suitbert. *Histoire de Bréviaire.* Translated by Reginald Biron. Paris: Letouzey et Ané, 1905.

Beal, Timothy K. "Ideology and Intertextuality: Surplus of Meaning and Controlling the Means of Production." Pages 27-39 in *Reading between texts: Intertextuality and the Hebrew Bible.* Edited by Danna N. Fewell. Louisville: Westminster John Knox, 1992.

Becker-Spörl, Silvia. *"Und Hanna betete, und sie sprach ..." Literarische Untersuchungen zu 1 Sam 1, 1-10.* Tübingen: Francke, 1992.

Beit-Arie, M.E. Silver, and T. Metzger, eds. *The Parma Psalter: A Thirteenth-Century Illuminated Hebrew Book of Psalms with a Commentary by Abraham Ibn Ezra.* London: Facsimile Editions Limited, 1996.

Berlin, Adele. *Biblical Poetry Through Medieval Jewish Eyes.* Bloomington: Indiana University Press, 1991.

———. *The Dynamics of Biblical Parallelism.* Revised and expanded. Grand Rapids: Eerdmans, 2008.

———. "The Message of Psalm 114." Pages 345-61 in *Birkat Shalom: Essays in Honor of Shalom Paul.* Edited by Chaim Cohen, Jeffrey Tigay, and Baruch Schwartz. Winona Lake: Eisenbrauns, 2008.

———. "On the Interpretation of Psalm 133." Pages 141-47 in *Directions in Biblical Hebrew Poetry.* Edited by Elaine R. Follis. Sheffield: Sheffield Academic, 1987.

———. "Rams and Lambs in Psalm 114:4 and 6: The Septuagint's Translation of X // בן Y Parallelisms." Pages 107-17 in *Textus* 24 (2009).

Berry, Wendell. "How to Be a Poet." *Poetry* (January 2001): 270.

———. *What Are People For?* New York: North Point Press, 1990.

Birkeland, Harris. "Die Einheitlichkeit von Ps 27," *ZAW* 51 (1933): 216-21.

Bjornard, Reidar B. "Hosea 11:8-9: God's Word or Man's Insight?" *BR* 27 (1982): 16-25.

Blaising, Craige A. and Carmen S. Hardin, eds. *Psalms 1-50*. ACCS 7. Downers Grove: InterVarsity Press, 2008.

Blenkinsopp, Joseph. *Isaiah 40-55*. AB 19A. London: Doubleday, 2000.

Blessing, Richard Allen. *Theodore Roethke's Dynamic Vision*. Bloomington: Indiana University Press, 1974.

Blidstein, Jacob (Gerald). "T'hillim 27." *Yavneh Review*, Spring 1965: 21-23.

Bogaert, Pierre-Maurice. "The Latin Bible." Pages 505-14 in *The New Cambridge History of the Bible: From the Beginnings to 600*. Edited by J. Carleton Paget and Joachim Schaper. Cambridge: Cambridge University Press, 2013.

Booth, Wayne C. "'Preserving the Exemplar': Or, How Not to Dig Our Own Graves," *CI* 3 (1977): 407-423.

Boulluec, Alain le and Pierre Sandevoir. *La Bible d'Alexandrie: L'Exode*. Paris: Cerf, 1989.

Breuer, Mordechai. *Pirqei Mo'adot* [Hebrew]. 2 vols. Jerusalem: Horeb, 1993.

Brodzki, Bella. "History, Cultural Memory, and the Tasks of Translation in T. Obinkaram Echewa's *I Saw the Sky Catch Fire*." *PMLA* 114 (1999): 207-20.

Brown, William P. *A Handbook to Old Testament Exegesis*. Louisville: Westminster John Knox, 2017.

Brueggemann, Walter. "Bounded by Obedience and Praise: The Psalms as Canon." *JSOT* 50 (1991): 63-92.

———. *Finally Comes the Poet: Daring Speech for Proclamation*. Minneapolis: Fortress Press, 1989.

———. "From Hurt to Joy, from Death to Life." *Int* 28 (1974): 3-19.

———. *The Message of the Psalms: A Theological Commentary* Minneapolis: Augsburg, 1984.

———. *Preaching from the Old Testament*. Minneapolis: Fortress Press, 2019.

Burrows, Mark S. "The Energy of Poetry in a Culture of Saturation." *ARTS* 24 (2013).

Buss, Martin J. *The Prophetic Word of Hosea*. Berlin: A. Toepelmann, 1969.

Byassee, Jason. *Northern Lights. Resurrecting Church in the North of England*. Eugene: Cascade Books, 2020.

Chalmers, R. Scott. *The Struggle of Yahweh and El for Hosea's Israel*. Sheffield: Sheffield Phoenix Press 2008.

Charles, Robert H. *A Critical and Exegetical Commentary on the Revelation of St. John*. 2 vols. Edinburgh: T&T Clark, 1920.

Carr, David M. "Reading Isaiah from Beginning (Isaiah 1) to End (Isaiah 65-66): Multiple Modern Possibilities." Pages 188-218 in *New Visions of Isaiah*. Edited by Roy F. Melugin and Marvin A. Sweeney. Sheffield: Sheffield Academic Press, 1996.

Charry, Ellen. *Psalms 1–50*. Grand Rapids: Brazos, 2015.

Cassuto, Umberto. *A Commentary on the Book of Exodus*. Translated by Israel Abrahams. Jerusalem: Magnes Press, 1967.

———. *Biblical and Oriental Studies*. Jerusalem: Magnes Press, 1973.

Chiang, Samuel E. "Editor's Note." *Orality Journal*, 2 (2013): 7–12.

Childs, Brevard S. "The Canonical Shape of Prophetic Literature." *Int* 32 (1978): 46–55.

———. *Introduction to the Old Testament as Scripture*. London: SCM Press, 1979.

deClaissé-Walford, Nancy Rolf Jacobson, and Beth LaNeel Tanner. *The Book of Psalms*. NICOT. Grand Rapids: Eerdmans, 2014.

Clements, Ronald E. "Patterns in the Prophetic Canon." Pages 42–55 in *Canon and Authority*. Edited by George W. Cots and Burke O. Long. Philadelphia: Fortress Press, 1977.

———. "Who is blind but my servant?" (Isaiah 42:19): how then shall we read Isaiah?" Pages 143–56 in *God in the Fray: A Tribute to Walter Brueggemann*. Edited by Tod E. Linafelt and Timothy K. Beal. Minneapolis: Fortress, 1998.

Clifford, Richard J. *Psalms 1–72*. Nashville: Abingdon, 2002.

———. *Psalms 73–150*. Nashville: Abingdon, 2003.

Clines, Francis X. "Poet of the Bogs," The New York Times Magazine, March 13, 1983. https://www.nytimes.com/1983/03/13/magazine/poet-of-the-bogs.html.

———. "Seamus Heaney, Poet of 'the Silent Things,'" The New York Times, August 30, 2013. https://www.nytimes.com/2013/08/31/opinion/seamus-heaney-poet-of-the-silent-things.html.

Cohen, A. *The Psalms*. Soncino Books of the Bible. 2nd ed. London: Soncino Press, 1992.

Cooper, Alan. "Biblical Poetics: A Linguistic Approach." Ph.D. dissertation, Yale University, 1976.

Couey, J. Blake and Elaine T. James, eds. *Biblical Poetry and the Art of Close Reading*. Cambridge: Cambridge University Press, 2018.

Craigie, Peter and Marvin Tate. *Psalms 1–50*. 2nd ed. WBC. Nashville: Thomas Nelson, 2004.

Craven, Toni. *The Book of Psalms*. Collegeville: Liturgical, 1992.

Cronin, Michael. "Translation Lecture 2." Paper given at Nida School of Translation Studies. Misano, Italy, 2016.

Cross, Frank Moore. *Canaanite Myth and Hebrew Epic: Essays in the History of the Religion of Israel*. Cambridge: Harvard University Press, 1973.

Culler, Jonathan. *Theory of the Lyric*. London: Harvard University Press, 2015.

Culley, Robert C. "Psalm 88 Among the Complaints." Pages 289–302 in *Ascribe to the Lord: Biblical and Other Studies in Memory of Peter C. Craigie*. Edited by Lyle Eslinger and Glen Taylor. Sheffield: JSOT, 1988.

Daniélou, Jean. *Sacramentum Futuri: Études sur les Origines de la Typologie Biblique*. Paris: Beauchesne, 1950.

——. *Théologie du Judéo-Christianisme*. Tournai: Desclée, 1958.

Darr, John A. *Herod the Fox: Audience Criticism and Lukan Characterization*. JSNTSup 163. Sheffield: Sheffield Academic, 1998.

Davidson, Robert. *The Vitalitz of Worship: A Commentarz on the Book of Psalms*. Grand Rapids: Eerdmans, 1998.

Davis, Ellen F. "Teaching the Bible Confessionally in the Church." Pages 311–30 in *The Art of Reading Scripture*. Edited by Ellen F. Davis and Richard B. Hays. Grand Rapids: Eerdmans, 2003.

Day, John. *God's Conflict with the Dragon and the Sea: Echoes of a Canaanite Myth in the Old Testament*. UCOP 35. Cambridge: Cambridge University Press, 1985.

Dearman, J. Andrew. *Hosea*. NICOT. Grand Rapids: Eerdmans, 2012.

Desnitsky, Andrei S. "Thread and Tracery, or Prose and Poetry in the Bible." *The Bible Translator* 57 (2006): 85–92.

Dickie, June F. "Psalm 133: Sacred Wisdom Interpreted by Contemporary South Africans." *JSem* 29 (2020): 1–16.

——. "Zulu Song, Oral Art, Performing the Psalms to Stir the Heart: Applying Indigenous Form to the Translation and Performance of Some Praise Psalms." PhD dissertation, University of KwaZulu-Natal, 2017.

Dietrich, Walter. *Samuel: Teilband I. 1 Sam 1–12*. BKAT 8/1. Neukirchner-Vluyn: Neukirchner Verlag, 2011.

——. "Stefan Heyms Ethan ben Hoshaja und der Hauptverfasser der Samuelbücher." Pages 3–40 in *The Books of Samuel: Stories—History—Reception History*. Edited by Walter Dietrich. BETL 284. Leuven: Peeters, 2016.

Dines, Jennifer M. *The Septuagint*. London: T&T Clark, 2004.

Dobbs-Allsopp, F.W. *On Biblical Poetry*. New York: Oxford University Press, 2015.

——. "Psalm 133: A (Close) Reading" *JHS* 8 (2008).

Donne, John. *The Sermons of John Donne*. 10 vols. Edited by George R. Potter and Evelyn M. Simpson. Berkeley: University of California Press, 1953–1962.

Doyle, Brian. "Metaphora Interrupta: Psalm 133." *ETL* 77 (2001): 5–22.

Duchesne, Louis. *Christian Worship: Its Origins and Evolution*. 5th ed. London: SPCK, 1919.

Eidevall, Göran. "Lions and Birds as Literature: Some Notes on Isaiah 31 and Hosea 11." *SJOT* 7 (1993): 78–87.

Elbogen, Ismar. *Jewish Liturgy: A Comprehensive History*. Translated by Raymond P. Scheindlin. Philadelphia: JPS, 1993.

Ellington, Scott A. *Risking Truth: Reshaping the World through Prayers of Lament*. Eugene: Pickwick, 2008.

Emmerson, Grace I. *Hosea: An Israelite Prophet in Judean Perspective*. Sheffield: JSOT, 1984.

Ernest Ansermet - Topic. "Symphony of Psalms: II. Psalm 40, Verses 2, 3, and 4." Video. YouTube, March 2, 2015. https://www.youtube.com/watch?v=h3Swan5TF_8.

EuroArtsChannel. "Händel: 'O Sing unto the Lord a New Song' Chandos Anthem HWV 249b." Video. YouTube, October 4, 2018. https://www.youtube.com/watch?v=N42nSAaeb9M.

Everson, David L. *The Vetus Latina and the Vulgate of the Book of Exodus*. Leiden: Brill, 2014.

Feb 1066, Psalter including Psalms 151 and the Book of Odes (Rahlfs 1088), MS 19352, British Library, London. http://www.bl.uk/manuscripts/Viewer.aspx?ref=add_ms_19352_f182r.

Feuer, Avrohom Chaim. *Tehillim: A New Translation with a Commentary Anthologized from Talmudic, Midrashic and Rabbinic Sources*. New York: Mesorah Publications, 2004.

Fiddes, Paul S. "G.M. Hopkins." Pages 563-76 in *The Blackwell Companion to the Bible in English Literature*. Edited by Rebecca Lemon et al. Chichester: Wiley-Blackwell, 2009.

Fields, Weston W. *Sodom and Gomorrah: History and Motif in Biblical Narrative*. Sheffield: Sheffield Academic Press, 1997.

Firth, David G. *1 & 2 Samuel*. AOTC. Nottingham: Apollos, 2009.

———. *1 & 2 Samuel: A Kingdom Comes*. London: Bloomsbury, 2017.

———. "Psalms of Testimony." *OTE* 12 (1999), 440-54.

———. "Shining the Lamp: The Rhetoric of 2 Samuel 5-24." *TynBul* 52 (2001): 203-24.

———. "The Teaching of the Psalms." Pages 164-74 in *Interpreting the Psalms: Issues and Approaches*. Edited by Philip S. Johnston and David G. Firth. Leicester: Apollos, 2005.

Fisch, Harold. *Poetry with a Purpose: Biblical Poetics and Interpretation*. Bloomington: Indiana University Press, 1988.

Foley, John Miles. *Immanent Art: From Structure to Meaning in Traditional Oral Epic*. Bloomington: Indiana University Press, 1991.

———. *Oral Tradition and the Internet: Pathways of the Mind*. Urbana: University of Illinois Press, 2012.

———. *The Singer of Tales in Performance*. Bloomington: Indiana University Press, 1995.

Fontaine, Carole R. "'Arrows of the Almighty' (Job 6:4): Perspectives on Pain." *AThR* 66 (1984): 243–48.

Foster, Benjamin. *Before the Muses: An Anthology of Akkadian Literature*. Bethesda: CDL Press, 1993.

Frankel, David. *The Land of Canaan and the Destiny of Israel: Theologies of Territory in the Hebrew Bible*. Winona Lake: Eisenbrauns, 2011.

Fretheim, Terence E. "The Authority of the Bible and the Imaging of God." Pages 45–52 in *Engaging Biblical Authority: Perspectives on the Bible as Scripture*. Edited by William P. Brown. Louisville: Westminster John Knox Press, 2007.

Fry, Euan McG. "Faithfulness: A Wider Perspective." Pages 7–27 in *Fidelity and Translation: Communicating the Bible in New Media*. Edited by Paul A. Soukup and Robert Hodgson. Franklin: Sheed & Ward; New York: American Bible Society, 1999.

Frye, Northrop. *Anatomy of Criticism: Four Essays*. Princeton: Princeton University Press, 1971.

Gadamer, Hans-Georg. *Truth and Method*. 2nd ed. Translated by J. Weinsheimer and Donald G. Marshall. Berkeley: University of California Press, 1991.

Gaines, Jason M.H. *The Poetic Priestly Source*. Minneapolis: Fortress Press, 2015.

Gelb, Ignace J., et al., eds. *The Assyrian Dictionary of the Oriental Institute of the University of Chicago*. 21 volumes. Chicago: The Oriental Institute of the University of Chicago, 1956–2010.

Geller, Stephen. *Parallelism in Early Biblical Poetry*. HSM 20. Missoula: Scholars Press, 1979.

———. "Were the Prophets Poets?" *Prooftexts* 3 (1983): 211–31.

Gentzler, Edwin. "Rethinking Translation and Rewriting Hamlet in China." Paper given at Nida School of Translation Studies. Misano, Italy, 2016.

Gera, Deborah. "Translating Hebrew Poetry into Greek Poetry: The Case of Exodus 15," *BIOSCS* 40 (2007): 107–20.

Gillingham, Susan. "Psalms of David, Psalms of Christ." Pages 69–85 in *Rooted and Grounded: Faith Formation and the Christian Tradition*. Edited by Steven Croft. Norwich: Canterbury Press, 2019.

———. *Psalms Through the Centuries: A Reception History Commentary*. 3 volumes. Blackwell Bible Commentaries. Oxford: Wiley-Blackwell 2008–2022.

Goh, Samuel T.S. *The Basics of Hebrew Poetry: Theory and Practice*. Eugene: Cascade Books, 2017.

Goldin, Judah. *The Song at the Sea*. New Haven: Yale University Press, 1971.

Goldingay, John. *Psalms 1–41*. BCOTWP. Grand Rapids: Baker Academic, 2006.

———. *Psalms, Volume 2: Psalms 42–89*. Grand Rapids: Baker Academic, 2007.

Goldingay, John and David Payne. *Isaiah 40–55*. 2 volumes. ICC. London: T&T Clark, 2006.

Goldschmidt, E.D. *Seder Rav Amram Gaon*. Jerusalem: Mosad Rav Kook, 1971.

Gordis, Robert. "Psalm 9–10: A Textual and Exegetical Study." *JQR* 48 (1957): 104–22.

Greenberg, Moshe. *Studies in the Bible and Jewish Thought*. Philadelphia: Jewish Publication Society, 1995.

Grossberg, Daniel. *Centripetal and Centrifugal Structures in Biblical Poetry*. SBLMS 39. Atlanta: Scholars Press, 1989.

Guite, Malcom. *Faith, Hope and Poetry: Theology and the Poetic Imagination*. London: Routledge, 2012.

Gunkel, Hermann. *Einleitung in die Psalmen: Die Gattungen der religiösen Lyrik Israels*. Götttingen: Vandenhoeck & Ruprecht, 1985.

———. *Die Psalmen*. HKAT. Volume 2. Göttingen: Vandenhoeck & Ruprecht, 1968.

Gunkel, Hermann and Joachim Begrich. *Introduction to Psalms: The Genres of the Religious Lyric of Israel*. Translated by James D. Nogalski. MLBS. Macon: Mercer University Press, 1998.

Gutt, Ernst-August. *Relevance Theory: A Guide to Successful Communication in Translation*. Dallas: Summer Institute of Linguistics; New York: United Bible Societies, 1992.

Hakham, Amos. *The Bible, Psalms with the Jerusalem Commentary*. Jerusalem: Mosad Harav Kook, 2003.

Harkins, Angela Kim. "The Performative Reading of the *Hodayot*: The Arousal of Emotions and the Exegetical Generation of Texts." *JSP* 21 (2011): 55–71

———. "The Emotional Re-Experiencing of the Hortatory Narratives Found in the Admonition of the *Damascus Document*." *DSD* 22 (2015): 285–307.

Harmon, Kathleen. "Growing in Our Understanding of the Psalms, Part 2: Persisting in Prayer when God is Silent." *Liturgical Ministry* 20 (2011): 52–54.

Hallamish, Moshe. *Studies in Kabbalah and Prayer* [in Hebrew]. Beer Sheva: Ben Gurion University Press, 2012.

Harper, William R. *Amos and Hosea*. ICC 13A.2. Edinburgh: T&T Clark, 1994.

Harris, Robert. *Discerning Parallelism: A Study in Northern French Medieval Jewish Biblical Exegesis*. Brown Judaic Studies 341. Providence: Brown Judaic Studies, 2004.

Hatim, Basil and Ian Mason. *Discourse and the Translator*. London: Longman, 1990.

———. *The Translator as Communicator*. London: Routledge, 1997.

Heaney, Seamus. *The Redress of Poetry*. London: Faber & Faber, 1995.

Heffelfinger, Katie M. *I Am Large, I Contain Multitudes: Lyric Cohesion and Conflict in Second Isaiah*. BIS 105. Leiden: Brill, 2011.

Heinemann, Joseph. *Prayer in the Talmud: Forms and Patterns*. Translated by Richard S. Sarason, SJ 9. Berlin: de Gruyter, 1977.

Held, Moshe. "A Faithful Lover in an Old Babylonian Dialogue." *JCS* 15 (1961): 1–26.

Held, Shai. *Abraham Joshua Heschel: The Call of Transcendence*. Bloomington: Indiana University Press, 2013.

Hermans, Theo. "Translation, Equivalence and Intertextuality." *Wasafiri*, 18 (2003): 39–41.

Heschel, Avraham Yehoshua. *Oheiv Yisroel* [in Hebrew]. Zhitomir, 1864.

Heschel, Abraham Joshua. *God in Search of Man. A Philosophy of Judaism*. New York: Farrar Straus and Giroux, 1955.

Hirsch, Edward. *How to Read a Poem: And Fall in Love with Poetry*. San Diego: Harvest Books/Harcourt, 2000.

Hirsch Jr., E.D. *The Aims of Interpretation*. Chicago: University of Chicago Press, 1976.

Hirshfield, Jane. *Hiddenness, Uncertainty, Surprise: Three Generative Energies of Poetry*. Newcastle: Bloodaxe, 2008.

de Hoop, Raymond. *Genesis 49 in its Literary and Historical Context*. OTS 39. Leiden: Brill, 1998.

Hossfeld, Frank-Lothar and Erich Zenger. *Psalms 2: A Commentary on Psalms 51–100*. Minneapolis: Fortress, 2005.

House, Humphry and Graham Storey, eds. *The Journals and Papers of Gerard Manley Hopkins*. London: Oxford University Press, 1959.

Howard, David M. Jr. "Psalm 88 and the Rhetoric of Lament." Pages 132–46 in *My Words Are Lovely: Studies in the Rhetoric of the Psalms*. Edited by Robert L. Foster and David M. Howard Jr. London: T&T Clark, 2008.

Hrushovski, Benjamin. "Prosody, Hebrew." Pages 1200–03 in Volume 13 of *Encyclopaedia Judaica*. Jerusalem: Keter.

Idelsohn, Abraham Z. *Jewish Liturgy and Its Development*. New York: Schocken Books, 1972.

———. "Impact." wycliffe.net. https://www.wycliffe.org.uk/about/our-impact/.

Illman, Karl-Johan "Psalm 88—A Lamentation without Answer." *SJOT* 1 (1991): 112–20.

Iser, Wolfgang. *The Implied Reader: Patterns of Communication in Prose Fiction from Bunyan to Beckett*. Baltimore: John Hopkins University Press, 1974.

Jakobson, Roman. "Grammatical Parallelism and Its Russian Facet." *Language* 42 (1966): 399–429.

———. "Linguistics and Poetics." Pages 350–77 in *Style in Language*. Edited by T. Sebeok. Cambridge: M.I.T. Press, 1968.

——. "Poetry of Grammar and Grammar of Poetry." *Lingua* 21 (1968): 597–609.

Janowski, Bernd. "Tempel und Schöpfung: Schöpfungsttheologische Aspekte der priesterschriftlichen Heiligtumskonzeption." *Jahrbuch für Biblische Theologie* 5 (1990): 11–36.

Jellicoe, Sidney. *The Septuagint and Modern Study.* Oxford: The Clarendon Press, 1968.

Johnson, Mark. *The Meaning of the Body: Aesthetics of Human Understanding.* London: University of Chicago Press, 2007.

Johnson, W.R. *The Idea of Lyric: Lyric Modes in Ancient and Modern Poetry.* Berkeley: University of California Press, 1982.

de Jong, Matthijs J. "A note on the meaning of *bᵉṣædæq* in Isaiah 42,6 and 45,13." *ZAW* 123 (2011): 259–262.

Joosten, Jan. "Targumic Aramaic a'wrm—'oppression' (Isa. XLVII 2, Hos. XI 7, Mic. VI 3)." *VT* 51 (2001): 552–55.

Kaduri, Yaakov. "Biblical Poetry: How Can It Be?" [in Hebrew]. Pages 287–306 in *The Literature of the Hebrew Bible: Introductions and Studies.* Edited by Zipora Talshir. Jerusalem: Yad Ben-Zvi Press, 2011.

Kinzie, Mary. *The Cure of Poetry in an Age of Prose: Moral Essays on the Poet's Calling.* London: University of Chicago Press, 1993.

Klein, Ralph W. *1 Samuel.* WBC 10. Waco: Word, 1983.

Klement, H.H. *2 Samuel 21–24: Context, Structure and Meaning in the Samuel Conclusion.* Bern: Peter Lang, 2000.

Kraus, Hans-Joachim. *Psalms 60–150: A Continental Commentary.* Translated by Hilton Oswald. Minneapolis: Fortress, 1993.

Kugel, James L. *The Idea of Biblical Poetry: Parallelism and Its History.* New Haven: Yale University Press, 1981.

——. *Traditions of the Bible: A Guide to the Bible As it Was at the Start of the Common Era.* Cambridge: Harvard University Press, 1998.

Kwakkel, Gert. "Exile in Hosea 9:3–6: Where and for What Purpose?" Pages 123–45 in *Exile and Suffering.* Bob Becking and Dirk J. Human. Leiden; Boston: Brill, 2009.

Landy, Francis. *Hosea.* NBC. Sheffield: Sheffield Academic Press, 1995.

Lefevere, André. *Translation, Rewriting, and the Manipulation of Literary Fame.* London: Routledge, 1992.

LeMon, Joel M. "Symphonizing the Psalms: Igor Stravinsky's Musical Exegesis." *Int* 71 (2017): 25–49.

Lenzi, Alan, ed. *Reading Akkadian Prayers and Hymns: An Introduction.* ANEM. Atlanta: Society of Biblical Literature, 2011.

Lewis, Theodore J. "The Textual History of the Song of Hannah: 1 Samuel ii 1–10." *VT* 44 (1994): 18–46.

Lichtenstein, Murray. "Biblical Poetry." Pages 105–28 in *Back to the Sources*. Edited by Barry Holtz. New York: Simon and Schuster, 2008.

Lieberman, Saul. *Hellenism in Jewish Palestine*. New York: Feldheim, 1950.

Lim, Timothy H. *The Holy Books of the Essenes and Therapeutae*. New Haven: Yale University Press, 2013.

Loewenstamm, Samuel E. *The Evolution of the Exodus Tradition*. Translated by Baruch Schwartz. Jerusalem: Magnes Press, 1992.

Lowth, Robert. *Lectures on the Sacred Poetry of the Hebrews*. Translated by G. Gregory. New York: Garland, 1971.

———. *Isaiah: A New Translation: With a Preliminary Dissertation, and Notes, Critical, Philological, and Explanatory*. 11th edition. Cambridge: James Munroe & Co., 1834.

Luther, Martin. *Lectures on Genesis 45–50*. Volume 8 of *Luther's Works*. Edited by Jaroslav Pelikan and Helmut T. Lehmann, American ed. Philadelphia: Muehlenberg and Fortress; St. Louis: Concordia, 1965.

Macchi, Jean-Daniel. *Israël et ses tribus selon Genèse 49*. OBO 171. Fribourg im Breisgau: Akademische Verlagsbuchhandlung; Göttingen: Vandenhoeck & Ruprecht, 1999.

Macintosh, Andrew A. *Hosea*. ICC 13A.1. Edinburgh: T&T Clark, 1997.

Mandolfo, Carleen. "Psalm 88 and the Holocaust: Lament in Search of a Divine Response." *BibInterp* 15 (2007): 151–70.

Maré, Leonard. "Facing the Deepest Darkness of Despair and Abandonment: Psalm 88 and the Life of Faith." *OTE* 27 (2014): 177–88.

Marty, Martin E. *A Cry of Absence: Reflections for the Winter of the Heart*. Grand Rapids: Eerdmans, 1997.

Maxey, James A. "Alternative Evaluative Concepts to the Trinity of Bible Translation." Pages 57–80 in *Translating Values: Evaluative Concepts in Translation*. Edited by Piotr Blumczynski and John Gillespie. New York: Palgrave Macmillan, 2016.

May, Herbert G. "Fertility Cult in Hosea." *AJSL* 48 (1932): 73–98.

———. "Some Cosmic Connotations of Mayim Rabbîm, 'Many Waters'." *JBL* 74 (1955): 9–21.

Mays, James L. *Hosea: A Commentary*, OTL 13A. Philadelphia: SCM, 1969.

McCann Jr., J. Clinton. "Psalms" in *The New Interpreter's Bible*. Volume 4. Edited by Leander E. Keck, et al. Nashville: Abingdon, 1996.

McCarter Jr., P. Kyle. *1 Samuel: A New Translation with Introduction and Commentary*. AB 8. Garden City: Doubleday, 1980.

McGilchrist, Iain. *The Master and His Emmisary: The Divided Brain and the Making of the Western World*. Expanded Edition. London: Yale University Press, 2019.

McKane, William. *A Critical and Exegetical Commentary on Jeremiah*. 2 volumes. London: Bloomsbury, 2014.

Mearns, James. *The Canticles of the Christian Church Eastern and Western in Early Mediaeval Times*. Cambridge: Cambridge University Press, 1914.

Milgrom, Jacob. *Leviticus 1–16*. AB 3. New York: Doubleday, 1991.

Miller, Patrick D. *Interpreting the Psalms*. Philadelphia: Fortress, 1986.

———. "The Theological Significance of Biblical Poetry." Pages 213–30 in *Language, Theology, and the Bible: Essays in Honor of James Barr*. Edited by John Barton and Samuel Balentine. Oxford: Oxford University Press, 1994.

Moberly, R.W.L. *The God of the Old Testament*. Grand Rapids: Baker Academic, 2020.

———. *Old Testament Theology: Reading the Hebrew Bible as Christian Scripture*. Grand Rapids: Baker, 2013.

Morris, Gerald P. *Prophecy, Poetry and Hosea*. Sheffield: Sheffield Academic Press, 1996.

Moyise, Steve. "Intertextuality and Biblical studies: a review." *Verbum et ecclesia* 23, no. 2 (2002): 418–31.

Mowinckel, Sigmund. *Psalmenstudien*. Volume 1. Amsterdam: P. Schippers, 1966.

Murray, Robert. *Symbols of Church and Kingdom: A Study in Early Syriac Tradition*. London: T&T Clark, 2006.

Naidoff, Bruce D. "The Two-fold Structure of Isaiah XLV 9–13." *VT* 31 (1981): 180–85.

Neale, Jason Mason and Richard Frederick Littledale, eds. *A Commentary on the Psalms from Primitive and Medieval Writers*. 2nd edition. 4 volumes. London: Masters, 1874–1879.

Nida, Eugene A. *Fascinated by Languages*. Amsterdam: John Benjamins, 2003.

Nida, Eugene A. and Charles R. Taber. *The Theory and Practice of Translation*. Helps for Translators 8. Leiden: Brill, 1969.

Nussbaum, Martha C. *Upheavals of Thought: The Intelligence of Emotions*. Cambridge: Cambridge University Press, 2001.

Oakley, Mark. *The Splash of Words: Believing in Poetry*. Norwich: Canterbury Press, 2016.

O'Donoghue, John, Anne F. Kelly, and Werner G. Jeanrond. "The Agenda for Theology in Ireland Today." *The Furrow* 42 (1991): 692–710.

Officium Majoris Hebdomadae et Octavae Paschae. Ratisbon: Pustet, 1923.

Oliver, Mary. *New and Selected Poems*. 2 volumes. Boston: Beacon, 2004–2005.

Orr, Gregory. *Poetry as Survival*. Athens: The University of Georgia Press, 2002.

O'Siadhail, Micheal. *Collected Poems*. Tarset: Bloodaxe Books, 2013.

———. *The Five Quintets*. Norwich: Canterbury Press, 2019.

———. *One Crimson Thread*. Hexham: Bloodaxe Books, 2015.

Parry, Robin. *Old Testament Story and Christian Ethics: The Rape of Dinah as a Case Study*. Milton Keynes: Paternoster, 2004.

Pilkington, Christine. "The Hidden God in Isaiah 45:15 – A Reflection from Holocaust Theology." *SJT* 48 (1995): 285–300.

Pius V., Clement VIII, and Urban VIII. *The Roman Breviary: Reformed by Order of the Holy Oecumenical Council of Trent*. 2 volumes. Translated by John, Marquess of Bute. Edinburgh and London: Blackwood, 1879.

Pyles, Anthony R. "Drowning in the Depths of Darkness: A Consideration of Psalm 88 with a New Translation." *Canadian Theological Review* 1 (2012): 13–28.

Pym, Anthony. *The Moving Text: Localization, Translation, and Distribution*. Philadelphia: John Benjamins, 2004.

von Rad, Gerhard. *Wisdom in Israel*. Translated by James D. Martin. London: SCM, 1972.

Ramakrishna, Shantha. "Cultural Transmission through Translation: An Indian Perspective." Pages 87–100 in *Changing the Terms: Translating in the Postcolonial Era*. Edited by Sherry Simon and Paul St-Pierre Simon. Ottawa: University of Ottawa Press, 2000.

Reif, Stefan C. *Judaism and Hebrew Prayer: New Perspectives on Jewish Liturgical History*. Cambridge: Cambridge University Press, 1993.

Rendsburg, Gary. Review of *Genesis 49 in its Literary and Historical Context*, by Raymond de Hoop, *JSS* 47 (2002): 138–41.

Rendtorff, Rolf. "Isaiah 56:1 as a Key to the Formation of the Book of Isaiah." Pages 181–94 in *Canon and Theology: Overtures to an Old Testament Theology*. Translated by Margaret Kohl. OBT. Minneapolis: Fortress, 1993.

Ricoeur, Paul. *The Rule of Metaphor: Multi-disciplinary Studies of the Creation of Meaning in Language*. Translated by Robert Czerny. London: University of Toronto Press, 1977.

Roberts, Michael Symmons. *Mancunia*. Cape Poetry. London: Jonathan Cape, 2017.

Roethke, Theodore. *Collected Poems of Theodore Roethke*. Garden City: Anchor Press/ Doubleday, 1975.

———. "On Identity." Page 42 in *On Poetry and Craft: Selected Prose of Theodore Roethke*. Port Townsend: Copper Canyon Press, 2001.

———. "On 'In a Dark Time.'" Pages 49–53 in *The Contemporary Poet as Artist and Critic: Eight Symposia*. Edited by Anthony Ostroff. Boston: Little Brown, 1965.

Rofé, Alexander. "Midrashic Traits in 4Q51 (so-called 4QSama)." Pages 75–89 in *Archaeology of the Books of Samuel*. Edited by Philippe Hugo and Adrian Schenker.

Rotelle, John E., ed. *The Works of Saint Augustine, A Translation for the 21st Century*. Translated by Maria Boulding. Hyde Park: New City Press, 2000.

Rowe, Gary R. "Fidelity and Access: Reclaiming the Bible with Personal Media,"
    Pages 47–63 in *Fidelity and Translation: Communicating the Bible in New Media*.
    Edited by Paul A. Soukup and Robert Hodgson. Franklin: Sheed & Ward;
    New York: American Bible Society, 1999.

Solms, Élisabeth de. *Bible Chrétienne V. Commentaires: Les Psaumes*. Quebec: Anne
    Signier, 2001.

Sanders, James A. *Torah and Canon*. Philadelphia: Fortress Press, 1972.

Sanzio, Rafaello. *Ecstasy of St. Cecilia*. 1518. Oil on wood transported on canvas,
    236 x 146 cm. Pinacotecca Nazionale Bologna. https://www.pinacoteca
    bologna.beniculturali.it/en/content_page/item/2811-st-cecilia-with-saints-
    paul-john-the-evangelist-augustine-and-mary-magdalen-ecstasy-of-st
    -cecilia.

Sarna, Nahum M. "Psalm XIX and the Near Eastern Sun-God Literature." Pages
    171–75 in *Fourth World Congress of Jewish Studies Papers*. Edited by Shaul
    Shaked, Y. Shenkman. Jerusalem: World Union of Jewish Studies, 1967.

———. *The JPS Torah Commentary: Exodus*. Philadelphia: JPS, 1991.

Sarna, Nahum, ed. *Olam Hatanakh: Tehillim* [in Hebrew]. 2 volumes. Tel Aviv:
    Dodezon-Itti, 1995.

Schäfer, Peter. *The Origins of Jewish Mysticism*. Princeton: Princeton University
    Press, 2009.

Scherman, Nosson, trans. *The Complete Art Scroll Siddur*, 2nd edition. New York:
    Mesorah Publications, 2003.

Schneider, Heinrich. *Die altlateinischen biblischen Cantica*. Beuron: Hohenzollern,
    1938.

———. "Die biblischen Oden in Jerusalem und Konstantinopel." *Biblica* 30 (1949):
    433–52.

Schökel, Luis Alonso. *A Manual of Hebrew Poetics*. Subsidia Biblica 11. Rome:
    Pontifical Biblical Institute, 1988.

Schürer, Emil. *The History of the Jewish People in the Age of Jesus Christ*. 5 volumes.
    Revised and edited by Geza Vermes, Fergus Millar, and Matthew Black.
    Edinburgh: T&T Clark, 1979.

Seitz, Christopher. *Word Without End: The Old Testament as Abiding Theological
    Witness*. Grand Rapids: Eerdmans, 1998.

Sherevsky, Esra. "Rashi and Christian Interpretations." *JQR* 61 (1971): 76–86.

Shirky, Clay. *Cognitive Surplus: Creativity and Generosity in a Connected Age*. New
    York: Penguin Press, 2010.

Siebert-Hommes, Jopie. "'With Bands of Love:' Hosea 11 as 'Recapitulation' of the
    Basic Themes in the Book of Hosea." Pages 167–74 in *Unless Some One Guide
    Me*. Edited by J.W. Dyk et al. Maastricht: Shaker, 2001.

Simon, Sherry. *Translating Montreal: Episodes in the Life of a Divided City*. Montreal: McGill-Queen's University Press, 2006.

Simon, Uriel. *Reading Prophetic Narratives*. Translated by L.J. Schramm. Bloomington: Indiana University Press, 1997.

Smith, Barbara Herrnstein. *Poetic Closure: A Study of How Poems End*. Chicago: University of Chicago Press, 1968.

Soloveitchik, Joseph B. "Redemption, Prayer, Talmud Torah." *Tradition* 17 (1978): 55–72.

Sommer, Benjamin D. *The Bodies of God and the World of Ancient Israel*. Cambridge: Cambridge University Press, 2009.

———. "Nature, Revelation, and Grace in Psalm 19: Towards a Theological Reading of Scripture." *HTR* 108 (2015): 376–401.

———. *A Prophet Reads Scripture: Allusion in Isaiah 40–66*. Stanford: Stanford University Press, 1998.

Soukup, Paul A. "Understanding Audience Understanding." Pages 91–107 in *From One Medium to Another: Communicating the Bible through Multimedia*. Edited by Paul A. Soukup and Robert Hodgson. Kansas City: Sheed & Ward, 1997.

Steiner, George. *Real Presences*. Chicago: University of Chicago Press, 1989.

Steinmann, Andrew E. *1 Samuel*. CC. St Louis: Concordia, 2016.

Stoebe, Hans Joachim. *Das erste Buch Samuelis*. KAT. Gütersloh: Gütersloher Verlagshaus Gerd Mohn, 1973.

Stökl Ben Ezra, Daniel. *The Impact of Yom Kippur on Christianity*. WUNT 163. Tübingen: Mohr Siebeck, 2003.

Stuart, Douglas K. *Hosea-Jonah*. WBC 31. Waco: Word Books, 1987.

Stuhlmueller, Carroll. "Deutero-Isaiah: Major Transitions in the Prophet's Theology and in Contemporary Scholarship." *CBQ* 42 (1980): 1–29.

Stulac, Daniel J. *History and Hope: The Agrarian Wisdom of Isaiah 28–35*. University Park: Eisenbrauns, 2018.

Suleiman, Susan Rubin "Introduction: Varieties of Audience-Oriented Criticism." Pages 1–45 in *The Reader in the Text: Essays on Audience and Interpretation*. Edited by Susan Rubin Suleiman and Inge Crosman. Princeton: Princeton University Press, 1980.

Swenson, Kristen M. *Living Through Pain: Psalms and the Search for Wholeness*. Waco: Baylor, 2005.

Taft, Robert. *The Liturgy of the Hours in East and West: The Origins of the Divine Office and Its Meaning for Today*. 2nd revised edition. Collegeville: The Liturgical Press, 1993.

Talmon, Shemaryahu. "The 'Desert Motif' in the Bible and in Qumran Literature." Pages 31–64 in *Biblical Motifs*. Edited by Alexander Altmann. Cambridge: Harvard University Press, 1966.

Tamez, Elsa. *When Horizons Close: Rereading Ecclesiastes*. Translated by Margaret Wilde. Maryknoll: Orbis, 2000.

Tanner, Beth. "Psalm 88." Pages 668–73 in *The Book of Psalms*. Edited by Nancy de-Claissé-Walford, Rolf A. Jacobson, and Beth Laneel Tanner. Grand Rapids: Eerdmans, 2014.

Tate, Marvin. *Psalms 51–100*. WBC 20. Dallas: Word Books, 1990.

———. "Psalm 88." *Review and Expositor* 87 (1990): 91–95.

Taylor, Joan E. *Jewish Women Philosophers of First Century Alexandria: Philo's 'Therapeutae' Reconsidered*. Oxford: Oxford University Press, 2003.

Thackeray, Henry St. J. *The Septuagint and Jewish Worship: A Study in Origins*, 2nd edition. London: Oxford University Press, 1923.

The Grail. "Psalm 96: O Sing A New Song." Revised Grail Psalms #706b, 1963. https://hymnary.org/hymn/HS1991/706b.

The Sixteen - Topic. "MacMillan: A New Song." Video. YouTube, September 15, 2018. https://www.youtube.com/watch?v=gwWM8Zth4ns.

Thornhill, A. Chadwick. "A Theology of Psalm 88." *EQ* 87 (2015): 45–57.

Tiemeyer, Lena-Sofia. "The Coming of the Lord–An Intertextual Reading of Isa 40:1–11; 52:7–10; 59:15b–20; 62:10–11 and 63:1–6." Pages 233–44 in *Let Us Go Up to Zion: Essays in Honour of H.G.M. Williamson on the Occasion of his sixty-fifth Birthday*. Edited by Iain W. Provan and Mark J. Boda. Leiden-Boston: Leiden, 2012.

———. "God's Hidden Compassion." *TynBul* 57 (2006): 191–213.

———. "When God Regrets." MA Thesis at Hebrew University; Jerusalem 1998.

Tomes, R. "Sing to the Lord a New Song." Pages 237–52 in *Psalms and Prayers. Papers Read at the Joint Meeting of the Society for Old Testament Study and Het Oud Testamentisch erkgezelschap in Nederland en België, Apeldoorn August 2006*. Oudtestamentische Studiën / Old Testament Studies 55. Leiden: Brill, 2007.

Toranova, Nadezhda and Erin-Lee McGuire. "The Kiev Psalter of 1397: An Analysis," Medievalists.net, 2003. https://www.medievalists.net/2009/06/the-kiev-psalter-of-1397-an-analysis/.

Tov, Emanuel. *Textual Criticism of the Hebrew Bible*. Minneapolis: Fortress Press, 1992.

Tsumura, David Toshio. *The First Book of Samuel*. NICOT. Grand Rapids: Eerdmans, 2007.

———. "TŌHÛ in Isaiah XLV 19." *VT* 38 (1988): 361–63.

Uffenheimer, Benjamin. "Amos and Hosea–Two Directions in Israel's Prophecy," Pages 294–98 in *Zer Li'Gevurot*. Edited by Ben-Zion Luria. Jerusalem: Kiryat-Sepher, 1972.

U2. "40." 10 *War*. Island Records, 1983. https://www.u2.com/music/lyrics/2.

Uyl, Anthony, ed. *Exposition on the Book of Psalms*. Woodstock: Devoted Publishing, 2017.

Vallejo, César. *The Complete Poetry*. Berkeley: University of California Press, 2007.

VanGemeren, Willem A. *Psalms*. Expositor's Bible Commentary 5. Grand Rapids: Zondervan, 2008.

Waard, Jan de and Eugene A. Nida. *From One Language to Another: Functional Equivalence in Bible Translating*. Nashville: Thomas Nelson, 1986.

Wacker, Marie T. "Father-God, Mother-God, and Beyond: Exegetical Constructions and Deconstructions of Hosea 11." *Lectio difficilior* 2 (2012).

Walsh, P.G., trans. *Cassiodorus, Volume One: Explanation of the Psalms 1–50*. Ancient Christian Writers 51. Mahwah, NJ: Paulist Press 1990.

———. *Cassiodorus, Volume Three: Explanation of the Psalms 101–150*. Ancient Christian Writers 53. Mahwah: Paulist Press, 1991.

Watson, Wilfred G.E. *Classical Hebrew Poetry: A Guide to Its Techniques*. JSOTSup. Sheffield: Sheffield Academic Press, 1984.

Watts, James W. *Psalms and Story: Inset Hymns in Hebrew Narrative*. Sheffield: JSOT, 1992.

———. "'This Song:' Conspicuous Poetry in Hebrew Prose." Pages 345–58 in *Verse in Ancient Near Eastern Prose*. Edited by Johannes C. de Moor and Wilfred G.E. Watson. Neukirchen-Vluyn: Neukirchener Verlag, 1993.

Watts, John D.W. *Isaiah 34–66*, WBC 25. Revised edition. Grand Rapids: Zondervan, 2005.

Wendland, Ernst R. "Bible Translations for the 21st Century." Paper presented at The Bjarne Wollan Teigen Reformation Lectures. Mankato, MN, October 25–26, 2012.

———. *LiFE-Style Translating*. SIL International Publications in Translation and Textlinguistics 2. Dallas: SIL International, 2006.

———. "Towards a 'Literary' Translation of the Scriptures: With Special Reference to a 'Poetic Rendition.'" *Acta Theologica* 22 (2002): 164–202.

Weil, Simone. *Waiting for God*. Translated by Emma Craufurd. New York: Perennial, 2001.

Weinfeld, Moshe. "Sabbath, Temple Building, and the Enthronement of the Lord." [in Hebrew]. *Beth Miqra* 69 (1977): 188–93.

Weiss, Meir. *The Bible from Within: The Method of Total Interpretation*. Publications of the Perry Foundation for Biblical Research in the Hebrew University of Jerusalem. Jerusalem: Magnes Press, 1984.

Weiser, Artur. *The Psalms: A Commentary*. Philadelphia: Westminster Press, 1962.

Wenham, Gordon J. *Story as Torah: Reading the Old Testament Ethically*. Grand Rapids: Baker Academic, 2000.

Wesselschmidt, Quentin F., ed. *Psalms 51–150*. ACCS 8. Downers Grove, IL: InterVarsity Press, 2007.

Westermann, Claus. *Praise and Lament in the Psalms*. Atlanta: John Knox, 1981.

———. "The Role of the Lament in the Theology of the Old Testament." *Int* 28 (1974): 20–38.

Wevers, John W. *Septuaginta: Vetus Testamentum Graecum Auctoritate Scientiarum Gottingensis editum II.1: Exodus*. Göttingen: Vandenhoeck & Ruprecht, 1991.

Whitman, Walt. "The Bible as Poetry." Pages 379–82 in *Complete Prose Works*. Philadelphia: David McKay, 1892.

Wicke, Donald J. "The Structure of 1 Samuel 3: Another View." *BZ* 30 (1986): 256–58.

Wilde, Oscar. *The Original Four-Act Version of the Importance of Being Earnest: A Trivial Comedy for Serious People*. London: Methuen, 1957.

Willey, Patricia Tull. *Remember the Former Things: The Recollection of Previous Texts in Second Isaiah*. SBLDS 161. Atlanta: Scholars, 1997.

Williamson, Hugh G.M. "Isaiah: Prophet of Weal or Woe?" Pages 273–300 in *"Thus Speaks Ishtar of Arbela:" Prophecy in Israel, Assyria, and Egypt in the Neo-Assyrian Period*. Edited by R.P. Gordon and Hans M. Barstad. Winona Lake: Eisenbrauns, 2013.

Willis, John T. "The Juxtaposition of Synonymous and Chiastic Parallelism in Tricola in Old Testament Hebrew Psalm Poetry." *VT* 29 (1979): 465–80.

Wolf, Michaela. *Changing the Terms: Translating in the Postcolonial Era*. Edited by Sherry Simon and Paul St-Pierre Simon. Ottawa: University of Ottawa Press, 2000.

Wolff, Hans W. *Hosea*. Hermemeia. Translated by G. Stansell. Philadelphia: Fortress Press, 1974.

Wragg, Arthur. *The Psalms for Modern Life*. New York: Claude Kendall, 1934.

van Wolde, Ellen. "Trendy Intertextuality." Pages 43–49 in *Intertextuality in Biblical Writings*. Edited by Sipke Draisma. Kampen: Kok, 1989.

Yee, Gale A. *Composition and Tradition in the Book of Hosea*. Atlanta: Scholars Press, 1987.

Yeivin, Israel. *Introduction to the Tiberian Masorah*. Translated by E.J. Revell. Masoretic Studies 5. Missoula: Scholars Press, 1980.

Zhang, Sarah. "How is a Love Poem (Song 4:1–7) Like the Beloved?" Pages 131–46 in *Biblical Poetry and the Art of Close Reading*. Edited by J. Blake Couey and Elaine T. James. Cambridge: Cambridge University Press, 2018.

Subject Index

Schroth, Elisa, 66
Scripture, 157–58, 159, 171–73
Second Temple period, 14, 117n30
 temple liturgy, 32–33, 39–40
Seinfeld, 242–43
Seitz, Christopher, 123
self, 55n39, 68, 75–76
 lament psalms, 60, 70–73, 234
 nafshi, 70–72, 73
 remembering, 61–62
 suffering, 64–65, 69–70
semantic parallelism, 108, 124, 126,
 131–32, 230
Septuagint (LXX), 19, 22, 117–18n30,
 131n61
 Hannah's Prayer, 45n11, 48n18
 Hosea, book of, 182n24
 Psalter, 33, 34–36, 40, 224
 Song of Miriam, 31n10
 Song of the Sea, 28–31, 33, 34–36,
  38–40, 231, 243–44
Shavuot, 139–40
Shema, 35–36, 40
Shirky, Clay, 87
silence, 59–60, 66, 150
Simeon, patriarch, 19, 24–25
Simon, Sherry, 88n25
sin, 61–63, 66, 179, 185
 betrayal of God, 180–82, 183, 185,
  188–89
 guilt, 62–63, 66
Sinai, Mount, 133–34, 135–36, 137, 139
Sisera, death of, 128–30
Smith, Barbara Herrnstein, 127, 140
Solomon, 9, 23, 109
Soloveitchik, Rabbi Joseph, 154–55
Sommer, Benjamin D., 3, 166n45, 197n5,
 213, 230, 235, 243
Song of the Sea, 2, 27–28, 41, 195–96,
 229, 231
 baptism, 37–40
 Catholic liturgical use, 28, 34, 36–41
 Jewish liturgical use, 28–29, 30–33,
  34–36, 39–40
Soukup, Paul A., 89

South Africa, 3, 92
 AIDS-support group, 97–99
 Zulu Bible translations, 3, 91–96,
  96–104, 231
specification, 108–10
stanzas, 114–19, 121–23, 140
Steiner, George, 57–58, 234
Stein, Jock, 204
Steinmann, Andrew E., 43n4
Stravinsky, Igor, 220
Stuart, Douglas K., 181n23, 182n26,
 182n29
Stulac, Daniel J., 175n2
suffering, 62–63, 64–66, 153, 154–55, 234
 chronic illness, 148–49, 150–51, 234
 social isolation, 150–51, 153
Swenson, Kristin M., 142n1, 155
synchronic-literary reading, 4–5

T
Taber, Charles R., 84–85
Talmon, Shemaryahu, 176n8
Tamez, Elsa, 16
Tanakh, 19–20
Tanner, Beth Laneel, 145n24
Tarfon, Rabbi, 120
Targums, 15, 19, 22
Tate, Marvin, 114n19, 115, 145, 146n26,
 147, 148n32
Taylor, Joan E., 33n18
temple, Jerusalem, 137–38
 liturgy, 32–33, 39–40
 Second, 14, 32–33, 39–40, 117n30
Thackeray, Henry St. J., 31n11
theophany, 133–35, 217
Therapeutae, 31–32, 33, 39, 40
Tiemeyer, Lena-Sofia, 180n20
time, 136–40
Tov, Emanuel, 117–18n30
trust, 117, 119, 121, 144–45, 151–52, 161,
 182–83
truth, 156–57, 166–67, 173
Tsumura, David Toshio, 170n64

Scripture & Extrabiblical Sources Index

Old Testament

New Testament

Dead Sea Scrolls

Early Jewish Works

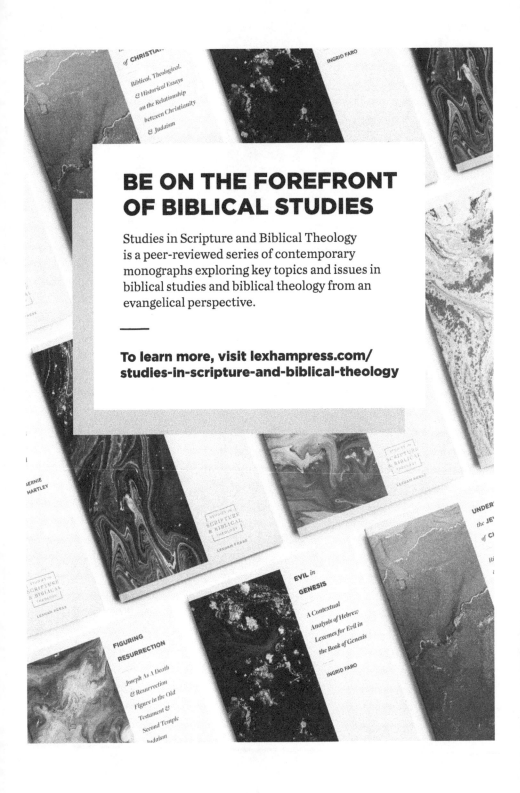